Portraying 9/11

Portraying 9/11

Essays on Representations in Comics, Literature, Film and Theatre

Edited by
Véronique Bragard,
Christophe Dony *and*
Warren Rosenberg

McFarland & Company, Inc., Publishers
Jefferson, North Carolina, and London

LIBRARY OF CONGRESS CATALOGUING-IN-PUBLICATION DATA

Portraying 9/11 : essays on representations in comics, literature, film and theatre / edited by Véronique Bragard, Christophe Dony and Warren Rosenberg.
p. cm.
Includes bibliographical references and index.

ISBN 978-0-7864-5950-6
softcover : 50# alkaline paper ∞

1. Comic books, strips, etc.— History and criticism   2. September 11 Terrorist Attacks, 2001—Caricatures and cartoons.   3. September 11 Terrorist Attacks, 2001, in literature.   4. September 11 Terrorist Attacks, 2001, in motion pictures.   5. September 11 Terrorist Attacks, 2001, in mass media.   6. Popular culture—Political aspects—United States—History—21st century.   I. Bragard, Véronique.   II. Dony, Christophe.   III. Rosenberg, Warren.   IV. Title: Portraying September 11.
PN6714.P67   2011   810.9'35873931—dc23   2011025615

BRITISH LIBRARY CATALOGUING DATA ARE AVAILABLE

© 2011 Véronique Bragard, Christophe Dony and Warren Rosenberg. All rights reserved

No part of this book may be reproduced or transmitted in any form or by any means, electronic or mechanical, including photocopying or recording, or by any information storage and retrieval system, without permission in writing from the publisher.

Front cover design by David K. Landis (Shake It Loose Graphics)

Manufactured in the United States of America

*McFarland & Company, Inc., Publishers
Box 611, Jefferson, North Carolina 28640
www.mcfarlandpub.com*

Table of Contents

Acknowledgments vii

Introduction
    Véronique Bragard, Christophe Dony *and* Warren Rosenberg 1

Part I: Comics

Covering 9/11: The *New Yorker*, Trauma Kitsch, and Popular Memory
    Timothy Krause 11

Spandex Agonistes: Superhero Comics Confront the War on Terror
    Matthew J. Costello 30

"Whose Side Are You On?" The Allegorization of 9/11 in Marvel's *Civil War*
    Stephan Packard 44

Part II: Literature

September 11 and Cold War Nostalgia
    Aaron DeRosa 58

Don DeLillo's *Falling Man*: Countering Post–9/11 Narratives of Heroic Masculinity
    Magali Cornier Michael 73

Misplaced Anxieties: Violence and Trauma in Ian McEwan's *Saturday*
    Ulrike Tancke 89

The Mediated Trauma of September 11, 2001, in William Gibson's *Pattern Recognition* and David Foster Wallace's "The Suffering Channel"
    Marc Oxoby 102

Part III: Performance

Terror and Mismemory: Resignifying September 11 in *World Trade Center* and *United 93*
    Gerry Canavan 118

From Flying Man to Falling Man: 9/11 Discourse in *Superman Returns* and *Batman Begins*
    Dan Hassler-Forest 134

Table of Contents

Authenticating the Reel: Realism, Simulation, and Trauma in *United 93*
    FRANCES PHEASANT-KELLY 147

Connecting in the Aftermath: Trauma, Performance, and Catharsis in
the Plays of Anne Nelson
    JAMES M. CHERRY 160

About the Contributors 173

Index 175

Acknowledgments

The volume you are holding in your hands has been an epic journey of reading, revising, and researching that started around 2009. The editors therefore express their gratitude to all contributors not only for their insightful research, but for their patience and the interest they have manifested in the volume since its earliest stages. We would also like to thank the reviewers Frédéric Verolleman and Virginie Housiaux for their work and kind cooperation as well as the INCAL (Institut des Civilisations, Arts, et Lettres). Additionally, we wish to thank Bénédicte Ledent and Mathilde Mergeai who provided invaluable help with revisions of the introduction and Corinne Rosenberg for her assistance in final editing. We would also like to thank Frédéric Debomy, Louis Joos, and the publishing house Glénat for allowing us to reproduce images from the comics album *Une Vie Silencieuse* (2006). Finally, the editors would like to thank each other for their work, patience, and friendship, without which this volume would not have existed.

INTRODUCTION
Véronique Bragard, Christophe Dony
and Warren Rosenberg

In "11 septembre," the opening story of the comics collection *Une Vie Silencieuse* (2006), Belgian artist Louis Joos and French scriptwriter Frédéric Debomy depict how a New York City taxi driver and amateur photographer, driving from one location to another, attempts to capture the essence of the city with his camera. The nameless protagonist apprehends New York City as a vast *mise-en-scène* too substantial to be framed into one single photograph, and as a result continually discovers new angles of approach and new compositions. After September 11, 2001, however, the photographer, facing adversity and torment, realizes that "something is missing" (6) and that he is unable to carry out his project in the same way as before. As he becomes aware of the impossibility of his artistic quest, he eventually gives up taking pictures of the American metropolis, deciding instead to turn to a more "powerful" photography directly representing the casualties of war and terror. Much as the protagonist in the story is conflicted, the panels from "11 septembre" reproduced here convey the double movement at the heart of any attempt to grasp the 9/11 catastrophe: the intense and sometimes cathartic need to record a reaction and the seeming impossibility of representing it. In both images, the strokes and scribbles on people's faces and the towers convey the physical, destructive explosion, as well as the artist's wish to wipe out his depiction of the catastrophe.

Clearly, this short graphic narrative demonstrates how difficult it is to mediate or even represent the overwhelming intensity of traumatic events and conforms with Cathy Caruth's claim that trauma "brings us to the limits of our understanding" (4). The mental, as opposed to the physical definition of trauma, is indeed a profound and lingering emotional reaction to events that can affect our ability to process and cope with them. Commentators or artists attempting to represent traumatic events therefore struggle to create meaning and achieve closure in the face of such powerful experiences. Because trauma exceeds experience and "cannot be placed within the schemes of prior knowledge" (Caruth: 153), it imposes a barrier between the imaginable and the expressible. As a result, many post-traumatic artistic responses to 9/11 also develop, as Richard Gray contends, an "aslant [...] approach," examining the cataclysmic events "by circuitous means, almost by stealth" (Gray: 136). In their turn, these oblique confrontations with the tragedy and the states of fear that followed considerably problematize any attempt to determine a 9/11 textual canon.

The date 9/11 can thus be considered a rupture that has paradoxically triggered an

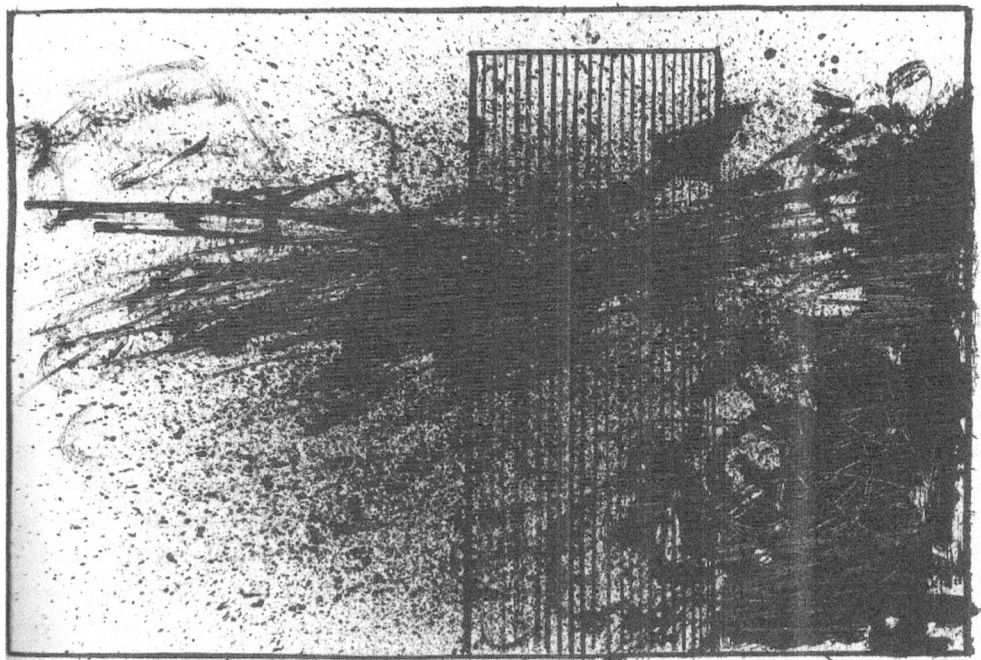

"11 septembre" panels from *Une Vie Silencieuse* by Frédéric Debomy and Louis Joos © Editions Glénat/Drugstore — 2006.

inflation of commemoration. In the early aftermath, for example, media pundits and government officials quickly attempted to commemorate the events within recognizable conventions, relying on notions such as heroism, nationalism, and patriotism. Next to these public remembering practices, many family members of the victims as well as a large number of people affected by the tragedy felt compelled to express their grief and, therefore, erected spontaneous memorials usually consisting of candles, flags, and posters of missing people. Yet, many of the creators of these memorials, whether official or spontaneous, were reluctant to display death and distress. Slavoj Žižek refers to this aesthetic (dis)inclination as the "'derealization' of the horror" and argues that it equates to an "ideological censorship" which is meant to maintain a "distance" between "Us" and "Them" (13).[1] Žižek's argument hints at the American, and possibly Western, domestication of "the attacks," leading to an evacuation of their political dimension. However, while early narratives attempting to address the tragedy presented cases of individual suffering, victimization, or sometimes revenge, the question of representation has taken on more weight with the distance and the time that are necessary to confront a traumatic catastrophe such as the moment the towers collapsed. As a result, multifarious representations of the events now challenge these "official" commemorative practices. A wide array of writers and artists have offered counter-narratives of 9/11 which reflect on and confront, in Richard Gray's words, "a yawning and possibly unbridgeable gap between before and after," as well as various other tensions that inform the (mis)representations of September 11, 2001 (130).

The sometimes precipitous need, both collective and individual, to frame the catastrophe within a larger picture — national, political, or even cultural — has also had the effect of overwhelming what some have called "the attacks" under a torrent of images and narratives attempting to capture their essence. As a result, a commemorative disjuncture between the events and eventness surfaced in the aftermath of 9/11. David Simpson, for example, claims that the commemorations of 9/11 "have been [...] urgent and perhaps untimely" and therefore "hurried along and even hijacked by a tide of secondary events" (4). In his contribution to this volume, which analyzes the controversial Marvel comics' series *Civil War* (2006-2007), Stephan Packard refers to this terminological profusion as the "semiotic greed" of 9/11 that has come to "envelop [...] more topics and events in its growing referential network." In other words, what we now commonly refer to as "9/11" is semantically surrounded by an almost infinite list of peripheral terms, events, and ideas including the War on Terror, imperialism, fundamentalism, globalization, as well as the East and the West. In short, the mnemonic fever of the aftermath has "conquered" trauma itself so that the expression "9/11" now gives rise to many interpretations resulting from the contexts in which it is scrutinized and functions, according to David Holloway, as a powerful and ever-expanding cultural "intertext."

These various interpretations may also be perceived in the many commemorating tensions informing September 11. As Stef Craps argues, "[T]he events of 11 September

INTRODUCTION

2001 caused a rupture not only in the normal order of things but also, and perhaps especially, in the signifying systems underwriting that order" (183). The spaces between "the real and the imagined, between image and trope, between the private realm of memory and the public realm of history" play a crucial role in the increasingly varied definitions of 9/11 (Keniston and Quinn: 2–3). As a shocking encounter with unexpected violence and brutal death, 9/11 triggered a range of responses at numerous levels, and in fact led to reconfigurations of many values, perspectives, and strategies in the U.S. and the world's social, political, and cultural fabric. In the public sphere, for example, U.S. foreign policy became harsher and national security more stringent, regional and individual perceptions by those in both the East and the West radically changed, while reconsiderations of American and Muslim cultures and identities surfaced on a global level. In more private and domestic spheres, terror shook the definition of the self and radically altered relationships among individuals, leaving behind not only grief and incomprehension but a range of other complex feelings as well such as fear, depression, and alienation from family and community.

It is not surprising, then, to observe that the events of 9/11, although barely ten years old, have led to a considerable number of academic investigations in various fields. Some commentators have approached the incidents in terms of politics, often discussing 9/11 in relation to the War on Terror and the U.S. military operations in Afghanistan and Iraq (Redfield, 2009). Others have examined them in terms of culture and commemorative practices (Simpson, 2006), or have discussed a range of cultural accounts and mediations of the tragedy (Keniston and Quinn, 2008). Both the singularity and the radical character of the disaster may partially account for this outpouring of analysis. But the ever-expanding intertextuality of 9/11 also partly explains this myriad of narratives, and more importantly, plays a crucial role in the present and future representations of the events. If one can conceive the existence of a so-called "9/11 literature," one must therefore acknowledge that it is vast, entails many permutations, and continues to expand. Whether approaching the calamities directly or via metonymy, in terms of trauma, culture or geopolitics, a multitude of artists, scholars and commentators are still engaged by these events, feeling compelled to confront the implications of that day and thereafter. In doing so, they reflect on the effects of both tragedy and oppression, shedding light on new elements surrounding the 9/11 events. Narratives such as Cormac McCarthy's *The Road* (2007), for example, convey America's fear of "falling" in the post–9/11 era. Depicting a devastated nation covered with ashes and dust, McCarthy's novel reflects the American anxiety over a potential nuclear Holocaust, a threat that has become steadily more menacing since 9/11. In a similar vein, the images of Ground Zero that the war veteran disappointingly discovers at the end of Wim Wender's *Land of Plenty* (2004) reveals how media images of the tragedy have created a range of needs and expectations. Narratives like these, whether sanitizing, containing, or aestheticizing the events, participate in the increasing development of the "9/11 intertext" and ultimately contribute to "memory in the making," that requires constant critical reassessment.

This collection participates in the reassessment of 9/11 memory-making, critically engaging its mediation in various genres and modes, including comics, literature, and performance. As such, this volume joins critical and insightful recent 9/11–related scholarship such as David Simpson's *9/11: The Culture of Commemoration* and Anne Keniston and Jeanne Quinn's edited collection of essays, *Literature after 9/11*. As these works seek to understand culture after 9/11, they "interrogate the mechanisms and ethics of witness[ing]" that surrounded the mnemonic fever engendered by 9/11 in various modes of storytelling (Keniston and Quinn: 6). The present collection is notable for its continuity with such works while it expands on the creation of a philosophical and aesthetic architecture of memory which, in contrast to the ideal of an objective and stable rendering of history, is dynamic. The essays in this volume thus constantly remind us that memory oscillates between remembering and forgetting and is therefore subject to assimilation, appropriation, and even distortion.

This scrutinizing of memory, along with the many and varied formal experiments that artists carried out as a result of their confrontation with the "unreal and unexpected," is the reason for the book's large scope of investigation. Consciously or not, the artists expand on the various commemorative tensions that 9/11 creates, and articulate them along various binary models such as before and after, individual and collective trauma and memory, reality and (the) spectacle (of mass media). Perhaps these tensions, as Gerry Canavan suggests in his contribution to this volume, are best symbolized in the "unparalleled imagistic power" of the Towers' twinness whose destruction "is central to many [...] texts written in the wake of 9/11" (Keniston and Quinn: 1). Art Spiegelman's "9/11/01" cover for the *New Yorker*, for example, which, as Timothy Krause argues in his contribution to this collection, presents the Towers in "stark silhouette, their jet-black, monolithic forms barely distinguishable against the only slightly lighter dark gray of the background," illustrates how the reflexive mirroring of the Towers now haunts many people with "an absent presence upon which any number of associations and memories can be projected" (Krause).[2] The contributors to this volume, however, do not read the tensions that inform 9/11 as simple binaries. Rather, they problematize them, criticize their incompleteness, and investigate how new implications surface at the crossroads and intersections of these models. In providing political, cultural, and theoretical approaches to the memory-making of 9/11, and applying them to specific modes of representations, the contributors offer a plurality of perspectives that deepen and expand upon the common stock of images from the mainstream news media and, taken together, establish a more nuanced and particularized view of the traumatic events of 9/11 after a decade.

The refusal to anchor the signification of the tragedy is also illustrated in the variety of critical approaches that the authors employ as they discuss how the disaster is constantly redefined or reinterpreted in specific media. In that way the contributors corroborate Jeffrey Melnick's claim that cultural critics, after 9/11, "will have to develop appropriate interpretive paradigms that may be more particular to this event and its fallout than the standard frameworks" (5). This unique collection, then, in addition to engaging with the memory-making of 9/11 and issues of gender, politics, and realism, among others, raises questions about the structural and generic possibilities of employing comics, literature, film, and performance to grasp the events of September 11. How and to what extent can these forms contribute to the ever changing construction of 9/11 memory? How is form transformed by trauma? What is the relationship between the events discussed and the codes used to refer to them? Can we critically examine the 9/11 events beyond the boundaries of genres? Or can we ultimately speak of a 9/11 genre? These are some of the questions at stake in the present book, and in the process of answering them the contributors suggest new paradigms for engaging with this threshold event in world history.

Although some thematic overlapping and methodological similarities surface in the essays, the present collection, for reasons of clarity and coherence, is divided into three parts whose titles refer to the medium they discuss: comics, literature, and performance. These sections merely offer a glimpse of what each medium has produced in terms of texts taking 9/11 as their starting point or backdrop and should therefore not be considered exhaustive.[3] Rather, each section considers the events of September 11 and its aftermath in unique ways that shed light on the possibilities, conventions, and means of production of the medium.

The chapter on comics groups three essays which approach, in different ways, issues of (dis)continuity and seriality in some early aftermath covers of the *New Yorker*[4] and various American superhero publications. Common to these pieces is their situating of the "texts" in the medium's cultural production, and their exploration of how these comics are inextricably bound up with the post–9/11 political and cultural context of state and society. Noted as well is the inclination of these texts to not explicitly refer to the tragedy — an omission which can be considered emblematic of the unreal character of trauma. Timothy Krause's essay, for example, reads the *New Yorker*'s covers as "operating between two poles of response" which he describes as "trauma kitsch" and "'legitimate' [...] memorialization." Matthew J. Costello discusses how various superhero texts challenge the orthodox commemorative mythology of 9/11 that media pundits and government officials rapidly constructed. In other words, "the 'official' [interpretative] story" of 9/11 (Leavey: 86, quoted in Costello), which was cast in a Manichean narrative and "laid the foundation for justifying an all-out military response," is questioned in narratives where costumed heroes are generally believed to defend the political *status quo*. Finally, Stephan Packard's essay focuses on the controversial comics crossover series *Civil War*. He argues that this narrative problematizes issues of (hyper)surveillance, and ultimately the very redemptive role of the superhero, while yet "contribut[ing] to the cohesion of the overarching post–9/11 discourse."

The second section examines 9/11–related novels and short stories by American and British authors such as Don DeLillo, Ian McEwan, David Foster Wallace, William Gibson, Ken Kalfus, and Jonathan Safran Foer. Similar to the comics analyses mentioned above, the essays of this section document the perceptions and interpretations of the

September 11 events and their aftermath, shedding light on the commemorative tensions inherent in remembering traumatic events. More precisely, each essay illustrates how trauma can impose a barrier between the imaginable and the expressible. Whereas comics metaphorically referred to "the attacks," the literary works discussed here reflect upon the limits of language and literature when confronted with the overwhelming intensity of the 9/11 events.

Aaron DeRosa's essay, for instance, which examines various American novels, establishes a linguistic and thematic "equivalency" between September 11 and America's fear of nuclear Holocaust in the Cold War. He argues that 9/11 has in part been "registered [...] as a traumatic repetition of the atomic blasts in America's cultural consciousness," which illustrates the difficulties that writers faced in appropriately describing the events. DeRosa further claims that the United States will never be able to fully "recover from" these traumas "until it recognizes their relationship to one another." As DeRosa's piece mirrors the tension between past and present while discussing 9/11 as "Cold War Nostalgia," Magali Cornier Michael's essay on Don DeLillo's *Falling Man* (2007) focuses on the disjunction between individual and collective memory, or between the public sphere of commemoration and the private need for healing. She suggests that DeLillo's novel intentionally focuses on the inner lives of one man and his wife living in post–9/11 Manhattan as they struggle to cope with the events in order to "counter" the public responses to 9/11. DeLillo's novel, she argues, challenges the (hyper)masculine responses to the attacks, which promoted a simplistic response of strength and dismissed the psychological distress that is the normal response to trauma, with devastating results. Finally, Marc Oxoby and Ulrike Tancke's pieces consider the tension between the dramatic reality of the events and the incomplete spectacle aesthetics of the mass media that sought to represent them. While acknowledging "the role of the media in 'fictionalizing' the attacks" and yet "reject[ing] the notion that 9/11 was merely a simulacra," Oxoby argues that William Gibson' *Pattern Recognition* (2003) and David Wallace's "The Suffering Channel" (2004) "problematize [...] the mediated experience(s) of 9/11." In this way Oxoby reflects on the creative potential of literature to interrogate more superficial media representations of reality. In a similar fashion, Tancke reads Ian McEwan's *Saturday* (2005) as a narrative challenging of "oft-met interpretations of 9/11 centering on collective experiences" which juxtaposes the public and individual realms of memory. In examining how many people were exposed to 9/11 through remote and often virtual means, Tancke suggests that *Saturday* "alerts us" to the media's (mis)representations of 9/11 and how we consume it as a "virtual reality."

The essays in the final section reflect on 9/11–related performance and explore various Hollywood films including *United 93* (Greengrass, 2006), *World Trade Center* (Stone, 2006), *Superman Returns* (Singer, 2006), and *Batman Begins* (Nolan, 2005), as well as two plays by Anne Nelson. In his contribution Gerry Canavan examines 9/11 as a "singularity," arguing that mass media and films such as *World Trade Center* and *United 93* have "distorted cultural memory by resignifying the disaster as a permanent state of emergency from which there is no possible relief or escape." Dan Hassler-Forest scrutinizes how allusions to 9/11 abound in superhero films such as *Superman Returns* and *Batman Begins*, yet claims that in dealing with the event these films "display ambivalent attitudes towards the narrative traditions of the superhero genre." In her analysis of *United 93*, Frances Pheasant-Kelly makes a similar point about genre modification, contending that Greengrass' movie adaptation "depart[s] from many of the usual spectacular devices of the Hollywood disaster film" to maintain "authenticity" and possibly function "as a mode of catharsis." Catharis is James M. Cherry's concern as well, as he critically examines how theatrical minimalism in two plays by Anne Nelson, *The Guys* (2001) and *Savages* (2007), "gesture[s] toward" a commemorative "aesthetic that seems appropriate for a post–9/11 America." In other words, Cherry sees "the lack of visual spectacle" in these plays as allowing the audience to connect more intimately with the actors' emotions and experiences, thereby offering the possibility of finding solace.

We believe that the essays collected here provide a representative sample of the contentious commemorative discourse emerging from the aesthetic responses to the events of 9/11. The editors of this book have brought together essays that address the historical, political, cultural, and personal meanings of the disaster and its aftermath, and have sought to explore a wide range of critical issues complicating the (mis)representations of 9/11 in various modes of storytelling. Taken together, however, the essays collected here respond to the political domestication of the events, that is, how America tends to unilaterally grasp the meaning and consequences of the tragedy of 9/11. With the exception of Ulrike Tancke's discussion of Ian McEwan's *Saturday*, all contributors discuss American-produced texts responding to the events. While several essays include remarks on how 9/11 is yoked with ideologies of "the Other," a majority of them suggests that September 11 has resulted in a crisis of sensibility in American life and values, including the shattering of ideals such as democratic exceptionalism and strength. In other words, the collection conveys that 9/11 has plunged America — and possibly the West — into a crisis of representation with itself, a crisis that inevitably contributes to and reinforces a war on terror mentality. As Joanne Faulkner puts it, "the attacks on the Twin Towers" have become "iconic images" of "planes perforating the clear, tranquil surface of those seemingly impenetrable buildings and thus *opening a rupture in the Western consciousness*, the reparation of which is not yet in sight" (67, emphasis added). While America may claim possession of the wound of 9/11, our study points to the need for a contrastive study with Arab- and Muslim-inspired works, among others, that may open up new postcolonial, transnational, and global perspectives on the events. Clearly, as an ever-expanding interest, 9/11 will render no definitive meanings. Only "the artist's conflicted response to [...] [the] extraordinary" (253), as David Foster Wallace describes it, can even begin to shape a culture's collective memory of such a traumatic event. As other studies of 9/11 surface, we hope that this collection will join them in usefully contributing to the very making of memory, and to the potential for healing, that we and others seek to articulate, explore, and effect.

Notes

1. While Žižek's "us versus them" dialectic initially opposes subaltern individuals vs. mainstream and dominant identities, its signification can also be extended to the attacked versus the attackers, or the survivors versus the Dead.
2. Spiegelman also rearticulates this tension between absence and presence in his later "comix" memoir of 9/11 tellingly entitled *In the Shadow of No Towers*.
3. For a substantial review of the immense production of 9/11–related art, literature and cinema, see the Lower Manhattan Project website, an excellent database that critically discusses the aestheticization of 9/11 in various media (http://lmp.uqam.ca/accueil).
4. Although the covers of the *New Yorker* may not be considered "comics" per se, their graphic composition shares similarities with the realm of comics.

Works Cited

Caruth, Cathy (Ed. and intro.). *Trauma: Explorations in Memory*. Baltimore: The John Hopkins University Press, 1995.
Craps, Stef. "Conjuring Trauma: The Naudet's Brothers' 9/11 Documentary." *Canadian Review of American Studies* 37.2 (2007): 183–204.
Debomy, Frédéric, and Louis Joos. *Une Vie Silencieuse*. Paris: Albin Michel, 2006.
Faulkner, Joanne. "Nietzsche, 9/11, and the 'Falling Man.'" *Journal of Nietzsche Studies* 35–36 (2008): 67–85.
Gray, Richard. "Open Doors, Closed Minds: American Prose Writing at a Time of Crisis." *American Literary History* 21.1 (2009): 128–151.
Holloway, David. "Cultural Politics After 9/11." Lecture presented at the conference The Depoliticization of 9/11. Newcastle University. November 6, 2010.
Keniston, Ann, and Jeanne Quinn (Eds.). *Literature after 9/11*. London and New York: Routledge, 2008.
McCarthy, Cormac. *The Road*. New York: Knopf, 2006.
Melnick, Jeffrey. *9/11 Culture*. West-Sussex: Wiley-Blackwell, 2009.
Redfield, Marc. *The Rhetoric of Terror: Reflections on 9/11 and the War on Terror*. New York: Fordham University Press, 2009.
Simpson, David. *9/11: The Culture of Commemoration*. Chicago: Chicago University Press, 2006.
Wallace, David Foster. "The Suffering Channel." *Oblivion, Stories*. New York: Little, Brown, 2004: 238–329.
Wenders, W. M. *Land of Plenty*. Emotion Pictures, InDigEnt, and Reverse Angle International, 2004.
Žižek, Slavoj. *Welcome to the Desert of the Real*. London and New York: Verso, 2002.

PART I: COMICS

COVERING 9/11
The New Yorker, *Trauma Kitsch, and Popular Memory*
Timothy Krause

The Fashion Issue: A Traumatic Introduction

On September 11, 2001, I watched the Twin Towers fall while standing at the corner of West and Green streets in Greenpoint, Brooklyn, staring southwest, transfixed, as a massive plume of smoke enveloped first the South Tower, then the North. The cloud consumed the Towers with a speed both instantaneous and agonizingly slow, with a dreamlike motion that reminded me then of time-lapse films of plants growing, as if some giant grey Venus fly-trap had swallowed the buildings. Like many traumatic events, the fall of the Towers seemed to open up a rent in reality itself, a space or gap between what was happening and my abilities to comprehend and narrate it.

Hours later, at home — after an endless televised fugue of planes striking, Towers falling, people running, a repeated cycle of traumatic imagery that had just begun to play itself out in the mass media and collective psyche — that week's copy of the *New Yorker* arrived: The Fashion Issue, dated September 17, 2001,[1] depicting on its cover the Statue of Liberty being cinched into an impossibly tight corset whose laces are the suspension cables of an anonymous, stylized bridge. The Statue's lips pucker, her eyes bulge, her torch hangs suspended in midair, dropped from her right hand: salaciously, Lady Liberty's breasts explode from the restrictive corset, whose embroidered edge exposes her green nipples. The cover image, "Yearning to Breathe Free" by Michael Roberts, is a typical *New Yorker* cover, mixing visual flair and arresting imagery with ironic wit and sophisticated detachment, qualities that had little purchase on the unfolding events of that day: indeed, in a grim historical irony, Fashion Week 2001 was canceled by 9/11, one of the many casualties of the terrorist attacks. The issue had already been marked and creased by the mail carrier's bag, its contents rendered relics by an unimaginable coincidence.

The image had become *outmoded*, to borrow the terminology of Hal Foster and, earlier, Walter Benjamin, who in his essay "Surrealism" defines the outmoded as

> the first iron constructions, the first factory building, the earliest photos, objects that have begun to be extinct, grand pianos, the dresses of five years ago, fashionable restaurants when the vogue has begun to ebb from them. [...] [The Surrealists] bring the

immense forces of "atmosphere" concealed in these things to the point of explosion [Benjamin: 210; Foster, *Design*: 137–39].

Interpreting Benjamin, Foster locates the Surrealists' power in what he calls the "nonsynchronous," the "hold[ing] together [of] markers of different times." He adds:

> This deployment of the nonsynchronous pressures the totalist assumptions of capitalist culture, and questions its claim to be timeless; it also challenges this culture with its own wish symbols, and asks it to recall its own forfeited dreams of liberty, equality, and fraternity [*Design*: 141, 139].

Thus the events of 9/11 not only rendered the *New Yorker*'s cover image of Lady Liberty surreal, *unheimlich*, a tad morbid or humorous; it opened a privileged gap, however infinitesimal, into the way culture works, how it is produced and consumed, and, most importantly, how cultural products are imbricated in their historical moment, how rapidly shifting historical contexts can imbue cultural products with a psychic life of their own — here, a *frisson* of artistic intent, the formal qualities of an image, and the ironies introduced by an unforeseen act of mass political terror.

The Benjaminian-Fosterian concepts of the "capitalist outmoded" (Foster, *Compulsive*: 162; cf. 156–91), the "profane illumination" (Benjamin: 209) — by which an outmoded object's latent historical energies are liberated — and the nonsynchronous are useful in looking at the subject of this essay: several covers run by the *New Yorker* from September to December 2001 that consciously commemorate the then-recent tragedy of 9/11, and in so doing attempt to mediate, through a mass visual medium, the traumas, individual and collective, public and private, caused on and by that day. For beginning immediately with Art Spiegelman's acclaimed "9/11/01" cover of September 24, 2001— which shows the Twin Towers in stark silhouette, their jet-black, monolithic forms barely distinguishable against the only slightly lighter dark gray of the background, an image at once graphically stunning and emotionally restrained, an absent presence upon which any number of associations and memories can be projected — the *New Yorker* made a quite visible intervention into the political-cultural discourse of 9/11, both in the months immediately following the attacks and repeatedly in the years thereafter.[2] These covers have been celebrated by both the magazine's audience and critics, but this mediation needs to be viewed critically, in the immediate context of the aftermath of the attacks, the unprocessed trauma and grief, resurgent American nationalism and bellicosity, and a newfound sense of historical vulnerability and existential fear that followed the events of September 11, 2001.

Many critics have called for such an analysis of the cultural artifacts produced by 9/11, noting the need for critical work as a counternarrative to the accepted version of events. One of them is Ann Cvetkovich, who writes:

> This approach is especially urgent for the task of building cultural memory around September 11 and resisting the momentum of the culture industry, which is eager to tell a story that glorifies heroes and stresses national unity. In the United States, September 11 has already joined the pantheon of great national traumas, and I fear that its many and

heterogeneous meanings (including the fact that it is a national trauma) will be displaced by a more singular and celebratory story [472].

Such official stories rely on what Janice Haaken terms "hysterical modes of storytelling — a reliance on dramatic, emotional accounts to communicate distress" (456); and they are meant to elicit particular responses from their audience, as Fritz Breithaupt notes: "the media's staging of trauma does not so much record the human suffering that has taken place but instead serves as the central axis of organizing the diverse information material in such a way to bring about the said response in the audience" (67). As Melani McAlister, working from Benedict Anderson's concept of amnesia, notes:

> Such narratives, born of amnesias, promise to stitch together a patchwork past. They are forged not just by policy makers, but at the intersection of news accounts, policy developments, and cultural texts such as films, novels, and even video games. Of course, the "memories" constructed and reconstructed in the public sphere are never distributed evenly or unproblematically. But they *are* powerful [McAlister: 440; Anderson: 187–206, esp. 204].

When such hysterical narratives are yoked to ideologies of patriotism, nationality, militarism, and the Other — as happened in America following September 11 — then painstaking critical work is necessary to expose their strange power, to provide formal readings of their complex imagery, and to uncover the subtle processes by which historical responses to traumatic events are mediated.

Following Benjamin's and Foster's examples, we must seek to go beyond the glossy surface of the covers and their imagery to expose the ideologies — nationalist, cultural, and aesthetic — that operate both within and behind them, that both visibly and invisibly construct their meaning(s). Far from being simple memorial images, the *New Yorker* covers under discussion reveal a complex array of assumptions and attitudes, a polyvalent web of signification that looks beyond straightforward commemoration to touch on issues of kitsch, mass-produced art, middlebrow culture, and the marketing of taste, consensus, community, and memory. As fictive images, they pose questions about themselves and the other images of their cultural moment, questions like those posed by Marianne Hirsch:

> [W]hat else will we get to see? How will these pictures be used? And what images have we not seen or will we never get to see? The debates about what is and is not appropriate to show to a public in mourning are as instructive as the images themselves [86].[3]

There's a lot under the covers, then, and only by looking at them with a dialectical, nonsynchronous, *traumatic* eye — a vantage point afforded by the intervening years, indeed, necessitated by the ruined wishes and "forfeited dreams" of the New American Century and the weakening of American political, economic, cultural, and military hegemony — can we peer past the surface sheen to see what lies beneath. As Lynn Meskell enjoins, we "can attempt to mediate between the numerous agendas and interest groups and mobilize the materials of the very recent past to confront religious, national and cultural difference, and to perform a service in the public sphere" (571): despite—indeed, precisely *because of*—their multiple and overdetermined ideologies, the *New Yorker* covers can be used as tools to aid in this effort.

Between Trauma Kitsch and Memorialization

I read the *New Yorker* covers as operating between two poles of response, both public and private, that have been theorized by researchers: that of trauma kitsch and that of "legitimate" (for lack of a better word) memorialization. The first of these poles, that of kitsch, has been outlined by Marita Sturken in *Tourists of History* (2007), where she embraces a reading of kitsch that is more complex and polyvalent than the aesthetically awful, politically disengaged kitsch usually signified by the term. Sturken's kitsch is one that interacts with its historical moment in sometimes banal and sentimental, sometimes fresh and creative, ways:

> Kitsch objects from the past can also be imbued with a kind of playful engagement with history, a kind of humorous pastiche. [...] When an object of the past is labeled kitsch, it can indicate a doubled reading; that is, an object is defined as kitsch when it is seen to have an original aesthetic status that is reread as being tasteless [...] but then is recorded as valuable. [...] The challenge to understanding how kitsch operates today is to see the range of responses that it produces, to consider how it can encourage both a prepackaged sentimental response and a playful engagement, simultaneously and to varying degrees, with history, innocence, and irony [*Tourists*: 21].

As Susie O'Brien notes, "Representation is notoriously slippery [...] and even the most careful stage management of images is powerless against an audience attuned to wayward significations" (162): thus even the kitsch that dare not speak its name can be ironized, dissected, explored in the light of its multiple, often contradictory, narratives.[4]

Following Sturken, I argue that many of the post–9/11 *New Yorker* covers, however seemingly simple in intention and effect, nevertheless allow for deeper readings that push behind the crisp visuals and readymade appeals to humor and goodwill: that, whatever their intentions are to entertain and reassure, they inevitably deconstruct themselves, and offer up — in fact, invite — politicized readings that are more complex and more disturbing. Despite the presence of these other readings, however, the dominant tone of many of the covers remains that of simple kitsch, apolitical and quiescent, mirroring bourgeois verities and the "truths" of American power and goodness — a departure from the traditional, pre–9/11 mood of so many of the *New Yorker*'s covers, which are generally rich in irony, holding up a loving-yet-critical satirical mirror to familiar aspects of American life. Sturken underscores the political dangers of such kitsch when she writes:

> Most kitsch conveys a kind of deliberate and highly constructed innocence, one that dictates particular kinds of sentimental responses and emotional registers. It is meant to

produce predetermined and conscribed emotional responses, to encourage pathos and sympathy, not anger and outrage. People can deploy a range of practices in relation to kitsch objects, yet even when a kitsch object might be used by someone in a nonkitsch way it is rarely an incitement to historical reflection or political engagement [*Tourists*: 21–22].

Whatever ironic messages one may find in the *New Yorker* covers, these are, after all, consumer objects, a hybrid of artisan labor (the unique work of a human artist or artists, done largely by hand) and mass production (the reduplication of the image in print and online). They are meant primarily as packaging, as advertisement for the magazine's contents, and as the sign and indication of the magazine's reputation for quality.

A further, final word from Sturken on the political dimensions of kitsch brings into focus the importance of the seemingly depoliticized, yet ideologically teeming, *New Yorker* covers — as consumer objects that aided in a complicity with the imperialist, security-state agendas of the George W. Bush administration:

Kitsch objects address consumers within a particular emotional register (including sympathy, sadness, comfort, and the reassurance of cuteness). On one hand, these objects skirt anger, since they are couched in terms of empathy and reassurance. [...] These forms of consumer culture enable a political acquiescence, in which consumers signal their "categorical agreement" through the purchase of tokens. [...] A kitsch image or object not only embodies a particular kind of prepackaged sentiment, but conveys the message that the sentiment is universally shared, that it is appropriate, and, importantly, that *it is enough*. When this takes place in the context of politically charged sites of violence, the effect is inevitably one that reduces political complexity to simplified notions of tragedy [*Tourists*: 25–26].[5]

Similarly, Christopher P. Campbell, reading an advertisement for Budweiser that aired during the 2002 Super Bowl — in which a team of Clydesdales "gracefully genuflect in unison, heads bowed toward the distant skyline" of lower Manhattan, the missing Twin Towers a haunting presence among the still-standing buildings — notes that "the myths that the commercials sustained contributed to a nationalistic political atmosphere that restricted discussion of U.S. foreign policy and the country's response to international terrorist activity" (49). Setha M. Low directly implicates the *New Yorker* in her critique of "memorial talk," which, she notes, threatens to "overwhelm the city and all of its media. Much of this 'talk' is channeled by the *New York Times* and the *New Yorker*, the official gatekeepers of what is known about the memorial process, but their renderings are limited and exclude local discourses that do not fit the media's representation" (327).

To be sure, it is difficult to explain the exact effect cultural products have on those who consume them, or what "mobile infinity of tactics" (de Certeau: 41) consumers use in interpreting and consuming culture: nevertheless, as McAlister notes:

[C]ulture is a crucial site for the negotiation of political and moral values and for the development of an often uneven and contested public understanding of history and its significance. Cultural texts do not inject ideologies into their audiences, but they do figure in the process of constructing frameworks that help policy make sense in a given moment [441].

The *New Yorker* covers posit their readers, not as active participants in the tragedy and memorialization of 9/11, but as passive consumers of the events: the sites of memorialization are moved from the streets and parks of Manhattan — the scenes of so many impromptu gatherings and mourning services, candlelit vigils and shouted debates, in the weeks following the attacks — to domestic spaces, the home, apartment, and living room. Collective tragedy is privatized, turned into aesthetic delectation: energies released by the events — traumatic, political, social — are channeled toward catharsis, and away from historical reflection and political engagement.

That said, to overemphasize the covers' status as kitsch objects would be to deny them their other set of valences, their other pole of signification, that of legitimate memorialization: an attempt to pay tribute to loss and tragedy, to make a public space for grief, and to remember the dead. We must ask ourselves the questions posited by Dana Heller in her study of the commercialization of 9/11:

> How might we understand the selling of 9/11 as *both* a cynical manipulation of consumers engineered by powerful corporate and political interests *and* a potentially liberating and authentic expression of the people's creative energies in the face of profound grief, genuine love of country, and sudden fear of national as well as global instability? How is the marketing of 9/11 indicative of an effort to construct an economy of symbolic goods that is aligned sympathetically, on one hand, with respect for human dignity and suffering, and on the other, with global capitalism's own successful reproduction and expansion? [5].[6]

For we must recognize the sincerity of the *New Yorker* images as well as their commercialism, their direct appeals to recent historical events and their audience's likely feelings about the same. Moreover, there are qualitative differences — in intention, subject matter, technique, and complexity — between the images, drawn by educated professionals for an audience of educated professionals, and the more popular expressions of trauma kitsch such as the WTC snowglobes and teddy bears that Sturken examines (*Tourists*: 1–9). While media images, the *New Yorker* covers are at times closer in spirit to the street memorials studied by E. Ann Kaplan:

> It became one vast communal outpouring of emotion and thought. The candles and the flowers took on many different forms, reminding one partly of 1960s protest culture, partly of memorials produced when Princess Diana died. And yet this was so different; this was personal and political in new ways. Different religions were represented. But despite all the differences in perspective that the artifacts showed, an apparent commonality reigned in the form of a respect for differences within a whole (the events) that we shared [12].

The products of professional artists, the covers must not be read conspiratorially: while their images may suggest complaisance and disengagement, we must read them as sincere attempts by well-meaning men and women, many of them New Yorkers, to offer solace for communal grief — the magazine's mass-media votary candle, if you will, placed, not at shrines in the public spaces of Manhattan, but in homes and mailboxes across America and around the world. McAlister's thoughts on the subtleties of culture's interactions with those who both make and consume it are again instructive:

> What I examine here is not a conspiracy nor a set of functionalist representations in the service of power, but a process of convergence, as historical events, overlapping representations, and diverse vested interests come together in a powerful, if historically contingent, accord that is productive of a new common sense. Cultural texts enter into that process: they are integral aspects of both history and politics [441].

Grief on the Ground: Urban Shrines and Make-Believe

As noted above, an immediate response to September 11 was the spontaneous building of shrines and memorials to the dead in the parks, streets, and other public places of New York. As James B. Gardner and Sarah M. Henry write,

> In the weeks after the attacks, parts of New York City had been literally blanketed with makeshift memorials. Union Square had become a sea of candles, photographs, poems, works of art, personal memorabilia, stuffed animals, and political manifestos. It had become a virtual civic church, a place of pilgrimage, prayer, and protest [40].

These democratic, haptic, non-monumental qualities are captured in "Street Scene," Edward Sorel's moving cover for the *New Yorker*'s October 1, 2001 issue, which presents an image that sidesteps both bathos and jingoism to give a ground-level view of grief: on a busy Manhattan street the legs of passersby frame, for a brief moment, a black-and-white photograph of a dead firefighter, who looks to the left, impassively, as if watching the living going about their business around him.[7] The passersby are anonymous, undifferentiated, shown from their shoulders down to their feet; headless, they contrast with the photographic bust of the fallen fireman, who alone has a face and, while unnamed, an identity. The living appear almost ghostly, their anonymity a foil for the firefighter's unique specificity, thus suggesting the surviving community's inability to totally comprehend the immensity of the loss of his life. The converse and dominant reading, however, is one of continuity amid tragedy: an individual has died, but the community lives on. This reading is underscored by Sorel's inclusion of elements of labor, race, and class in the image, with the survivors — a white businesswoman with her bag, an African American laborer pushing a handcart — forming a cross-class, multiethnic, harmoniously functioning whole, and metonymically standing in for the cosmopolitan metropolis of New York. While this is of course an idealization, it is neither a noxious, or even particularly objectionable, one: it prettifies, but does not overlook New York's differences while portraying its post–9/11 solidarity, that spirit of shared civic renewal and concern felt by so many after the attacks. Viewed in this light, the grieved-for firefighter becomes, like Milton's Lycidas, a tutelary spirit, the genius of the Manhattan shore, watchfully guarding, like a household god or working-class Lares, his striving descendants.[8] Loss is recuperated as memory, the absent human being removed by death aesthetically reconfigured as a living, vital presence.

"Local Heroes," the October 29, 2001, cover by Peter de Sève, presents a different scene of communal mourning and memory: a group of children trick-or-treat on a city street, all of them dressed, incongruously, as either New York City firefighters or police officers. This improbability is, of course, the cover's point: rather than dress individually, the kids have all embraced the costumes of working-class heroes, most likely not as conscious acts of mourning, but through sheer childlike emulative wonder. Another quality of the dead is thus shown to have been transmitted to the survivors: not, as in Sorel's cover, the memory of an individual, but the communal roles the dead once inhabited and performed, which are at once shown to be functioning and to have been sacralized, made objects of veneration and adoration. But they are also objects of consumption, symbols bought and worn, and perforce imperfectly internalized: these are kids, after all. As Fritz Breithaupt notes of similar totemic images, "Obviously, images are not therapy. [...] [T]here is what seems to be the opposite of consciousness: a surface, a mere static image, a reflecting shield" (77).

De Sève's cover is problematic due to the discrepancy in its subject matter (the never-made-explicit events of 9/11) and its execution, especially the tone of the image. The kids' smiling, cherubic faces seem inappropriate as markers of communal loss: a romanticized angelic choir of lovably multiethnic ragamuffin boys and girls rather than realistically depicted children, it is difficult to credit them as real, as believable survivors of 9/11 who are now acting out the roles of their newfound heroes. The image is infantilizing, especially if the kids are not considered *qua* kids, but as surrogates or stand-ins for the adult community viewing the image, weary of trauma and uncertainty and hungry for such readymade examples of "comfort culture" and its simplifications and fictions: its privileging of immediacy and sentiment, its cutesiness, its disavowal of responsibility (Sturken, *Tourists*: 5–9, *passim*). The kids' costumes thus evoke their real-life costumic counterparts, the hundreds of thousands of NYPD and NYFD t-shirts and other memorabilia sold immediately after 9/11, a vast paroxysm of identification-through-consumption, sentimental memorialization, and commercialized grief. The gap between sign and symbol, the complex, recalcitrant trauma of 9/11 and its banal commercial manifestations as trinkets and items of clothing, suggest the gaps between our own experience of trauma and our ongoing attempts to narrate, mediate, and tame it. Nevertheless, de Sève's cover fails to make productive use of this gap, opting for the safely sentimentalized, innocently beaming kids playing make-believe rather than a dialectical, more self-aware study of community, identity, and memory.

Targeting the Other

The *New Yorker*'s cover of November 5, Carter Goodrich's "What So Proudly We Hailed," is both richer and more disquieting than the previous ones. Changing focus from a wounded America to America's Other, the cover raises questions of nationalism, xenophobia, and tolerance that make a straightforward comic or consolatory reading impossible. The image shows an iconic New York City yellow cab, driven by yet another New York icon: the non–Anglo, or "foreign," cabdriver, here (determined by the narrative of 9/11) a bearded Muslim man wearing a turban and a long-sleeved robe. The cabdriver hunches low in his seat; his eyes, wide with fear, stare directly at the viewer. The cab is festooned with American flags, their suctioned-cupped staves bristling from its back like a forest of spears or some nightmarish protective armor; a similar welter of American flag stickers adorns the cab's door and body. The image of commodified patriotic memorabilia, of flags and flag stickers, repurposed as apotropaic devices to ward off xenophobic retribution is a stroke of ironic genius, although Goodrich does not carry his critique to other opportunistic consumer-displayers of nationalist symbols. The foreign Other is singled out for attention, an aesthetic strategy eerily at one with both the hyper-aggressive police actions taken against Muslims, Arabs, and other "non–Westerners" directly after 9/11, as well as with the many acts of hate crimes, harassment, and other acts of victimization (Ahmad; Leonard; Moore; Hassan). There is no broader context given that would show the cabdriver acting with the crowd, of assuming the garb of patriotic display, like so many Washington politicians donning flag pins. Indeed, what is interesting, given the general "United We Stand" tenor of the mass media after 9/11, is that there is no suggestion that the cabdriver's show of patriotism, however overdone, might be *genuine*, that he, like many Americans and citizens of other nations, ranging across cultural and ideological spectrums, spontaneously embraced these patriotic tokens as visible signs of pride in the United States. If *Le Monde*'s front-page editorial of September 12 read "Nous sommes tous Américains," clearly by November 5 United States citizens were thinking differently, and were participating cross-culturally, across a wide variety of discourses, in a conversation about America and its Others, who was in and who was out, who was, in the words of President George W. Bush, "with us" and who was against.

Questions about Goodrich's sympathies toward the cabdriver, and related questions about our own, also intrude on "What So Proudly We Hailed," further complicating it, further revealing it as a contested site of cultural and ideological ambiguities. Are we meant to empathize with the cabdriver's obvious fear? Or are we meant to laugh at his plight? Is his overcompensating for his non-white American appearance in the form of hyper–American ostentatious consumption supposed to be funny, touching, sad, or a combination of all three? Is the cabdriver a United States citizen, and how might we know this? Are we perhaps meant to fear the cabdriver, to read in his fear not the signs of affrighted innocence but a look of terrified guilt: is he another Mohammed Atta, hiding in plain sight while waiting, patiently, to strike? These questions are obviously unanswerable from the data presented by the image, but such is the overdetermined role of the Muslim male in American society — as outsider, as threat, as Other — that the cabdriver becomes a kind of reflector of our own cultural prejudices: not a blank slate onto which we project anything we want, but a kind of composite of our already-formed, inherited cultural prejudices, from which we take those elements that seem uppermost. What is certain is that the image exhibits a marked lack of empathy for the cabdriver, and thus suggests a similar lack of identification on the part of the viewer. Whatever his motivations, the cabdriver is portrayed as a dissimulator, a faker, a fraud, i.e., not "one of us," not one of the "real" Americans grieving communally over a shared trauma. He remains outside the focus of our sympathies but is made a conscious target of our attention as a possible threat and a tantalizing ambiguity. The ambiguity extends even to Goodrich's title, either a grudging nod to cabdrivers' continued usefulness, or an outright mockery of the driver's pretensions to Americanness: are we really proud to hail the driver, to recognize in him our double, our secret sharer across national and cultural boundaries? Is our hailing of him a simple command to a servile Other, or is it a recognition of our shared humanity with the Other? Goodrich's image refuses to decide, and its ambivalence remains interpretable as a sign of aesthetic richness, a guarded show of tolerance, or a crass display of xenophobia — or even some hybrid of all three.

Escape from "New Yorkistan"

Certainly the richest, most polyvalent, and most potentially disturbing of the post 9/11 *New Yorker* covers is also the most famous: the much-celebrated "New Yorkistan" cover for December 10, 2001, in which collaborators Maira Kalman and Rick Meyerowitz refashion the wounded city as a cross between New York City and Afghanistan, the American-led invasion of which latter had begun, with much public approval, on October 7. The first stage of the American invasion was well over by the issue's publication date, the decisive Battle of Mazar-I Sharif having been won in November, with the capital, Kabul, falling to Western forces shortly thereafter. According to a *New York Times* article from December 10, "The five-year rule of the Taliban, exceptionally harsh even in a land governed for decades by bloodletting, came to an official end today as the last Afghan province slipped from their control" (Rohde and Schmitt). A few days after the issue's publication, Osama bin Laden would elude American forces through the complex cave systems of Tora-Bora. The cover appeared at a critical time in American history, with the shock and grief occasioned on September 11 still fresh in the public mind, but with many of the issues that would come to dominate the political discourse of the next decade — the projection of American power abroad, for reasons of both expansion and security; the nation's embrace, if not totally of its imperial destiny, then largely of its imperialistic activities; debates over the use of "hard" over "soft" power; and so on — beginning to form in public discourse (LaFeber).

"New Yorkistan" is thus a pivotal, liminal document that records an ambivalent response to September 11 and its attendant events, one that uses the optic of imaginary cartography to address a set of very real and very troubling issues. It is an uncanny doc-

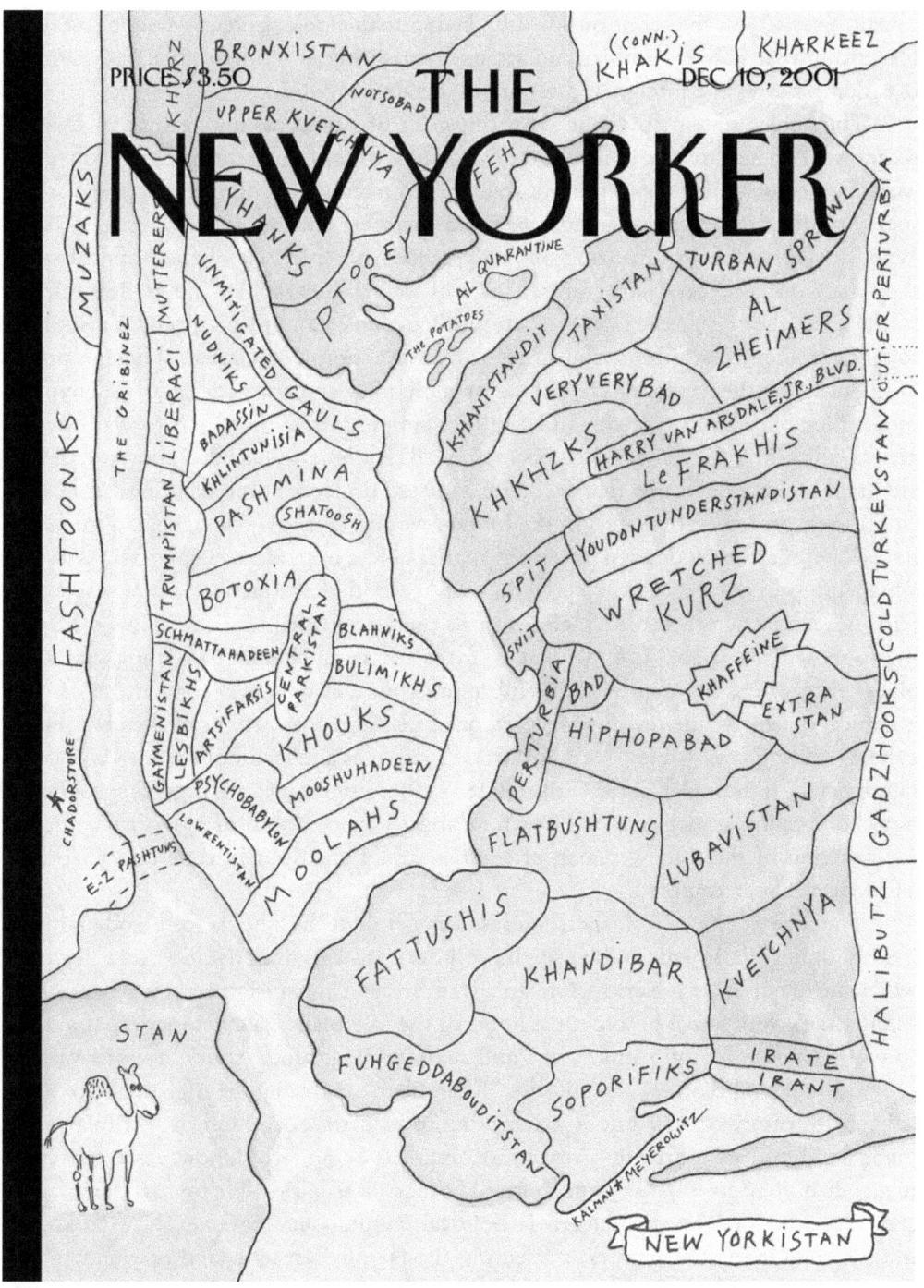

"New Yorkistan," the most famous *The New Yorker* cover of December 12, 2001. Drawing by Kalman & Meyerowitz, © Condé Nast Publications.

ument, precisely in the terms outlined by Heischman's look at Freud's famous essay on the uncanny: it is both familiar and strange, reassuring and provocative, a document that domesticates the foreign and estranges the already known.

The choice of a map as the cover image is of particular importance in light of recent work that scholars of maps and cartography have done in the field, and what this work has demonstrated about the culturally constructed nature of maps and the work — social, political, ideological — such maps do for their creators (Harley, esp.: 149–68; Wood). Maps are far from being perfectly objective depictions of the physical space they chart; rather, they chart cultural space as well as geographic, and are less mirrors to the lands they represent than they are aesthetic lenses and ideological prisms, prone to exaggerations, distortions, and other narrative fictions. As Graham Huggan points out, "maps, by their very nature, are never more than approximations of the environments they purport to represent" (3); in the "simple formulation" put forward by the general editors of *The History of Cartography*, J. B. Harley and David Woodward, "Maps are graphic representations that facilitate a spatial understanding of things, concepts, conditions, processes, or events in the human world" (xvi). As Thongchai Winichakul notes, "[A] map is a code for a presumed spatial object in modern geography. As a sign, a map appropriates a spatial object by its own method of abstraction in a new sign system. A map encodes a space which, in turn, can be decoded to disclose knowledge of the supposed real space" (54–5), that is, maps tell as much about their makers as the places they ostensibly depict, depicting more contours of power than those of geographical space.[9] While the obvious cartoonishness and abstractions of the map render a literal reading impossible, "New Yorkistan"'s status as a reflector of the corrosive community created through trauma (Erikson: 188–90) is important: this is psychogeography, not chorography, a map, not of New York and its exurbia, but of a particular mental construction of the same — a map of trauma, and a snapshot in time of a particular effort to reconcile trauma.[10]

The joke of "New Yorkistan," and its key comic technique, is to re-code familiar New York neighborhoods and boroughs with foreign-sounding names, the majority of which are drawn from America's foreign adventures in Afghanistan and elsewhere: thus, Manhattan's Wall Street becomes the home of the "Moolahs," a combination of *moolah* (literally "money," origin unknown) and *mullah* (an Islamic cleric); a vast swath of central Brooklyn becomes, inexplicably, "Khandibar," marrying the Afghan city of Kandahar with candy bars. While it is tempting to read the cover and its wordplay as so much good fun, as a normally-isolationist America's being forced, however unwillingly, to glance beyond its linguistic and cultural borders, it is impossible to miss the imagery and text's other valences, particularly its political-cultural ones. For one, "New Yorkistan" is a heavily Orientalizing work, presenting the far-off East as a land of wonders and dangers, of exoticism and adventure, "the site of dreams, images, fantasies, myths, obsessions, and requirements" (Bhabha: 71; Said).[11] It is also a site of Otherness, here presented comically in the welter of supposedly funny non–English toponyms. This linguistic-cultural Otherness is domesticated by the semantic root of each name, which all bespeak a locality that is irreducibly American and New Yorkish. The cover invites us to look at the once-familiar locations of New York through a scrim of the foreign, the places retaining their uniquely American stamp yet inflected with a taste of the exotic Other. In a superficial sense, the Other has invaded the space of America, as the terrorists violated American security with the destruction of the Twin Towers: but in a far more important sense, the image suggests that the Other has been tamed, domesticated, imported, Americanized.

Like any Orientalizing work, "New Yorkistan" must be read with an eye toward colonial and postcolonial ideologies, as a map, not of the "real" New York or the "real" Afghanistan, but of an imaginary intermixture of the same, a colonialist pastiche of the newly conquered foreign lands inflecting the homeland with their captured spice and richness. As Alfred Hiatt notes, "[I]f maps are the measure of the colony — if they both serve and enable colonial vision — they are also colonialism's detritus, what is left behind for the postcolony to work with, to redraw, and to comprehend itself" (48): "New Yorkistan," then, as both America's greeting-card and surrender-leaflet, the imagistic counterpart to the 2,400,000 Pop-Tarts (ersatz food, colonialist and nutritive "detritus") dropped on starving Afghanis during the invasion from the American bombers flying overhead (Harper's Index).[12] This pastiche of colonialist-imperialist synthesis fails, historical ironies to which we are privy suggesting that this uneasy alliance of empire with Other will not last. From the vantage point of 2010, "New Yorkistan" appears far less the cosmopolitan metropolis of the twentieth century — the "actual," historical New York — or as the utopian global American Empire foreseen by neoconservatives. Instead, "New Yorkistan" reminds us of the partitioned, war-scarred, tribalized dystopian city of the new millennium: not the Big Apple (however Orientalized) but Grozny, Kabul, Baghdad.

While it would be unfair to overstate or to actively misread the overdetermined fictions of "New Yorkistan" as an active embrace of the attitudes displayed therein, the presence and formal functioning of these ambiguities needs to be discussed, especially because of the image's public canonization as beyond politics. It needs to be noted that these ambiguities have been disavowed by one of the cover's artists, Maira Kalman, whose statements about "New Yorkistan," consciously or not, have framed the image as mere entertainment and reassurance. At a New York Public Library lecture on April 1, 2002,[13] she noted that the cover "was a lot of fun to do," and dispensed a homespun nostrum concerning the need for humor in adverse situations:

> It was the ability to be able to say, at a moment when things were very grave and really dismal, that there's never ever a time when humor doesn't help you through. I mean, the worse things get, the more you need your sense of humor. And that's probably one of the most important messages that I have in my books — if you don't have humor, you're dead. So this cover, we got hundreds and hundreds of letters and e-mails, and, of course, they made a poster out of it, and most people really thought it was very funny; only a few people said, "How dare you, how dare you make fun at a time like this," and I think, My God, that's a terrible thing to hear [Kalman].

The typing of criticism as always already ignorant carping, as self-evidently "terrible," is telling, a personally aggrieved response that functions to exclude politics from the debate. A *New York Times* review of Kalman's work echoes her unreflecting, keep-your-chin-up tone, noting that "her depictions here of radiant fruit bowls, pink bedrooms and people in flamboyant hats make the case that our consolations for loss, bewilderment and impending death are beauty, humor and surprise," and lauding her for being "very witty, particularly in the face of the grim and the unsolvable." With the article's crediting "New Yorkistan" as "the first joke that was funny after 9/11" (Levy) the apotheosis is complete: the image has been removed from the immediate contexts of the politics of trauma, memory, and mourning, and translated to the realm of classic works of art, a pioneering joke that ushered in a new sensibility for a troubled age — a sensibility curiously nostalgic and incurious about its own constructed origins, a pastiche of nativism, nationalism, exoticism, and sentimentalism, but a sensibility nevertheless.

"New Yorkistan" was an immediate success, both popularly and critically, yet there was something uncritical about all the adoration: a *New York Times* article from December 8, 2001 gushes, "When their cover came out, suddenly a dark cloud seemed to lift. New Yorkers were mad for the map. They laughed. They shared it" (Boxer). Indeed, "they shared it" in more ways than one, with the Cartoon Bank — the *New Yorker*'s online image service — quickly offering poster reproductions of the cover in both unframed and framed versions; these were followed by the "New Yorkistan" shower curtain, jigsaw puzzle, t-shirt, notecards (personalized or non-), even an eponymous jazz song.[14] "New Yorkistan"'s polymorphous ability to reproduce itself across media is only partly attributable to its popularity, however; clearly, its "flat and naïve" (Boxer) aesthetic, visual simplicity, and its steadfast refusal of the political all allow its commercial metamorphosis into new, unforeseen, hopelessly kitschy manifestations. As Benedict Anderson notes, colonial maps made similar journeys, going from models of the real world to become "pure sign, no longer compass to the world. In this shape, the map entered an infinitely reproducible series, available for transfer to posters, official seals, letterheads, magazine and textbook covers, tablecloths, and hotel walls" (175). As Meskell notes:

> We are witnessing the desire for grounded materiality at a staggering rapidity, to apprehend the objects and physical signs of a newfound heritage in real and tangible ways. This familiar desire for material commemoration and the physical marking of the event is juxtaposed against the realization that the attacks (and the subsequent war on Afghanistan) have been experienced through virtual means [559].

The officially-licensed shower curtain is a perfect symbol of this process, and an ironic comment on the uneasy marriage of mass-produced capitalist art with America's post–9/11 security craze: a domestic hygienic-prophylactic device, designed to keep stray water, soap, hair, and other detritus off the bathroom rugs and tiles, on which is printed a similarly prophylactic symbolic image, one designed to channel anxiety and political uncertainty humor, acceptance, and quiescence.

Conclusion

The commercial cross-platforming of this "all is well" message is another kitsch moment, with the "New Yorkistan" image proliferating almost to the point of self-parody, its original messages buried beneath the weight of their various reproductions. Note again the limiting of available responses to consumption, from sharing an image and discussing it — a not necessarily political act, but at least a start — to mere owning.[15] What Sturken has called the "tyranny of meaning" ("Aesthetics": 312) surrounding 9/11 has become the tyranny of non-meaning, of meanings suffocated by nostalgic kitsch and the blandishments of mass consumption. We are left to grapple with the groundlessness, resistance to closure, and mediatedness of our postmodern traumatic grief, left, as Frederic Jameson writes, "to seek History by way of our own pop images and simulacra of that history, which itself remains forever out of reach" (25). Decoding the *New Yorker* covers and their attendant consumer artifacts provides, if not a way to combat directly the simulacra created by power and ideology, then at least a way to show how simulacra operate, an exposure of their highly fictive claims to represent reality. What we do with this knowledge — whether we use it to make similar critical readings of our own present-day simulacra, fictions, deceptions, and outright lies, or whether we are content merely to consume our own critiques, removed from the broader discourses surrounding our work — is up to us.

One way forward is suggested by the furor surrounding another *New Yorker* cover, Barry Blitt's July 28, 2008, parody of the controversy surrounding Barack and Michelle Obama's famous "terrorist fist dap." In the image Barack Obama is wearing Muslim clothes, Michelle Obama the militant style of the 1960s Black Panthers, both costume Blitt's biting commentary on the slew of nativist and racist invective that swarmed around Senator Obama during the election. The image generated a firestorm of controversy, with Blitt's and the *New Yorker*'s editors criticized for, if not outright endorsing, then uncomfortably depicting, the stereotypical, denigratory images of the Other with which the American Right mocked the candidate. Remnick's response to the criticism is instructive:

> Obviously I wouldn't have run a cover just to get attention — I ran the cover because I thought it had something to say. What I think it does is hold up a mirror to the prejudice and dark imaginings about Barack Obama's — both Obamas' — past, and their politics. I can't speak for anyone else's interpretations, all I can say is that it combines a number of images that have been propagated, not by everyone on the right but by some, about Obama's supposed "lack of patriotism" or his being "soft on terrorism" or the idiotic notion that somehow Michelle Obama is the second coming of the Weathermen or most violent Black Panthers. That somehow all this is going to come to the Oval Office. [...] This is saying a particular thing at a particular time, when these imaginings and dark fantasies and misconceptions about Obama exist. And we're putting it all together in one image and holding a mirror up to it and showing it for it for the absurdity that it is [Sklar].

If, then, the 9/11 *New Yorker* covers failed to receive the kind of wide public attention that Blitt's "terrorist" cover did, there is nothing necessary or predetermined about this. Certainly the variables between the two cases — a time of national crisis versus a national election; an issue, 9/11, on which there was near-total uniformity, at least of sentiment, among Americans versus one, Barack Obama's legitimacy and patriotism, about which there were (and still are) multiple contradictory, at times clashing, viewpoints; the vaguer, safer, simpler truths of nationalism, homeland, and country versus the disturbing, uncomfortable, complex questions of race, ethnicity, and gender; the powerful but still growing Internet of 2001 versus the ubiquitous social media of the Web 2.0 in 2008 — played a large part in the reception of the 9/11 covers and the "terrorist" one. Taken as a whole, both receptions suggest — one negatively, the other hopefully — the multiple ways in which imagery, politics, ideology, consumption, and critique co-existed and interacted in a single form of mass media during the first decade of the twenty-first century.

Notes

1. Like many weekly magazines, the *New Yorker* is on sale and delivered to subscribers about a week in advance of its cover date.

2. It has become a staple of the magazine to commemorate the anniversary of 9/11 with a cover specifically devoted to the attacks: due to considerations of space, these annual commemorative covers will not be discussed in this essay. The 9/11 covers, taken as a whole, constitute a rare and remarkable exception to the standard style of *New Yorker* covers — ironic, emotionally distant, satirical, even arch — a standard that was quickly resumed, and has been largely followed, since 2002, some three months after 9/11. See, for example, the cover of February 10, 2003, or of December 19, 2005: while still humorous, these images continue the vein of pathos, patriotism, and pride so noticeable in the 9/11 covers.

3. While Hirsch is discussing photography, her questions apply equally as well to other kinds of images.

4. This is especially the case for an audience such as the *New Yorker*'s, one attuned to and appreciative of irony, nuance, and wit, and one open to arguments and opinions coming from the left of the political spectrum. Note, however, that the *New Yorker*'s cover images have a much wider cultural orbit than the magazine's contents, and are seen — on newsstands, in reproductions, on the Internet — by many viewers who might never read the magazine itself.

5. Italics in the original. This is not to suggest that the *New Yorker*'s editors or staff were explicitly or implicitly acting in support of the Bush Administration, only that the covers under discussion were part of the outpouring of sentimentalized, jingoistic, America-first propaganda that dominated the media after 9/11, and that (much of it intentionally, much of it not) directly and indirectly supported the Bush regime's political and military goals. Certainly David Remnick, the *New Yorker*'s editor, has often been critical of the Bush regime, as in his response to the furor surrounding Barry Blitt's 2008 cover depicting Barack and Michelle Obama as terrorists. "We've run many many satirical political covers. Ask the Bush administration how many" (Sklar).

6. Italics in the original.

7. Copyright and image-reproduction costs prevent many of the images discussed in this article from being reproduced here. Readers are encouraged to look up the covers in on an online search engine.

8. Cf. Whitman's sympathetic assumption of the persona of an injured firefighter in the 1855 *Leaves of Grass*:

> I am the mash'd fireman with breast-bone broken,
> Tumbling walls buried me in their debris,
> Heat and smoke I inspired, I heard the yelling shouts of my comrades,
> I heard the distant click of their picks and shovels,
> They have clear'd the beams away, they tenderly lift me forth. [...]
> Distant and dead resuscitate,
> They show as the dial or move as the hands of me,
> I am the clock myself.

In both the cover image and in Milton's and Whitman's poems, loss is recuperated by an act of aesthetic imagination that is grounded in a spirit of communal poetics.

9. The use of maps as tools of power and empire must be stressed here, particularly the defining turn toward scientific cartography during the beginning of European colonialism in the early modern period. "New Yorkistan" thus suggests itself as a map, not only of the fear and anxiety of the postcolonial Other that invaded the United States after 9/11—imaged here in the exotic names, on which more below—but also of the "imperial conquest" of the United States by its own unbridled power and expansionist policies post–9/11.

10. For more on *psychogeography*, cf. Debord: 5: "*Psychogeography* could set for itself the study of the precise laws and specific effects of the geographical environment, consciously organized or not, on the emotions and behavior of individuals. The adjective *psychogeographical*, retaining a rather pleasing vagueness, can thus be applied to the findings arrived at by this type of investigation, to their influence on human feelings, and even more generally to any situation or conduct that seems to reflect the same spirit of discovery."

11. In this "New Yorkistan" joins a long line of *New Yorker* covers, most famously Saul Steinberg's "View of the World from Ninth Avenue" (March 29, 1976), which shows New York the way a hypothetical *echt* New Yorker would see it: as the cosmopolitan mecca of the world, with the rest of North America a thin strip of arid land bounded on the west by the Pacific Ocean. Thus "New Yorkistan" also manages to satirize New Yorkers' pretensions to centrality and uniqueness even as it seeks to mediate their shock and grief over 9/11.

12. Harpers' Index cites the "Defense Security Cooperation Agency (Arlington, Va.)" as their source for the two-million-plus Pop-Tarts. Cf. O'Brien: 162–63: "In media reports of the conflict in Afghanistan, one of the representations that proved least amenable to state control was the image of Western aid efforts in the form of massive food drops. Notwithstanding earnest efforts to paint the relationship between charity and war as not contradictory but complementary, in their mutual goal of liberating the Afghan people from the scourges of hunger and fundamentalism, the image of women and children tiptoeing through fields laced with landmines to pick up their rations of Pop-Tarts and peanut butter *resonates with meanings that the official frame cannot finally contain. The only way we can begin to read the significance of these pictures is by adopting an ironic perspective*" (my italics).

13. The *New Yorker* website erroneously dates the lecture as having happened in 2001, which would make it too early for the events of 9/11, and thus too early for "New Yorkistan." The New York Public Library's own Press Information correctly dates the event: http://www.nypl.org/press/2002/pepspring2002.cfm.

14. Kalman herself has stated that Remnick owns the original of "New Yorkistan" (Harmanci). Remnick's advocacy and eventual ownership of the image suggests an identification with and interest in the cover that goes beyond the simply editorial. As Francoise Mouly, the *New Yorker*'s art editor, recalls, "I showed ['New Yorkistan'] to David Remnick ... *and he said it was so great that we should put it on the cover*" (Herschthal: italics mine).

15. Note, however, that "New Yorkistan"'s transmigration from magazine cover to shower curtain, does not mean that the image was read uncritically in its original form, or even in its later, more commodified ones. But it certainly suggests a moving from a paradigm of consumption as aesthetic delectation, critique, and debate (the cover) to a paradigm of consumption as commerce, ownership, and daily use (the shower curtain). One might indeed critically parse the "New Yorkistan" shower curtain during one's daily ablutions, but this is not likely the primary use its owners have for it.

Works Cited

Ahmad, Muneer. "Homeland Insecurities: Racial Violence the Day after September 11." *Social Text* 72 (2002): 101–15.

Anderson, Benedict. *Imagined Communities*. (2nd ed.). New York: Verso Books, 1999.

Benjamin, Walter. "Surrealism: The Last Snapshot of the European Intelligentsia." *In* Michael W. Jennings, Howard Eiland, and Gary Smith (Eds.). Rodney Livingstone, et al. (Trans.). *Selected Writings, Volume 2: 1927–1934*. Cambridge: The Belknap Press of Harvard University Press, 1999: 207–21.

Bhabha, Homi K. *The Location of Culture*. London: Routledge, 1994.

Boxer, Sarah. "A Funny New Yorker Map Is Again the Best Defense." *The New York Times*. December 8, 2001. July 29, 2009. http://www.nytimes.com/2001/12/08/arts/design/08NOTE.html?ex=1008820507&ei=1.

Breithaupt, Fritz. "Rituals of Trauma: How the Media Fabricated September 11." *In* Steven Chermak, Frankie Y. Bailey, and Michelle Brown (Eds.). *Media Representations of September 11*. Westport, CT: Praeger, 2003: 67–81.

Campbell, Christopher P. "Commodifying September 11: Advertising, Myth, and Hegemony." *In* Steven Chermak, Frankie Y. Bailey, and Michelle Brown (Eds.). *Media Representations of September 11*. Westport, CT: Praeger, 2003: 47–65.

Certeau, Michel de. *The Practice of Everyday Life*. Steven Rendall (Trans.). Berkeley: University of California Press, 1984.

Cvetkovich, Ann. "9–11 Every Day." *Signs 28.1, Gender and Cultural Memory* (2002): 471–473.

Debord, Guy. "Introduction to a Critique of Urban Geography." *In* Ken Knabb (Ed. and Trans). *Situationist International Anthology*. Berkeley: The Bureau of Public Secrets, 1981: 5–8.

Erikson, Kai. "Notes on Trauma and Community." *In* Cathy Caruth (Ed.). *Trauma: Explorations in Memory*. Baltimore: The Johns Hopkins University Press, 1995: 183–199.

Foster, Hal. *Compulsive Beauty*. Cambridge: The MIT Press, 1993.

_____. *Design and Crime (and Other Diatribes)*. New York: Verso Books, 2003.

Haaken, Janice. "Cultural Amnesia: Memory, Trauma, and War." *Signs 28.1, Gender and Cultural Memory* (2002): 455–457.

Harley, J. B., and David Woodward. "Preface." *In* J.B. Harley, and David Woodward (Eds.). *The History of Cartography, Volume One: Cartography in Prehistoric, Ancient and Medieval Europe and the Mediterranean*. Chicago: University of Chicago Press, 1987: xv–xxi.

Harley, J. B., and Paul Laxton (Eds.). *The New Nature of Maps: Essays in the History of Cartography*. Baltimore: The Johns Hopkins University Press, 2001.

Harmanci, Reyhan. "Maira Kalman: Artist, Journalist, British Pea Enthusiast." *The Bay Citizen*. July 1, 2010. July 30, 2010. http://www.baycitizen.org/blogs/pulse-of-the-bay/maira-kalman-someone-bring-lady-can-peas/.

Harper's Index. January 2002. July 29, 2009. http://harpers.org/index/2002/1/39.

Hassan, Salah D. "Arabs, Race and the Post–September 11 National Security State." *Middle East Report* 224 (2002): 16–21.

Heischman, Daniel R. "The Uncanniness of September 11th." *Journal of Religion and Health* 41.3 (2002): 197–205.

Heller, Dana. "Introduction: Consuming 9/11." *In* Dana Heller. *The Selling of 9/11: How a National Tragedy Became a Commodity*. New York: Palgrave Macmillan, 2005: 1–26.

Herschthal, Eric. "The Pursuits of Maira Kalman." *The Jewish Week*. April 7, 2010. July 30, 2010. http://www.thejewishweek.com/arts/arts_guide/pursuits_maira_kalman.

Hirsch, Marianne. "I Took Pictures: September 2001 and Beyond." *In* Judith Greenberg (Ed.). *Trauma at Home: After 9/11*. Lincoln: University of Nebraska Press, 2003: 69–86.

Huggan, Graham. *Territorial Disputes: Maps and Mapping Strategies in Contemporary Canadian and Australian Fiction*. Toronto: University of Toronto Press, 1994.

Jameson, Fredric. *Posmodernism, or, The Cultural Logic of Late Capitalism*. Durham: Duke University Press, 1991.

Kalman, Maira. "How to Conquer Stupidity." *The New Yorker Online.* May 7, 2001, misdated. July 29, 2009. http://www.newyorker.com/archive/2001/05/07/slideshow_010506?slide=17#showHeader.

Kaplan, E. Ann. *Trauma Culture: The Politics of Terror and Loss in Media and Literature.* New Brunswick, NJ: Rutgers University Press, 2005.

LaFeber, Walter. "The Post–September 11 Debate Over Empire, Globalization, and Fragmentation." *Political Science Quarterly* 117.1 (2002): 1–17.

Leonard, Karen. "American Muslims, before and after September 11, 2001." *Economic and Political Weekly* 37.24 (2002): 2293–2297, 2299–2302.

Levy, Ariel. "Painted Whimsies." *The New York Times.* February 17, 2008. July 29, 2009. http://www.nytimes.com/2008/02/17/books/review/Levy-t.html?_r=1&scp=1&sq=painted%20whimsies&st=cse.

Low, Setha M. "The Memorialization of September 11: Dominant and Local Discourses on the Rebuilding of the World Trade Center Site." *American Ethnologist* 31.3 (2004): 326–339.

McAlister, Melani. "A Cultural History of the War without End." *The Journal of American History* 89.2, *History and September 11: A Special Issue* (2002): 439–455.

Meskell, Lynn. "Negative Heritage and Past Mastering in Archaeology." *Anthropological Quarterly* 75.3 (2002): 557–74.

Moore, Kathleen. "A Part of U.S. or Apart from U.S.?: Post–September 11 Attitudes toward Muslims and Civil Liberties." *Middle East Report* 224 (2002): 32–35.

O'Brien, Susie. "On Death and Donuts: Irony and Ecology After September 11." *Cultural Critique* 58 (2004): 148–67.

Rohde, David, and Eric Schmitt. "Taliban Give Way in Final Province Where They Ruled." *The New York Times.* December 10, 2001. July 29, 2009. http://www.nytimes.com/2001/12/10/world/nation-challenged-ground-war-taliban-give-way-final-province-where-they-ruled.html?scp=1&sq=ground&st=nyt.

Said, Edward W. *Orientalism.* New York: Vintage Books, 1979.

Sklar, Rachel. "David Remnick on that New Yorker Cover: It's Satire, Meant to Target 'Distortions and Misconceptions and Prejudices' about Obama." *The Huffington Post.* July 21, 2008. July 30, 2010. http://www.huffingtonpost.com/2008/07/13/david-remnick-on-emnew-yo_n_112456.html.

Sturken, Marita. "The Aesthetics of Absence: Rebuilding Ground Zero." *American Ethnologist* 31.3 (2004): 311–25.

_____. *Tourists of History: Memory, Kitsch, and Consumerism from Oklahoma City to Ground Zero.* Durham: Duke University Press, 2007.

Winichakul, Thongchai. *Siam Mapped: A History of the Geo-Body of a Nation.* Honolulu: University of Hawai'i Press, 1997.

Wood, Denis. *The Power of Maps.* New York: The Guilford Press, 1992.

Spandex Agonistes
Superhero Comics Confront the War on Terror
Matthew J. Costello

The 9/11 attacks on the World Trade Center and Pentagon were immediately seen as a major event fraught with cultural significance, and have become what Jan Assman calls a "figure of memory," a "fateful event [...] of the past" whose "memory is maintained through cultural formation [...] and institutional communication" (129). Such figures of memory become cultural battlegrounds for competing visions of national identity, redefining the present by constructing a memory of the past. This is particularly important in moments of national crisis, because, as Wulf Kansteiner suggests, "memory is valorized where identity is problematized" (184). It was in such a moment of identity crisis that the attacks occurred. A decade after the collapse of the Soviet Union, the United States was still searching to define itself globally without the communist other serving as its justification. The attacks seemed to provide the occasion for redefining the global role of the U.S.; containing communism would be replaced by the War on Terror as the driving force behind America's global policy.

Attributing such a meaning to the events of 9/11 became a preoccupation of officials almost immediately after the attacks. Patricia Leavy argues that a hegemonic definition of the attacks was created by the Bush administration and a compliant media. "The most relevant dimension of 9/11 reporting is the extent to which it reinforced and legitimized the 'official story' constructed by the Bush administration. [...] [J]ournalists reported on the event within a socio-political context in which dissent was viewed as unpatriotic" (86). This "official story" was one of senseless violence perpetrated by evildoers against the good Americans (92). Such a characterization, she claims, rendered the attacks outside the realm of politics, and made it impossible to question the extent to which American foreign policy might have provoked the attacks (93).

Leavy may be too hard on the media, casting them as co-conspirators in the government's definition of the significance of 9/11. She notes that the creation of collective memory of events is linked to the narratives of national identity that are constantly being renegotiated (90). It is likely, then, that the media would draw on existing identity constructs to frame the 9/11 narrative. Tom Engelhardt identifies the one key narrative of American national identity as the American war story. In this story a community of innocents suffers a massacre at the hands of (generally non-white) barbarians. The community then rises up in its holy wrath to wreck vengeance on the attackers, utterly destroying them. Lawrence and Jewitt offer a similar narrative of national identity in their "American heroic monomyth." The attacks of 9/11 and the early government and popular response to the events clearly had attributes of this story. Elements of these narratives of innocence versus savagery, of a virtuous "us" versus an immoral "them" appear in President Bush's televised address of 9/11, 2001, in which he identified the perpetrators of the attacks as "evil-doers" who struck at an innocent America of "moms and dads, neighbors and friends," because it was "the brightest beacon for freedom and opportunity in the world," followed by an extended reference to the 23rd Psalm (Bush). This Manichean construct of the events laid the foundation for justifying an all-out military response.

Leavy's "official" story, however, was not common to all media, and the continuing conflict over the meaning of the 9/11 attacks suggests that how 9/11 is remembered remains contested terrain. Superhero comic books early and consistently cast doubts on this portrayal of both the attacks and the chauvinistic, nationalist response that Leavy sees as the media's story. Superhero comics developed a 9/11 narrative that specifically challenged this story in two key aspects. First, the attacks are not characterized as a blameless massacre of innocents by savages; instead the American government is often implicated in the attacks, either through explicit action or through accumulated grievances. This renders ambiguous the moral role of America and generates the second challenge — the portrayal of the American response not as a morally righteous act, but as the product of nationalist hubris. Confronting a post-national conflict in terms of nation and state creates a contradiction at the very heart of cultural constructs of the 9/11 attacks and war on terror, making it difficult to sustain the myth of national exceptionalism and moral virtue. These two elements — U.S. culpability in the 9/11 attacks and the problematic nationalist response — are central to how superhero comics remember 9/11.

This essay examines several popular superhero comic books in the wake of the 9/11 attacks. Drawn from both major (Marvel and DC) and less well known publishers, the books reflect the breadth of the contemporary field of superhero comics. The emphasis will be largely on the narrative elements of the story rather than the art, since the ideological component of the stories is more directly offered in the speech of the characters. By examining the way the attacks of 9/11 are remembered in this broad selection of texts, this essay will demonstrate the challenge posed to Leary's "official story" within superhero comics.

Superheroes and National Security Crusades

Superhero comics have had their greatest popularity as chauvinistic supporters of national security crusades. Early superhero comics, originating during the Great Depression (notably Superman) often expressed a populist and libertarian disdain for the rich and the powerful. The stories quickly developed a nationalist stance as the medium's popularity exploded during the Second World War, often leading the calls for American intervention.[1] The two periods of greatest popularity of the superhero comic — the 1940s and the late 1960s and early 1970s — coincide with the two great national security crusades of the mid-to-late twentieth century — World War II and the Cold War. While comic books grew increasingly critical of American society in the 1970s, they rarely veered from their nationalist support for Cold War policies (see Costello). This nationalist impulse in superhero comics was reflected in the earliest treatments of 9/11, portraying the attacks as a national tragedy in some of the stories and in a series of books issued to raise money for the victims of the attacks (see Jenkins). Within the books themselves, however, 9/11 was set in the context of the subsequent War on Terror and used narratively and metaphorically to question the very socio-political context that Leavy claims was outside the realm of political discourse. While the comics themselves faced some of this labeling (Medved), there was much less support for the "official story" and more willingness to challenge the actions that followed the event.

Within superhero comics, a common narrative developed in the early treatments of 9/11 as real and metaphorical events. The elements of this narrative included an attack on American innocents by a foreign entity causing great damage and/or many deaths. Government responses proved inadequate, and the superheroes needed to intervene to defend against further attacks. This narrative bears a resemblance to Jewitt and Lawrence's American heroic monomyth, but with profound differences. Where Jewitt and Lawrence see the heroic narrative as leading ultimately to the redemption of the virtuous American community, rarely is redemption achieved in the 9/11 narrative. This failure to redeem reflects the conflict between assertions of mythic American innocence and virtue and the reality of a half century global actions from Guatemala to Iran to Vietnam to Chile in pursuit of containing communism. In the 9/11 superhero narrative, rather than being innocent, the Americans are portrayed as complicit in the attacks. This often takes the form of product of U.S. militarism, which manufactures the technology by which the attacks are carried out. The stories often reference past actions of the U.S. government — particularly global interventions during the Cold War — as generating the grievances of the attackers. The intervention of the superhero is often cast in ambiguous terms. Rather than redeeming the nation, heroes' nationalist responses are often counterproductive. Only some form of multilateral action, and one based on understanding the foe rather than vilifying him as a barbarian, can prove successful. The culpability of the U.S. and the failure of nationalist responses suggest that there can be no redemption for the American nation, leaving the moral outcome of the narrative ambiguous.

The 9/11 Narrative in Superhero Comics: U.S. Culpability and the Loss of American Innocence

"Enemy" was the first story arc in the rebooted *Captain America* volume 4, beginning in 2002. Writer John Ney Rieber was influenced by the attacks of September 11 and wanted the first story to raise questions about America in their wake (Bartle). The story opens with Captain America's alter ego, Steve Rogers, sifting through the rubble of the World Trade Center, looking for survivors. When asked by superspy Nick Fury where he was when the attacks happened Rogers replies, "Not here." Captain America is subsequently drawn into a hunt for a group of terrorists led by the mastermind al Tariq that has taken a small town hostage. The story takes Captain America from New York to Nebraska to Dresden, Germany for a final confrontation with and the defeat of al Tariq.[2]

The story constantly challenges the portrayal of the U.S. as innocent victim in the attacks. The primary employer in the town al Tariq has taken hostage is a munitions factory that manufactures cluster bombs. When Captain America comes to the town he battles the youthful followers of al Tariq, all of whom have prosthetic limbs, victims of land mines and cluster bombs left behind by the American army in various military actions. The soldiers of Al Tariq, his prosthetic wearing victims of American weapons, are offered to suggest that U.S. militarism may well be a source of the terrorist threat. Al Tariq describes his own history as a product of U.S. anticommunist military actions that killed his parents and left him disfigured. In doing so, Al Tariq challenges Captain America to identify his nationality:

> You know your history, Captain America. Tell your monster where he's from. You can't answer me[...]. You played that game in too many places[...]. The sun never set on your political chessboard — your empire of blood. In Africa, Asia, South America, we died.

Not only are the terrorists a product of U.S. military actions, their army is actually made possible by U.S. military technology. Al Tariq's followers are linked and controlled by a piece of technology developed by the U.S. military called a CATtag. The CATtag is essentially a biometric monitor that also allows a form of mind control over the wearer. The Secretary of Defense had attempted to get Captain America to wear one, but he had refused.

Beyond the military actions and military technology that produced the terrorist army, the U.S. is further implicated in the technique of terrorism. Captain America's visit to Dresden evokes the fire-bombing of that city during World War II, which Captain America sees in retrospect as an act of terrorism. The equation of the U.S. fire-bombing of Dresden with the 9/11 attacks against the World Trade Center undermines the role of the U.S. as innocent victim by rehearsing a major act of terrorism committed by the U.S.

Captain America's doubts will be a consistent theme throughout the 50 issues of volume 4, cast against the backdrop of the 9/11 attacks. In "The Extremists" (Rieber, Hairsine and Miki), Captain America must face a threat posed by a Native American shaman, Inali Redpath, who controls the weather and seeks to return America to Native Americans. When faced with Redpath's argument that America was forcibly taken from the natives and built with slave labor, Captain America responds, "I'm tired of people trashing this country." Yet even in what seems a clear chauvinistic turn, Captain America must doubt his cause and his moral role. Government superagent Nick Fury tells him, "Ever since 9/11 you've been challenged to be something you don't want to be and it's making you nuts" (Rieber et al., April 2003). After defeating Redpath, Captain America muses:

> I remember a time when it was easy to feel pride in "this" country. When "this" country celebrated the victories of its loyal soldiers. When "this" country was my country right or wrong — and most of the time it was right. But times have changed haven't they. The battles are less clear, the wars less noble, the cause less right, even in the shadow of 9/11 [Rieber et al., "The Extremists"].

While he reasserts his pride in his country, he also recognizes the complexity of the context, the issues and the responses. Even the common national security threat defined by 9/11 is insufficient to reconcile the conflict between nationalist acts and their global consequences. The assertion of American morality conflicts with the reality of genocide against native Americans and global adventurism during the Cold War. As the avatar of the American mission and the American creed, Captain America must be plagued by doubts arising from this conflict, and this agon dominates the story-line. Torn between the chauvinistic nationalism of his costume and the reality of his history, Captain America is not sure who he is, what he wants, or where he is going.

U.S. complicity in the terrorist attacks is not confined to the pages of Captain America comics. The Superman story "The Harvest" (2003) has him confronting an fake superman who offers a history of himself as the product of Cold War competition between the U.S. and the Soviet Union. Here the metaphorical 9/11 attack is a biological terrorist attack that has activated super-powered mutations in millions of Americans, often with disastrous results. Superman discovers that the only way to halt the mutations is to turn the Earth's yellow sunlight red, which will render him powerless. When he does so, he finds that this was a plot by the leader of the nation of Pokolistan, who is sort of an anti–Superman; where yellow sunlight gives Superman power, the red sunlight empowers his enemy. With the sunlight changed to red, the Pokolistan leader can take over the world.

The allegory to 9/11 is made explicit in several ways. The initial attack is against an innocent American community. President Lex Luthor is in a secure bunker. At the end of the day, an advisor tells Luthor, "You asked me earlier today if the U.S. was under attack." Pointing to a strategic map of the U.S. pinpointing sites of contagion she continues, "There is your answer." This echoes the dialogue between President Bush and Terrorism Czar Richard Clarke as offered in Clarke's memoirs (Clarke). The attack is not from the Pokolistan government, but from a rogue, third-party state called Bialya, which has been given the weapons by the Pokolistani leader.

The history of the Pokolistan leader is a counter history to the well-known origins of Superman. Raised in an Eastern European country under totalitarian rule, he is reared by the government to become the communist answer to Superman in a metaphoric superpowered arms race.[3] After the collapse of the USSR, he takes control of Pokolistan, setting his sights on defeating the man he was meant to oppose from the cradle. He has had himself genetically altered to look like Superman and takes Superman's place. Posing as the real man of steel, he convinces the United Nations and the United States to put him in charge of military forces invading Bialya. When he receives this authority, he uses it to destroy Bialya; dressed as Superman, but with an American flag draped over his shoulder, he leads the UN–sponsored invasion. He then makes a deal with U.S. President Luthor, which allows him to gain control over the U.S. nuclear arsenal which he uses to conquer the world. While the U.S. president is not here seen as aware of the duplicity, President Luthor seeks to use the opportunity provided by the attacks for his own militaristic ends. In this instance, the self-interest of the politician and nationalist ideologies lead the rulers of the world to accept that the morally pure, mighty hero is best suited to solve their problems. But inverting the result, rather than saving the nation, he subverts it in his own dream of world conquest. Superman finally defeats the false Superman by freeing all of the supervillains imprisoned on a satellite to serve as his army to defend the world. As Captain America must travel across the globe to fight global terrorism, so must Superman build a coalition of the good and the evil to defeat his terrorist.

As in "Enemy" U.S. Cold War actions, proliferation of military technologies, and nationalist responses are indicted in "Harvest." Superman's initial reaction is to assume that the U.S. is complicit in the attacks. He accuses President Luthor of engineering the biological weapon. The battle against the Bialyans is led by the imposter Superman, his cape replaced by an American flag, highlighting the nationalism of the response. This very nationalism, however, is what lets the false Superman into the heart of the U.S. military establishment, where he takes control of the U.S. nuclear arsenal to hold the world hostage. Al Tariq and the false Superman both define themselves and their actions in relation to U.S. global military actions from the Cold War. The Cold War was the first period in which the U.S. took a global forward military position rather than retreating from the conflicts of "petty tyrannies" as George Washington termed them in his farewell address. In so doing, something appears to have been lost—the ability to assert that the American nation is an innocent victim. Both Engelhardt's war story and Jewitt and Lawrence's American monomyth require that the victims of the massacre be blameless. These stories reject that characterization and thus undermine the very heart of both the War Story and of the 9/11 narrative described by Leavy. This loss of innocence is reflected in the self-interested actions of the government officials portrayed in the stories. The Secretary of Defense in "Enemy" wants to maintain his own deniability in the production and sale of the CATtags; in "Harvest" President Lex Luthor seeks to further his own anti–Superman agenda. In neither story is the government portrayed as concerned with public service.

Wild Storm comics' miniseries called *Coup D'État* (2004) crosses over its various titles to tell a story in which the U.S. government exploits alien technology for weapons research, inadvertently killing a large portion of an alien race, whose survivors then declare war on the Earth. In response the superhero group, the Authority, decide to take over the USA to avoid global destruction. The story opens with images of fiery destruction of skyscrapers as a giant alien vessel disintegrates over Florida. The images are reminiscent of the footage of the destruction of the twin towers. Most of Florida is destroyed, with millions of people killed. When the Authority discover that this disaster is the product of the U.S. government trying to modify alien technology for military purposes, they decide to stage a coup to forestall an invasion by the aliens whose ship was destroyed.

As in the previous stories, the superheroes must step in to save the world from this threat and finally take the stand of replacing the politicians who instigated the crisis. As the coup settles and the Authority take control, they assure the other nations of the world that they seek no national power but only to improve the lives of all humanity. This position, however, is fraught with ambiguity, as the coup perpetrated by the Authority is opposed by other groups of heroes (Stormwatch and the Wildcats). The Authority have proven themselves as biased and unaware as the politicians they replace. They have mistaken a dictator taken captive by Stormwatch under UN authority for a victim of torture. They have manipulated footage of the U.S. President, making him appear more intentionally culpable than he was, to convince the aliens that the perpetrator of the attack on them has been brought to justice. Having assumed control and assured the world of their good intentions, one member of the group, Midnighter, asks the others, "What the fuck do we do now?"

Other comic book stories also raised questions about U.S. culpability, often more directly. In the Avengers story "Red Zone" (2003) a bio-weapons attack is made on Mount Rushmore. This attack, portrayed as a terrorist action, echoes the attacks of 9/11, causing great destruction at a famous American landmark. It is revealed that the weapons were designed by the U.S. military and released on order of Secretary of Defense Dell Rusk, who is, in fact, Captain America's World War II nemesis the Red Skull (of which Dell Rusk is an anagram). When revealed, the Red Skull says that he has given up his dreams of reviving the Nazi regime, seeing America as ripe for global conquest if only it fears more. The military cannot stop the spread of the bioweapon and need the Avengers to solve the problem, although there is much conflict between the American military and the UN–sanctioned Avengers in the process. A key sub-plot involves the distrust between U.S. entrepreneur Tony Stark, who is the hero Iron Man, and T'challa, king of the African nation of Wakanda and also the hero Black Panther. Both espouse a nationalist position and have a strong distrust of each other. This distrust initially prevents them from cooperating in the development of an antidote to the plague that has been unleashed. Facing the Red Skull's fascistic racism, both learn the perils of nationalist hubris, overcome their difference, and eventually cooperate.

This story presents a vision of political failure that permits the evil to grow within the bosom of government. The fascistic Red Skull, operating within the center of U.S. power, is an unknown threat from within that leads the U.S. government ultimately to launch an attack on its own people. The Skull suggests that America is ripe for a fascist takeover, since after 9/11 "freedom knows fear." The ideological conflict between Iron Man and the Black Panther — both arguing from a nationalist position — demonstrates the potential of the fascistic response.

Unlike the other stories, "Red Zone" ends on a redemptive note, with the Skull stopped, the plague destroyed, and the threatened life of a young child saved. Iron Man and the Black Panther put aside their nationalist conflict to cooperate on developing an antidote for the plague. Captain America tells the president that he wants to be sure that all other bio-weapons labs are destroyed, and the president agrees, stating that if he fails, he wants the Avengers there to help him succeed. Still, the weapons lab under Mount Rushmore is number 13 (suggesting there are at least 12 more), and the president seems to imply that he will need the Avengers if he is to shut down the others successfully, indicating that he may not have control over his own government.

Each of these stories follows the same narrative structure. A devastating attack against America kills thousands of people. Normal systems of response fail, and superheroes need to save the community from this attack. Nonetheless, the normal channels of authority share some level of responsibility for the attack, and the aftermath of the events suggest that things will never be the same. Even in the story that seems the most redemptive, "Red Zone," questions linger. Why did no one in the government note that the Secretary of Defense was a Nazi super-villain? The She-hulk, infected by the virus, has left on a violent rampage, and it will require another story arc to subdue her. While the president has claimed to be in the process of shutting down other labs, he makes this claim only after Captain America insists that they be shut down. In none of these stories is the moral virtue of the U.S. asserted unambiguously, while in all of them the attacks are some form of blow-back, a reaction to some previous act of the U.S. This is a far cry from the moral certainty of the U.S. virtue against the Nazis or Soviets of four decades past. It reflects an underlying ambiguity concerning the American national identity in the post–Cold War world, an agon of conflicting identities. In the globalized world of the twenty-first century, it is increasingly difficult to define the American nation, and actions based on an assumption of nationalism will only prove counter-productive.

The Legacy of the 9/11 Narrative: Hubris and the Limits of Nationalism

The elements of the 9/11 narrative constructed in superhero comics between 2002 and 2004 have marked the interpretation of the War on Terror in these books. In particular, the narrative's dismissal of claims of American innocence and virtue, and the questioning of the nationalist response to the attacks have created an assumption of hubris on the part of authorities and an ambiguous stance toward the morality of nationalism as an approach to global problems. These limits of hubristic nationalism and unilateralism continue to be a common feature of many stories. The potential for a fascistic nationalism in response to the attacks suggested in "Red Zone" points in this direction. A more common strategy is to displace the hubris of nationalism onto the superhero, questioning the very possibility of moral action in the contemporary global order.

In "The Best Defense" (2003-04) Iron Man's alter ego Tony Stark is nominated for Secretary of Defense, and his Senate confirmation hearings consistently note that Stark acts on his own initiative, often ignoring the will of others. One Senator claims, "You think the smartest guy should be in charge — and that guy is you[...]. You're too smart for school, Mr. Stark. You make up your own rules" (Miller and Lucas). In "Letting Go" (Jurgens and Mandrake) the Mighty Thor has moved Asgard to Earth and begun to intervene directly in human affairs, finally trying to raise a human child from the dead. For his hubris, he faces the destruction of Asgard and loses the ability to lift his mystical hammer, which can only be raised by one who is morally pure. Both of these stories problematize what is usually an accepted staple of the superhero narrative — the fundamental correctness of the inner-directed morality of the hero. Displacing the moral claims of the U.S. onto superheroes, these narratives question the virtue of the motives of actors. Is Tony Stark acting in the country's best interest or his own? Is Thor helping mankind or merely celebrating his own godhood? Is George Bush really seeking to promote freedom and democracy, or is there a more self-serving agenda? As the post–9/11 superhero narrative questioned the innocence and virtue of the U.S., it also challenged the moral certainty of the U.S. mission; what previous generations might have characterized as manifest virtue was now offered as hubris.

The questioning of motives lies at the core of "Black Reign" (Johns et al.) a tale that crosses over the DC titles *Justice Society of America* (JSA) and *Hawkman*. In this story an anti-hero from Captain Marvel comics, Black Adam, assembles a group of morally questionable heroes to take control of his native Middle Eastern country of Kandhaq from its brutal dictator. The Justice Society and Hawkman oppose this action, claiming that it is not the role of superheroes to use their powers to topple governments, even evil ones. Hawkman's actions, wresting control of the Justice Society from its elected President to lead the counteroffensive against Black Adam, are equated with Black Adam's wresting control from the leader of Kandhaq. In the end, the Justice Society leaves Kandhaq with Black Adam still in charge, welcomed by the people of Kandhaq as a liberator. The nationalist visions of the JSA would leave the people of Kandhaq to suffer, while the vigilantism of Black Adam violates norms of sovereignty that are the basis of international affairs. The moral value of the invasion of Kandhaq is left an open question, while the hubris of Black Adam and Hawkman is clearly offered as morally wrong.

Another comic book that extends notions of government culpability to a conspiracy involving government, corporations, and superheroes is *The Boys*. "The Boys" of the title refer to an international team of human agents who intervene between superheroes and humans when the heroes begin to act excessively. The need for the boys stems from the hubris of the superheroes, who act with no regard for civilian damage (the first issue opens with a gruesome killing of an innocent bystander by a superhero chasing a super villain). Identifying clearly which nation acts hubristically, the boys are French, English, Irish and Scottish, while the superheroes in this book are all Americans, created, funded, and directed by a giant American corporate conglomerate, Vought-American. Closely tied to certain sectors of the U.S. government, Vought-American seeks to extend its own power. The hubris of the American government here extends to corporations and the superheroes. In a recent, adult oriented and unapologetically pornographic spinoff from this series, *Herogasm* (2009), the hubris of the heroes is central. The title refers to an annual week-long superhero orgy of sex and drugs, a superheroes-only vacation where they can blow off steam.[4] In the midst of this story the 9/11 attacks are explicitly identified as a product of the U.S. government and military contractors who facilitate the 9/11 attacks to create a climate of fear which will further these ends. With full knowledge that an attack is coming, the President orders the Air Force to shoot down the civilian aircraft. He is knocked unconscious by his Vice President — a Vought-American stooge — who orders the Air Force to stand down (Ennis, McCrea and Burns).

Marvel's year-long "Civil War" story-line (2006-2007) also questioned the motives of government and heroes. The eponymous Civil War is a product of the government's attempt to regulate superheroes through registration after a disaster in a small Connecticut town kills over six-hundred civilians. Iron Man led the pro-registration government forces and Captain America led the anti-registration underground. Captain America's argument was that registration would make him an agent of the government, incapable of following his internal moral compass, while Iron Man argued that most lacked that moral compass and acted mainly from hubris. As in "Black Reign," while the issue was raised it remained unresolved as the Civil War ground on for over a year, culminating in Captain America's surrender to stop the harming of innocents.

None of these stories offers the moral claims of the hero or the government unambiguously. Unlike earlier national security crusades, where the U.S. was presented as absolutely right and the enemy — nazi or communist — absolutely wrong, these stories question the very morality of the U.S. position, and displace that questioning onto the possibility of heroism.

In all of these stories, ranging from 2002 to the present, the actions of the U.S.— direct and indirect — are identified as either a precondition or cause of the terrorist attacks of 9/11. Rather than supporting the "official story" as Leavy suggests all media do, this medium treats America as at least morally complicit in creating the conditions or such terrorist acts as those of 9/11. In this context, the war story of Engelhart or the monomyth of Lawrence and Jewitt cannot be invoked without irony; the U.S. was not the innocent victim of massacre, these works suggest, but the victim of blowback from its own actions abroad, its citizens' failure to be a vigilant check on government, its veneration of style and celebrity over moral values and substance. To the extent that the U.S. is not merely an innocent victim but morally culpable, any nationalist, militaristic response to the attacks must be questioned.

An Exception

One unique series that has explicitly and continuously defined itself in relation to the attacks of 9/11 is *Ex Machina* by Brian Vaughn and Tony Harris, which began in 2004. *Ex Machina* is the story of Mitchell Hundred, a civil engineer in New York City who, in 1999, is exposed to some kind of alien technology that imbues him with the power to give orders to machines. Working with former naval captain turned government agent Bradbury and a Russian immigrant called Kremlin, he develops a costume with a jetpack and becomes a hero called the Great Machine. His heroic actions, however, often backfire, resulting in as much harm as good. After consulting with the New York City Police Commissioner he decides to quit being a hero and run for mayor as an independent. His campaign is barely getting off the ground in 2001 when the terrorist attacks of the World Trade Center occur. After using his abilities to stop the second plane and save one of the twin towers his campaign in galvanized, and he is elected mayor of New York City.

This is where the story begins. Each story arc refers in flashback to the period before the September 11th attacks, establishing the moment as transformative, creating a new beginning. This new beginning is the inauguration of a centrist politics of pragmatism. As Mayor Hundred confronts a series of issues that are relatively mundane compared to terrorist attacks, he must also confront more super-heroic problems. Thus the first story arc concerns someone who is killing city workers, while the mayor is concerned primarily with a controversial art exhibit that is being funded with tax dollars. Later he must confront a subway monster, produced by the same artifact that gave him his powers, while also dealing with the issues of gay marriage and education. The book is notable for its sophisticated discussion of complex issues, including school vouchers, decriminalizing marijuana, gay marriage, and state-church separation, among others. Mayor Hundred sees all of these from a pragmatic, centrist position, eschewing ideological extremes. He stands between the U.S. government agent Bradbury and the unreformed Soviet, Kremlin. Much of the political conflict in the book is the mayor trying to steer public policy in a rational direction in the face of ideological opposition.

In its own way, *Ex Machina* offers a very similar criticism of the "official story." *Ex Machina* reverses the basic elements of the superhero narrative, and leads the reader in a direction opposite to that of the more common superhero narrative. In that narrative superheroes taking on the role of public authorities and acting unilaterally is challenged as hubristic, and the moral codes under which both heroes and nations operate are rendered problematic. In *Ex Machina* Mitchell Hundred rejects the role of superhero for elected official; rather than continue to act with his own inner-directed morality, he chooses to follow the dictates of democratic elections. Rather than follow his own beliefs to resolve issues irrespective of the ideas of others, Mayor Hundred searches for pragmatic solutions that are broadly acceptable to his electorate. While *Ex Machina* does not posit government complicity in the attacks of 9/11, it does indict the unilateralism and chauvinism of the nationalist response. Mitchell Hundred is specifically not a politician. He continually fights with his own staff of career politicos to get his pragmatic agenda pushed through. He is non-ideological, willing to champion such liberal causes as gay marriage, but maintaining an ambiguous position on abortion, willing to speak at the Republican national convention, yet pro-legalization of marijuana. He has reversed the superhero narrative in profound ways; rather than the hero swooping in to save the world when established authorities fail, he quits his superhero costume to enter those formal channels to meet his community's needs. Unlike the other superhero 9/11 narrative in superhero comics, *Ex Machina* exhorts its readers to take control of the system from politicians to produce a politics of pragmatism that will benefit the community as a whole.

Conclusion

The terrorist attacks of 9/11 remain culturally contested terrain. While the "official story" identified by Leavy may have been the dominant interpretation, it was not hegemonic to all media. Superhero comics early and consistently took a skeptical position on the meaning of the 9/11 attacks. Developing a common narrative that challenged notions of U.S. innocence and the appropriateness of a nationalist response, the books challenged the dominant interpretations coming from mainstream media, interest groups, and government. Even in *Ex Machina*, there is a challenge to nationalism and the ability of formal authorities to address the problems that beset America, although the book makes the argument by inverting the superhero narrative.

With this narrative as backdrop, it is unsurprising that superhero comics continue to cast doubts on the moral mission of America. In recent books from each of the major publishers, evil rather than good seems to be triumphant. Marvel's Civil War was followed by "Secret Invasion," in which shape-shifting aliens infiltrated the superhero community to conquer the world. While finally defeated, the invasion discredited the superhero community, and Norman Osborn (the Green Goblin from Spiderman comics) was placed in charge of superhero registration. He immediately began to replace all of the heroes with villains who pose as heroes, inverting conventional identities as villains are heroes and the heroes become villains. Various story-lines at DC comics have left Batman dead, Superman exiled from Earth and under close supervision by the U.S. military, and the Green Lantern Corps, the galaxy's police force, under siege and in disarray, a situation brought on by the increasing centralization of power within the Corps.

At Wildstorm comics, government sponsored superhuman experiments led to a global catastrophe that destroyed most of the world and killed most of the population. While not all of this is directly related to the attacks of 9/11, it grows out of the same crisis of identity that rendered superhero comics incapable of developing a narrative of innocence and national virtue in the wake of 9/11. Rather than re-affirming an identity of a morally virtuous American nation beset by senseless evil, superhero comics — and the nation at large — continue to confront a world in which American virtue is questioned and nationalism seems an inadequate and counterproductive response to globalized problems. The official story that Leavy sees as a hegemonic discourse in reporting did not extend to superhero comics. The memory of 9/11 offered in superhero comics does not affirm a nationalist mission, but produces anxiety in the definition of an American self, an American hero, and an American mission.

Notes

1. The famous cover of the first issue of *Captain America Comics* — depicting the red, white, and blue hero punching Hitler — was dated March 1940 (released in February 1940), thus pre-dating America's entry into the war by nearly a year.
2. See Ditmer (2005) for an interesting discussion of geography, politics, and 9/11 in *Captain America*.
3. DC Comics also ran a story imagining what the world would have been like had a rocketship from Krypton landed in the Ukraine rather than Kansas in *Superman: Red Son* (2003). Rendering Superman a communist was another form of challenging the moral superiority of the United States in the post–Cold War world.
4. The cover story for their absence from their normal societies is that they are fighting some intergalactic menace; this is a joke, mocking the annual summer cross-over "event" stories that have become a staple to superhero books over the last several decades.

Works Cited

Assman, Jan, and John Czaplicka (Trans.). "Collective Memory and Cultural Identity." *New German Critique* 65 (1995): 125–133.
Bartle, Jeff. "John Ney Rieber Interview." *Comics Journal* 241 (February 2002): 88.
Brubaker, Ed, Joe Casey, Robbie Morrison, and Micah Ian Wright (w), Carlos D'Anda, Jim Lee, Whilce Portacio, and Trevor Scott (p), David Baron, Randy Mayor, Alex Sinclair, and Carrie Strachan (i). *Coup d'Etat* 1–4 (April 2004). Wildstorm Publications.
Bush, George W. "Address to the Nation, 11 September 2001." September 11, 2001. September 29, 2009. http://www.americanrhetoric.com/speeches/gwbush911addresstothe nation.htm.
Clarke, Richard. *Against All Enemies: Inside America's War on Terror*. New York: Free Press, 2004.
Costello, Matthew J. *Secret Identity Crisis: Comic Books and the Unmasking of the American Cold War*. New York: Continuum Books, 2009.
Dittmer, Jason. "Captain America's Empire: Reflections on Identity, Popular Culture, and Post–9/11 Geopolitics." *Annals of the Association of American Geographers* 95.3 (2005): 626–643.
Engelhardt, Tom. *The End of Victory Culture: Cold War America and the Disillusioning of a Generation*. New York: Basic Books, 1995.

Ennis, Garth (w), John McRea, and Keith Burns (a). *Herogasm* (2009). Dynamite Entertainment.

Ennis, Garth (w), and Darick Robertson (a). *The Boys* 1–6 (October 2006–February 2007). Wildstorm Publications; 7–present (2007–present). Dynamite Entertainment.

Jenkins, Henry. "Captain America Sheds His Mighty Tears: Comics and September 11." *In* Daniel Sherman and Terry Nardin (Eds.). *Terror, Culture, Politics: Rethinking 9/11*. Bloomington: Indiana University Press, 2006: 69–102.

Johns, Geoff (w), Don Kramer (p), and Keith Chaampaigne (i). "Black Reign, Parts 1, 3 and 5." *JSA* 56–58 (Early March–April 2004). DC Comics.

Johns, Geoff (w), Olivier Coipel (p), and Andy Lanning (i). "Red Zone." *The Avengers* vol. 3, nos. 65–70 (May–October 2003). Marvel Comics.

Johns, Geoff (w), Rags Morales (p), Michael Bair, and John Dell (i). "Black Reign: Parts 2, 4 and 6." *Hawkman* 23–25 (Early March–April 2004). DC Comics.

Jurgens, Dan (w), Scott Eaton (p), and Drew Geraci (i). "Letting Go." *The Mighty Thor 2*, no. 79 (June 2004). Marvel Comics.

Kansteiner, Wulf. "Finding Meaning in Memory: A Methodological Critique of Collective Memory Studies." *History and Theory* 41.2 (2002): 179–197.

Kelly, Joe (w), Tom Derenick, Pascual Ferry, and Tom Raney (p), and Bob Petreca, Norm Rapamund, Cam Smith, and Walden Wong (i). "The Harvest." *Action Comics* 801–805 (May–September 2003). DC Comics.

Lawrence, John Shelton, and Thomas Jewitt. *The Myth of the American Superhero*. Grand Rapids: W. B. Eerdmans, 2002.

Leavy, Patricia. "Writing 9/11 Memory: American Journalists and Special Interest Groups as Complicit Partners in 9/11 Political Appropriation." *Journal of Military Sociology* 35.1 (2007): 85–101.

Medved, Michael. "Captain America, Traitor?" *The National Review Online*. April 4, 2003. June 15, 2007. www.nationalreview.com/comment/comment-medved040403.asp.

Millar, Mark (w), Dave Johnson, and Killian Plunkett (p), Andrew Robinson, and Walden Wong (i). *Superman: Red Son* (1–3, 2003). DC Comics.

Millar, Mark (w), Steve McNiven (p), and Dexter Vines (i). *Civil War* 1–7 (June 2006–January 2007). Marvel Comics.

Miller, John J. (w), and Jorge Lucas (a). "The Best Defense." *Invincible Iron Man 3*, nos. 73–78 (December 2003–May 2004). Marvel Comics.

Rieber, John Ney (w), and John Cassady (a). "Enemy." *Captain America 4*, nos. 1–6 (June–December 2002). Marvel Comics.

Rieber, John Ney (w), Trevor Hairsine (p), and Danny Miki (1). "The Extremists." *Captain America 4*, nos. 7–11 (February–May 2003). Marvel Comics.

Sherman, Daniel, and Terry Nardin (Eds.). *Terror, Culture, Politics: Rethinking 9/11*. Bloomington: University of Indiana Press, 2006.

"Whose Side Are You On?"
The Allegorization of 9/11 in Marvel's Civil War
Stephan Packard

Civil War is the title of a Marvel multi-volume superhero narrative, a major "crossover" event spanning numerous established comic book series, protagonists and antagonists, as well as two new dedicated serials. Cross-overs enjoy considerable popularity within the genre and emphasize the unity of the one fictitious universe that supposedly contains the events of all the different series. While also motivating readers of some series to buy additional episodes from other lines that tell further parts of the shared story, massive cross-overs respond to certain codes and have developed specific aesthetic techniques. All of its parts taken together, *Civil War* was published over a period of almost one year between 2006 and 2007, and covers the work of roughly 20 different authors and 40 pencillers in 25 serials, 60 comic books, and 1500 comic pages.[1]

The story of *Civil War* shows essential similarities to political events and debates that have taken place in the United States since September 11, 2001. In the small town of Stamford, some superheroes and villains trigger an explosion that kills 600 civilians, many of them children. The government reacts by introducing a Superhero Registration Act (SRA), mandating that superheroes register their special abilities as well as their secret identities with the authorities, and sometimes recruiting them for a centrally controlled security organization overseen by the U.S. government. This law divides what is now referred to as the "superhero community." While some support their government — most notably Iron Man, whose civilian identity, Tony Stark, is a plutocrat and weapons manufacturer — others refuse to abide by the SRA's rules. The latter anti–SRA group is led into the eponymous "civil war" among superheroes by Captain America, a stars-and-stripes-clad U.S. hero celebrated ever since the time of the Second World War.

Repeatedly asking the reader, "Whose Side Are You On?," *Civil War* caught the attention of audiences beyond regular comic book readership. News media and political commentators discussed the series and connected its story to contemporary real world controversies (Ari; McCrae). It seems obvious that the narrative is partially designed with just that intention. The plot offers itself as an allegory to the events of September 11 and to ensuing discussions that have often pitted concerns for national safety against individual liberties. *Civil War*'s leading author Mark Millar has described his work as "a story where a guy wrapped in the American flag is in chains as the people swap freedom for security" ("Mark Millar's Civil War Post-Game Show").

While there have been many other reactions to 9/11 within the art form, I will show that *Civil War* fulfils a unique function by means of a specific type of allegory. As opposed to an otherwise common depiction of September 11 as an interruptive suspension and inconceivably event-like other, this series accomplishes a re-discursivation of that perceived. An exploration of this process can yield some preliminary and admittedly partially genre-specific answers to central questions regarding the cultural treatment of 9/11: What mechanisms have contributed to the cohesive unity of a continuous post–9/11 discourse? How is it possible that such discourse often goes beyond the direct reference to the events of 9/11 and includes other topics, such as the war in Iraq, the introduction of new techniques for investigation and interrogation, and even hurricane Katrina, and implicitly or explicitly connects them and many others to the destruction of the World Trade Center? What pre–9/11 cultural tendencies and conditions made the special rhetorical and aesthetic construction of these events possible? And what specific role did the current convergence of historiography and visual media play in the post–9/11 discourse? (Chute: 268).

In the following pages, I show that the *Civil War* narrative inscribes the aesthetic treatment of 9/11 into a continued discourse by superimposing a mediating regularity based in popular genre conventions; that this contributes to the cohesion of the overarching post–9/11 discourse; and that this process employs an aesthetic appreciation for contiguous storytelling that began in the 1990s. Starting with some features from a paradigmatic depiction of 9/11 as an ultimate interruption that forbids any discursive continuity, I will discuss alternative treatments of what I will refer to by the general term *caesuras* from a semiotic point of view in the context of established mainstream representations of 9/11. Beyond iconic and deictic assimilations, *Civil War* can then be characterized by a large-scale allegorization of September 11, utilizing the provocative potential of narrative irreversibility within the superhero genre as an opportunity for a special aesthetic significance and demarcation.

9/11 Interrupts

It is especially during the first two years after the attacks that several avant-garde (e.g., Spiegelman; Kuper; Fleiss; and Lisner) as well as popular (e.g., *Heroes*; "9-11"; Rieber and Cassaday; and Vaughn) comic books presented treatments of the events of September 11. Almost all of them have in common that they reconstruct the attacks and the collapse of the WTC's towers as a catastrophe suspending conventional patterns of genre, form, and thought; as an inexplicable and ultimate other and thus as the realization of the oft-quoted incursion of the real into the orders of the imaginary and the symbolic. According to that point of view, the attacks feature such an immediate experience of death, of pain, of danger, of violence, or simply of a basic political force suspending policy, that the discourses usually ordering our experiences are unable to represent and come to terms with their content. This would either doom them to traumatically repeat or to altogether avoid the attacks as a topic; at the same time, it might promise a dimension of authenticity, even of escape from the power distributions of the established symbolic order. But such claims are themselves difficult to verify and ultimately dubious, as they will typically serve other purposes entangled in their own orders of policy and power (Žižek).

Immediately after 9/11, J. Michael Straczynski and John Romita, Jr.'s famed "black issue" of *Amazing Spider-Man* (2.36) established a paradigm for these aesthetics of suspension. The completely black cover is followed by a likewise black first page, with a short boxed caption at its centre: "We interrupt our regularly scheduled program to bring you the following Special Bulletin" (1). That phrase reproduces the stereotypical introduction of TV and radio reports covering the attacks, and marks this comic book as an exception. The actions depicted on the following pages have no place in the unity of Marvel's fictitious universe; they are neither temporarily nor causally related to other events in the protagonist's life. As a tribute to the attacks, as well as an immediate attempt at handling their emotional impact, the issue stands alone, and it draws its primary rhetorical demarcation from this conspicuous break with the serial form. What follows, we understand, is so extraordinary that it puts the narrative conventions of *Spider-Man* on hold. On the next few pages, it quickly becomes clear that some of the rules governing the fictitious universe have also been discontinued. Spider-Man and numerous other Marvel heroes appear notably weaker than they usually are, their helplessness in the face of two collapsing towers allowing them only to save a very few injured survivors with extreme effort. On the one hand, this renegotiates the border between fiction and reality, offering an implausible but all the more easily sublimated answer to that obvious question: How can catastrophes like these occur in a world where superheroes are ready to thwart all attacks? "You cannot hear us for the cries, but we are here" (8), claims Spider-Man, explaining the apparent lack of superheroes during the crisis. On the other hand, Straczynski connects the fictional border defining the genre with the topical suffering of 9/11, and places the heroes' absence in the context of the sublime, by moving them to a place severed from sensible perception by the experienced pain. In a page-sized macropanel, John Romita, Jr., draws Spider-Man among the ruins of the WTC, bent under the weight of an over-dimensioned steel beam. Throughout the issue, superheroes are depicted as small, taking up little space within the large macropanels, and confronted with enormous representations of destruction. They are often shown from behind or in profile in almost stationary poses that are either passive or strained; their gaze is usually turned upwards towards the surrounding and overbearingly gigantic rubble. In addition to its size, it is the architecture of the wreckage that sustains the impression of sublimity. Many of the burst walls, cracked foundations and splintered pieces of furniture are reminiscent of cathedrals with Gothic pointed arches, galleries and detailed stained-glass windows.

While Spider-Man's internally focalized report in the caption boxes reinforces the evaluation of this event as unimaginable, inexplicable, and overwhelming, the same view is also confirmed by a group of superheroes who join our hero's amazement over the extent of the destruction. Even Dr. Doom, for example, who has repeatedly depopulated whole planets with devastating weaponry in the history of the Marvel universe, succumbs to emotion in the face of the attacks on Manhattan. As Spiderman observes:

> Even those we thought our enemies are here. Because some things surpass rivalries and borders. Because the story of humanity is written not in towers but in tears. In the common coin of blood and bone. In the voice that speaks within even the worst of us, and says This Is Not Right! Because even the worst of us, however scarred, are still human. Still feel. Still mourn the random death of innocents [9].

In three vertically arranged, broad panels, the frame closes in on Doom's face, pointing out the tears in the eye-holes of his horrid metallic facial mask. Such pathos, which suits genre conventions but might seem difficult to accept with regards to 9/11 given a current retrospective, was at the time readily approved by many readers and reviewers (cf. the numerous reviews listed at marvel.com as of March 3, 2008). This is probably due not only to the close temporal proximity to the attacks, but also because of the marked violation of generic and formal expectations. The suspension of familiar structures is transformed into an experience of the sublime, as Spider-Man and other superhuman characters take the reader's place in perceiving, and failing to conceptualize, that which is only presented as the limit of semiosis and as surpassing the faculty of sensual perception (Hertz: chap. 10). The direct address: "You cannot hear us..." grammatically divides the world into common mortals ("you") and superheroes ("we"), who confront the former at the limits of the imaginable and thus circumscribe a space in which everyday humans may become heroes: "We stand blinded," Spider-Man's inner monologue continues, "by the light of your unbroken will. Before that light, no darkness can prevail" (14). But in another part of the same issue, we see the first signs of a changed rhetoric and a very different perspective. For besides being addressed in the second person, human beings without super powers appear in one other function: As children who are discussed in the third person: "What do we tell the children? [...] Perhaps we tell them that we are sorry. Sorry that we were not able to deliver unto them the world we wished them to have" (21). In this unfulfilled aspiration to shape the world for those to whom the powerful refer in the third person, the genre's typical role for their protagonists signals its return. A few years later, *Civil War* will begin to reinscribe into a continuous discourse the very topic that leads to a complete suspension of discursive conventions in the "black issue," and the role of superheroes as active shapers of common man's world is essential to that process.

Short Semiotics of Caesura

To better understand that change of positions, a rough typology of alternative semiotic realizations of caesura is helpful. Whether a psychological, cultural or factual caesura actually took place on 9/11 is a question we may suspend for the moment, concentrating instead on the various ways that a caesura can be explicitly denoted or indirectly expressed by a certain set of semiotic operations. A basic differentiation of such operations is offered by Charles S. Peirce distinction of icon, index and symbol and the corresponding categorical trichotomy of firstness, secondness and thirdness (Peirce, 1887).

I suggest that two minimal semiotic conditions define a caesura. It has to be isolated from its surroundings, by virtue of representing an external object (secondness), a deviant mode of representation (thirdness), or a differently structured sign surface (firstness), so that it might be perceived as a caesura among other significations; and it has to serve as a point of reference for the continuous chain of signification, introducing new possibilities for indication, or transforming old ones, so that it might unfold some semiotic effect.

Such a combination of isolation and relevance can be thought of as what Peirce repeatedly calls a "degenerated" thirdness, where the fully functional and connected triad of the sign, the object and their mediation is reduced to the secondness of mere sign-object relations or to the firstness of purely monadic signs. The most typically described reduction in this context is that to secondness, which is to conceive of 9/11 as a caesura in the sense of the incontrovertible factuality of the event, where symbolic discourse is reduced to a binary, direct and inescapable relation between a trivially receptive, passive observer, indistinguishable from a sign, and its immutable object. This conception corresponds with those interpretations that ascribe to the event a traumatic force and an indexical reference to the real. However, this sense of interruption is rivaled by another mode of suspension, in which the sign of 9/11 is reduced to a firstness, i.e. an iconic representation not of a real object, but of a mere quality, an isolated image. This interpretation emphasizes the self-referentiality of the comparatively small set of repeated visuals depicting 9/11, and holds that this constitutes 9/11 as an opaque sign without an exterior object in many discourses, often because that object is again severed from signification by the sublimity of the attached pain. The pertinent photographs and TV images have become common knowledge and are easily recalled by a few key

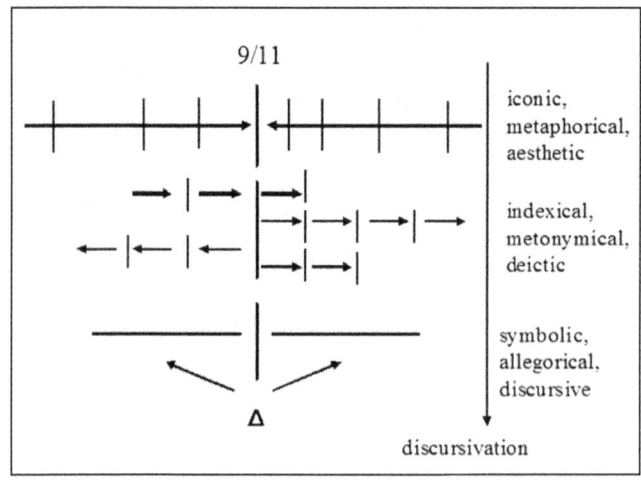

A short semiotics of caesura.

phrases: "The towers," "smoke," "second plane," "falling man," and so forth. Taking their cue from well-established and emphatically aesthetic depictions of the World Trade Center before the attacks, which often repeat the already twinned towers yet again in their reflection in the waters adjacent to Manhattan, these isolated images are also infinitely repeated and reflected, from full color pictures through silhouettes to abstract double rectangles, to the point where such similar repetition replaces objective reference as well as subjective interpretation. These icons identify the constructed object with its sign on screens and canvasses, so that the real does not suspend the imaginary so much as it becomes the imaginary and suspends the symbolic order of referential discourse. 9/11 reaches its most extreme semiotic isolation not in the trauma of its sudden factuality, but in the ideology of its image. It is the perfect example of "the unity of the real relations and the imaginary relations between men and women and the real conditions of their existence" that make up the ideology of cinema — and, by extension, of the popular images discussed here — by Stephen Heath's definition (Heath: 5). This differentiation between 9/11 as trauma and as ideology calls for a more detailed examination; but for the scope of this article, it will suffice to point out the manifold recurrence of 9/11 icons as a phenomenon that cannot be ignored (Packard, "Die Rede von der Zäsur").

This pictorial isolation of the event 9/11 as a section cut from the continuous chain of signification produces a suspension, but it also allows the production of further iconic signs for the caesura: the images that endlessly repeat the same quality after the event, in similar form and with constant reference to the event, still continue the circulation of signs. In the same way, an iconic anticipation of 9/11 can be recognized in pictures from before 9/11, and it is one of the most striking features of 9/11 imagery that it seems to have been prepared in various popular depictions of collapsing sky-scrapers from *Fight Club* to *Independence-Day* (Scheffer). These iconic representations ascribe aesthetic, partially sublime qualities to the caesura and generally offer themselves to visually metaphorical restatements[2] and approximations, such as the light installations at Ground Zero or the transparent shapes of the missing towers on recent New York postcards. As this isolated iconic sign is limited to the pictorial shape, the shape of an absent can advance to the form of the picture.

The other perhaps more commonly discussed but less commonly reproduced form of isolation reduces discourse to a secondness, not evading reality as much as succumbing to its shocking presence. Such representations of 9/11 employ indices rather than icons and work in a completely different way. Compared to the ideological identification of the event with its image, the causal integration of September 11 and the combination of its mere shape with a concrete factuality marks a first step towards re-discursivation. Where the image has become indistinguishable from its opaque object, the introduction of an additional, causal reality can re-differentiate the signification, adding the complexity of real, dynamic objects to the merely qualitative content of the isolated image. Indexical signs might point to the primarily isolated event by immediate deictic reference, by establishing causal connections of the event with its causes and consequences, and especially by a metonymical replacement of 9/11 by one of its roots or effects. The degeneration of such signs then makes it possible to combine an iconic representation of 9/11 with other, concrete objects and events, metonymically presenting them as a causal relation even when that causality cannot be explicitly argued: this is the case in the many political caricatures showing the towers at the centre of a flooded New Orleans. The earliest might have been Steve Bell's drawing "The Spirit of 9/11" in the *Guardian* on November 12, 2005, which shows two towers with the faces of President Bush and Vice President Cheney standing in masses of water. The caption has Bush saying: "It's time to declare war on wet people!" By a similar degeneration, events that preceded 9/11 can be connected to the caesura not only as its causes, but even as its consequences when presented as apocalyptic anticipations, which Žižek refers to as "symptoms returning from the future."

Ideological icons and traumatic indices both refuse the symbolic whole that is the hallmark of fully connected and connectable semiosis, of functional and mediated discourse. Discourse requires an interpretant position to complement the isolated elements, a regulatory third instance. The various imaginable forms of such regulation all begin by observing a difference Δ, which wraps the abstract idea of caesura into the distinction of the times and spaces that the caesura separates. The events of 9/11 can then be thought of as one realization of that general rule, confirming rather than interrupting discourse. The observer's point Δ is removed from the bidirectional line of events and discerns a qualitative change of that sequence at its caesura. Elevating the otherwise reduced caesura to the set of regularly denoted objects, the emergent speech can talk of this as of any other element from its discursive universe, describing differences introduced by the event as intelligible occurrences in a common temporal sequence, and subjecting them to the same judgments as any other part of semiosis. In Peircean terms, the pictorial quality of firstness and the factual moment of secondness are combined by such regularity to a well-formed thirdness, and fully integrated into the semiotic process.

As semiosis closes around the represented caesura, it separates it once more from its unapproachable real. The representation can then be considered as an allegory, where any reference, no matter how explicit, always speaks of something other than its ultimate reality, of which it cannot speak without reduction. To distinguish this allegory, we might call it an allegorical assimilation, as opposed to the allegorical dissimilations in fully-developed metaphors that were common in European narratives following 9/11, and that would speak of other factual or fictitious events instead of the attacks. Examples include parts of Frédéric Beigbeder's *Windows on the World* (2003), Luc Lang's *11 septembre mon amour* (2003), and Y.B.'s *Allah Superstar* (2003). These formats as well as the reduced ideological and traumatic representations that are their alternative eventually seem to yield to the allegorical assimilation showcased by *Civil War*: It is from the "black issue" and its dominantly aestheticized depictions, and through some later and increasingly indexical references to 9/11, that Marvel's superhero comics gradually introduce an allegorical mastery of the caesura.

Iconic and Indexical Integrations

After the "black issue," Straczynski continues the previous narrative of Spider-Man in more usual episodes. While Spider-Man's experiences on September 11 remain suspended and are never specifically acknowledged, Peter Parker and the other protagonists live in an America that shows increasing signs of having suffered 9/11. Long before *Civil War* begins in 2006, several opportunities to reference the attacks are welcomed. However, they are never used to repeat the radical interruption of narrative. Rather, these allusions are introduced through a gradual integration and commentary in the comic books' plots and depictions.

An early example occurs in *Amazing Spider-Man* 2.43, from July 2002, as Peter Parker tries to take a plane from New York to the West coast. As some parts of his packed Spider-Man costume trigger the sensors, Peter, his aunt May and his luggage undergo scrutiny from two security officers. 9/11 is not mentioned by any of the characters, but a framed poster on the wall behind the guards shows the rough rectangular shape of the towers and the caption "Never forget" (11–2). That Peter has trouble hiding his secret identity is a well-established topos of the series. But here, that standardized scene alludes to post–9/11 America without ever turning it into a major plot element. The repeated iconic form suffices. Not only is the image of 9/11 repeated on the poster, the poster is itself repeated in several panels, and the vertical rectangles on the poster are echoed by its shape as well as by the shape of two of the comic panels in this sequence. While the frame around the poster can be seen as a repetition of the panels' surrounding gutter, the same form is echoed in the two tall, slim officers — demonstrating the pervasiveness of the continued allusion.

On the one hand, this iconic integration underscores the ubiquitous aesthetics of the infinitely repeated and reflected picture of 9/11. But on the other hand, the allusive aesthetic is refracted by its inclusion into the sequence of the comic panels and the margins of the plot. Although the ever-mirrored icon infects several shapes in the comic page, it is also subjected to the rules of the sequential art and the gazes of the characters that coordinate the pictorial elements of the comic. The same guided gaze of the comic-book characters' cartoon drawings is central to the main technique for indexical integration at the heart of *Civil War*, where omnipresent motifs of 9/11 are quoted but then reframed in new regularities and added relations that dissolve their isolation (McCloud: esp. chap. 2 and Packard, *Anatomie des Comics*). They perform a reversal of the main structures in the "black issue." There, Spider-Man and other heroes stood small and help-less against gigantic monuments of destruction, and the hero's inner monologue de-scribed equally well the state of other characters loosely placed next to and behind each other: Their "you" was directed at common mortals suffering under the events or reading the comic. At the beginning of *Civil War*, a parallel destruction is represented in a very different way. In the first issue of the dedicated serial (Millar, *Cival War* 1), the main story — following a short prologue — starts with a two-page macropanel depicting the ruins of

Stamford along with the main titles. But this time, penciller Steve McNiven chooses a perspective diagonally looking down at the site, over several superheroes' shoulders. Some of them are flying down from above, others are drawn large in the foreground, pointing at the debris on the ground and discussing it among themselves. Instead of the passive voice directed at the "you" of humans without special abilities, this image as well as its text boasts a confident first person speaking for a community. Beyond this new "we," common people and their destroyed livelihood are relegated to a third person, Iron Man's outstretched finger pointing them out to Captain America's gaze. "What will we tell them?" had been the question concerning the children, which interrupted the address to common men in the "black issue." Its deixis resurfaces here as the orientation for the new narrative of a superhero "we," from which are recruited the cartoons whose gaze orders the panel. They decide over the "them" of the administrated citizens, who appear in much the same role as the children did before:

"I'm told they've got a lead[...]" (Iron Man).
"Does it matter? All these children, Tony. The F.E.M.A. chief said there could be eight or nine hundred casualties[...]" (Captain America).
"They should have called us [..., they] knew they were out of their league" (Iron Man) [10].

And, in anticipation of the Superhero Registration Act, another superhero observes: "They'll be coming after us with torches and pitchforks" (12).

Every so often, subsequent issues do present the image of a small superhero in the foreground passively looking up: But then his gaze is not met by an overwhelming image of human suffering, but by the gaze of a more powerful hero looking down. One instance of this is Captain America's depiction as an enormous incorporation of the American flag, who draws the admiring attention of Peter Parker and lectures him with a long patriotic speech, emphasizing his stance in favor of liberty and against totalitarian tendencies of the government; yet he does so by redefining said government alongside its subjects as "they," over whom heroes — and the narrative perspective — soar:

Doesn't matter what the press says. Doesn't matter what the politicians or the mobs say. Doesn't matter if the whole country decides that something wrong is something right. This nation was founded on one principle above all else: The requirement that we stand up for what we believe. No matter the odds or the consequences. When the mob and the press and the whole world tell you to move, your job is to plant yourself like a tree beside the river of truth, and tell the whole world — "No, you move" [Straczynski, *Amazing Spider-Man* 1.537:14].

This changed deixis turns those events that allegorically refer to 9/11 into objects that can be denoted and commented upon by a separate and ongoing discourse. For while mortals are confined to the third person, readers are not; they follow the gaze and communications of the heroes, whose gaze in turn meets theirs and whose speech they read. The discourse of this superior community constitutes precisely that of the narrative, engaging the reader not in the sense of naïve identification, but of participation in a reinstated circulation of signs.

Symbolic Discursivation

While Captain America's speech is an emphatic denouncement of the security-focused politics of his government-abiding opponents, in *Civil War* every plea for one side is answered by a counter argument. This can be considered the main regulative device, the first rule of *Civil War*: The *dramatis personae* are not divided into heroes and villains; instead, Marvel's most popular published protagonists and authors take different sides. That it is Captain America of all people who leads the resistance against America's government is an ironic punchline; but the other camp is supported by characters who are no less popular, and whose actions are presented with an equal amount of sympathy. Tony Stark, Reed Richards and others hold the rule of democratically legitimized law, the security of the citizenry, and not least the unity of the nation (whose precariousness is signaled by the historical allusion in the series' title) to be more important than the individual superhero's freedom to dispense anonymous vigilante justice.

"Whose Side Are You On?"—Yellow banderols on the covers of the *Civil War*-comics challenge readers to decide the dichotomy for themselves. What the text offers them is a presentation of the operative difference as such, which identifies the distinction between the time before and after the attacks with the binary of political conflict. To live after 9/11 is to be confronted with a division of popular opinion that cannot be evaded any more than there could be a return to the time before the caesura. That border is as impossible to cross as the limits of discourse that separate it from the construed reality of the attacks, which was shortly glimpsed in ideology and trauma and then lost again.

Rather, the seamless continuation of discourse defies the caesura. One important topical as well as aesthetic function in this process is performed by a strong historiographical tendency, which is no less prominent in *Civil War* than in most non-genre reactions to 9/11 in comic books. As much as Art Spiegelman quotes, paraphrases, and parodies comic strips from the turn of the previous century in his *In the Shadow of No Towers*, drawing attention to the origins of his sequential art and continuing the search for a form that is adequate to treat the events of 9/11, *Civil War* recurs to the history and prehistory of its heroes, to obsolete print formats and previous styles of drawing. In issue 25 of *Captain America*, in which the plot of *Civil War* culminates, Ed Brubaker recapitulates the origin of his hero in World War II. Retellings of the hero's origin are common in superhero stories, but Steve Epting's sepia-colored panels elude such conventions. Reminiscent of old photographs and playfully evoking a documentary stance, they do not rediscover the protagonist's origin as an ever-renewable and basically valid narrative, but as a past that stands in contrast to a very different present. Quoting the styles of several earlier pencillers of *Captain America* comics, most of all those by the famous Jack Kirby, Epting expands this attention to history to cover not only fiction, but the evolution of the genre.

In many other instances of such retrospectives, specific tropes connect the allegorical tale with September 11, while combining it with other topics and events to a newly constituted whole. One of the superheroes involved in the massacre at Stamford finds himself a prisoner at a camp that alludes to Guantanamo Bay by some of its visuals and some conspicuous choices in naming. The highly controversial imprisonment of "enemy combatants" is metonymically presented as a direct consequence of Stamford, and thus of 9/11 (Jenkins, "[Untitled]": 30–33). In another, untitled lyrical comic scripted by Paul Jenkins, Kei Kobayashi's drawings in every panel superimpose a motif from the ongoing civil war among superheroes with pictures from American internment camps for Japanese citizens in World War II, and with pictures of a Japanese-American and his son in the present, remembering his own internment. Caption boxes present an anonymous poem written in the camps in 1943. There is a fissure here between what is shown by the drawing and what is visible in the fictitious world. The visual metaphor takes up once more the ideologically isolated iconic imagery of 9/11, but replaces it with a different, discursive ideology. No longer an inconceivable unique event, it is now connected to numerous similar or related, historical or current experiences. The ambivalent argument of *Civil War* demonstrates the variability and flexibility of this discursive ideology, but also its semiotic greed that envelops ever more topics and events in its growing referential network. They all become parts of one symbolic monolith that seems to be completely identifiable with 9/11, without naming reasons for this subsumption beyond the workings of the discourse itself.

This strategy employs the dichotomy of the caesura to close its discourse against the incursion of the real. The absolute distinction between before and after is transformed into a regular and mediated experience of difference on this side of the distinction. The irreversibility that marks caesura re-emerges at other places, where it contributes to rather than suspends the continued circulation of signs. It does so in the inescapable ubiquitous challenge to choose a side, a choice that is simultaneously made impossible by the equable presentation of either party, in the shortcomings of the merely indirectly referenced historical event beyond the allegory, in the improper qualities of metonymical and metaphorical mechanisms that guarantee discursive cohesion, and in the strange manner with which fictitious and stylistic comic history re-enters its own textual surface.

But the provocation of this irreversibility aspires to become a genre feature itself. And it is in this aspect that the main strategy of *Civil War* is facilitated by changes in genre conventions hailing back to the late 1980s and the 1990s, developments in popular storytelling that have prepared this special semiotic treatment of caesura. Ever since the two first massive cross-over events in superhero comics, DC's *Crisis on Infinite Earths* (1985) and Marvel's *Secret War* (1984), the interest in the amalgamation of numerous serials to one coherent fictitious universe is also focused on the ruptures and problems introduced by these combinations. There are at least two kinds. First, the different serials resist their joining in various ways. Second, the continuous progression of irreversible events contradicts laws that previously seemed to be unshakeable in popular episodic storytelling. As each episode should be of equal value to every other, the starting conditions for each issue had to be the same, so that new and irregular readers could easily find their way, and regular readers could be sure to find more of the same material that they had come to appreciate. And so every story had to essentially return to its point of origin. This restriction of seriality to similarity gradually yielded to a fascination with contiguity in comics as well as in movie, TV and computer game serials during the last two decades. Special episodes were marked as important because they changed the status quo — at least for a while, for a short- or mid-term story arc (Johnson: 85–96). Marriage, incontrovertible change and even death started happening to protagonists in episodes that the audience felt they had to read or watch in order to follow the ongoing series. Increasingly, change became the new rule, and today's popular series often imply voluminous previous knowledge for each episode and only approach a very loose general form of a standardized episode cyclically and asymptotically. Increasingly, then, popular series of the late 1990s consider those events worthy of narration "after which nothing will be the same as before"— the very form of caesura by which 9/11 has been described. As the discursive treatment of 9/11 makes use of an intense experience of irreversibility, the preceding popular tendency towards this form might even be considered to be a cultural expectation for such caesuras, and count among the many preconditions and facilitators for the corresponding interpretation of 9/11.

Conclusion

The irreversibility of caesura is among the basic foundations upon which *Civil War* is built, both in its aesthetic presentation as well as in the logic of its narrative development. At its very end, however, the defeat and ultimately the death of Captain America add a decisive quality to the contiguous style of storytelling. At this point, the event caught the attention of news media and political pundits once again. While everyone seemed quick to accept the comic as a sharp commentary on present political conflicts, controversial interpretations could not agree whether it was an indictment of "the toxic state of Bush and Cheney's America" (Emanuel) or a symbol for the ruin of a nation "that has been hijacked by liberalism and is slowly being destroyed by democrat-ick socialism, [...] the acceptance of atheism and the homosexual agenda" (McCrae) — two of many different answers to *Civil War*'s sustained motto: "Whose Side Are You On?"

Either way, the politically ambivalent allegory is unequivocally connected to contemporary political discourse[3] and ends in yet another repetition of the irreversible caesura, and yet again turns it into a model for the ongoing productivity of the overarching discourse. Captain America surrenders amidst the ruins of Manhattan, reminiscent of 9/11, but destroyed by the battle of warring superheroes. Once more, the wrecked buildings are shown from above (Millar, *Civil War* 7: 20) but this time, the hero is one tiny detail among the rubble; in the following panels, the reader gazes down upon his upturned face. The series named after *Captain America* continued publication — with growing readership — for almost two years without its dead protagonist, celebrating irreversible change as a motivator for rather than an interruption of discourse. The unchanged title of the Captain America series relates to the past caesura, which no longer suspends, but drives the narrative.

(A German version of this article was previously published as "Whose Side Are You On?— Zur Allegorisierung von 9/11 in Marvels Civil War*—comics," 9/11 als Kulturelle Zäzur. Repräsentationen des 11 September 2001 in Kulturellen Diskursen, Literatur und visuellen Medien, ed. Sascha Seiler et al. [Bielefield: Transcript, 2009], 317–336.)*

Notes

1. The corpus follows the "Civil War Checklist" as published by Marvel, but also includes preparations and continuations in other episodes from the series included in the cross-over, especially the previous issues scripted by J. Michael Straczynski in *Amazing Spider-Man* and *Fantastic Four*, as well as the later issues of *Fantastic Four* scripted by Dwayne McDuffie and those of *Captain America* scripted by Ed Brubaker.
2. Metaphor, metonymy, and eventually allegory are used here in the sense given to these terms by French psychoanalysis, and connected with the corresponding Peircean categories (Lacan and Packard: "Anatomie des Comics," chap. 1 and 6).
3. It is this persuasive allegory that had probably impressed that pundit on Fox News who criticized the death of Captain America with a somewhat surprising claim to the realism of superheroes on March 8, 2007: "Comic books sell because they are somewhat realistic. [...] My point is, you should not kill Captain America while we're at war."

Works Cited

Bell, Steve. "The Spirit of 9/11." *The Guardian*. November 12, 2005.
Brubaker, Ed. *Captain America* 25. New York: Marvel, 2007.
Chute, Hillary. "Ragtime, Kavalier & Clay, and the Framing of Comics." *Modern Fiction Studies* 54.2 (2008): 268–301.
"Civil War Checklist." "Civil War (Comic Book)." *Wikipedia*. March 21, 2008. April 17, 2009. en.wikipedia.org/wiki/Civil_War_(comic_book).
Emanuel, Ari. "Did Bush and Cheney Kill Captain America?" *Huffington Post*. March 8, 2007. April 8, 2009. www.huffingtonpost.com/ari-emanuel/did-bush-and-cheney-kill-_b_42967.html.
Fleiss, Elein. *Septembre*. Paris: Onestar, 2002.
Heath, Stephen. *Questions of Cinema*. Bloomington: Indiana University Press, 1981.
Heroes: The World's Greates Superhero Creators Honor the World's Greatest Heroes 9/11/2001. New York: Marvel, 2001.
Hertz, Neil. *The End of the Line: Essays on Psychanalysis and the Sublime*. New York: Columbia University Press, 1985.
Jenkins, Paul. "The Accused." *Civil War Frontline* 2. New York: Marvel, 2007: 15–24.
_____. "[Untitled.]" *Civil War Frontline* 1. New York: Marvel, 2006: 30–33.
Johnson, Steven. *Everything Bad Is Good for You. How Popular Culture Is Actually Making Us Smarter*. New York: Riverhead, 2005.

Kuper, Peter. *Stop Forgetting to Remember: The Autobiography of Walter Kurtz*. New York: Crown, 2007.
Lacan, Jacques. "L'instance de la lettre dans l'inconscient ou la raison depuis Freud." *Écrits: Le champ freudien*. Paris: Seuil, 1966: 493–528.
Levitz, Paul (Ed.). *9-11: The World's Finest Comic Book Writers & Artists Tell Stories to Remember*. New York: DC, 2002.
Lisner, Joseph Michael. *I Love New York*. 2002. March 18, 2009. April 20, 2009. Lisner.com.
"Mark Millar's Civil War Post-Game Show." *Newsarama*, February 26, 2007. February 17, 2009. www.newsarama.com/marvelnew/CivilWar/millar_final.html.
McCloud, Scott. *Understanding Comics. The Invisible Art*. New York: HarperCollins, 1994.
McCrae, Michael John. "Captain America, the Death of a Republic." *The Conservative Voice*. March 8, 2007. May 4, 2009. www.theconservativevoice.com/article/23328.html.
Millar, Mark. *Civil War* 1. New York: Marvel, 2006.
_____. *Civil War* 7. New York: Marvel, 2007.
Packard, Stephan. *Anatomie des Comics: Psychosemiotische Medienanalyse*. Göttingen: Wallstein, 2006.
_____. "Die Rede von der Zäsur. Ein Versuch anhand von Nietzsches neuer Bildlichkeit." *In* Sascha Seiler et al. (Eds.). *Von Zäsuren und Ereignissen*. Bielefeld: Transcript, 2010 (forthcoming).
_____. "Reflections of the Cartoon." *International Journal of Comic Art* 8.2 (2006): 113–125.
_____. "Whose Side Are You On?—Zur Allegorisierung von 9/11 in Marvels Civil War—Comics." *In* Sascha Seiler et al. (Eds.). *9/11 als kulturelle Zäsur. Repräsentationen des 11. September 2001 in kulturellen Diskursen, Literatur und visuellen Medien*. Bielefeld: Transcript, 2009:317–336.
Peirce, Charles Sanders. "A Guess at the Riddle" (1887–8). *In* Pierce Edition Project: Max H. Fisch et al. (Eds.). *Writings of Charles S. Peirce: A Chronological Edition*. Bloomington: Indiana University Press, 1982. Vol. VI. 166–210.
Rieber, John Ney, and John Cassaday. *Captain America: The New Deal*. New York: Marvel, 2003.
Scheffer, Bernd. "'...wie im Film.' Der 11. September und die USA als Teil Hollywoods." *In* Mathias N. Lorenz (Ed.). *Narrative des Entsetzens. Künstlerische medial und intellektuelle Deutungen des 11. September 2001*. Würzburg: Königshausen & Neumann, 2004: 81–103.
Spiegelman, Art. *In the Shadow of No Towers*. New York: Pantheon Books, 2004 [2001–2].
Straczynski, J. Michael. *Amazing Spider-Man* 1.537. New York: Marvel, 2007.
_____. *Amazing Spider-Man* 2.36. New York: Marvel, 2001.
_____. *Amazing Spider-Man* 2.43. New York: Marvel, 2002.
Vaughn, Brian K. *Ex Machina*. New York: DC/Wildstorm, 2004.
Žižek, Slavoj. *Welcome to the Desert of the Real! Five Essays on September 11 and Related Dates*. London: Verso, 2002.

PART II: LITERATURE

SEPTEMBER 11 AND COLD WAR NOSTALGIA
Aaron DeRosa

These are the days after. Everything now is measured by after.
Don DeLillo, *Falling Man*

Introduction

In 1950, just five years after the atomic bombs brought World War II to a welcomed but tragic close, William Faulkner traveled to Stockholm, Sweden, to accept the Nobel Prize for Literature. "Our tragedy today," he told the assembly, "is a general and universal physical fear so long sustained by now that we can even bear it. There are no longer problems of the spirit. There is only one question: When will I be blown up?" ("Banquet Speech"). Widely praised, Faulkner's address cut to the spirit of the Cold War era. A year earlier, the increasingly aggressive Soviet Union successfully tested its first atomic bomb, justifying Americans' widespread terror felt after the first nuclear detonations in 1945. By the time the first *thermo*nuclear bomb was tested and information leaked about persistent radioactive fallout, it was well understood that the bomb was "no longer a weapon of war, but a means of extermination of whole populations" (qtd. in Boyer: 344).

These anxieties were not limited to the worried few. The invention of the ICBM in the late 50s, satellite photographs of missiles in Cuba in 1963, persistent nuclear detonations in the "Atomic Southwest" (Nevada alone would see over 1,000 detonations before 1992), nuclear proliferation in China (1964), India (1974), and Pakistan (1998), and the expansion of the nuclear power industry alongside the disasters at Three Mile Island and Chernobyl justified the pervasive sense of impending doom throughout the 20th century. This nuclear fear has ebbed and flowed with spikes in the 50s and early 60s leading up to the Cuban Missile Crisis, the late 70s and early 80s with increased Soviet aggression, and again in the late 90s and early 2000s with another wave of nuclear expansion.[1] As a result, America, it seems, has spent much of the last sixty years struggling to break free from the apocalyptic nightmare of nuclear weapons.

It is within this historical trajectory that the reaction to the events of September 11, 2001, needs to be understood. Although the tragedy of that day was drastically different in size, scope, and implications from the 1945 bombing of Hiroshima and

Nagasaki, America has come to imagine them through the same lens of national trauma. Certainly both events were traumatic in the sense that they were "sudden, comprehensive, fundamental, and unexpected" shocks to the country (Sztompka: 159). Reflecting on the immediate post–Hiroshima years, historian Paul Boyer suggested that "the entire basis of [the United States'] existence [had been] fundamentally altered" by the bomb (3). Don DeLillo made a similar assertion regarding the World Trade Center attacks, stating it would change "the way we think and act, moment to moment, week to week, for unknown weeks and months to come, and steely years" ("Ruins": 33). Indeed, the threat of a cultural trauma as we will see rests not just in its suddenness, but in its ability to radically alter the trajectory of cultural institutions and social interaction across generations.

However, to say that America was traumatized in 1945 and again in 2001 is to miss how the response to the latter is intimately woven with that of the former. Not only did the literary and political discourses surrounding September 11 establish an equivalency between these two moments, but they have imagined the terrorist attacks as the realization of the apocalyptic fear that Faulkner warned about after World War II. Put another way, September 11 registered, in part, as a traumatic repetition of the atomic blasts in America's cultural consciousness, a trauma from which America can never fully recover until it recognizes the true relationship of these events to one another. Healing America's cultural wounds is not something that simply happens over time, but requires what Dominic LaCapra calls "an articulatory practice" of "working through" that allows one to "distinguish between past and present and to recall in memory that something happened to one (or one's people) back then while realizing that one is living here and now with openings to the future" (22). That is, traumatic repetition must be recognized *as repetition* rather than reality. The importance of such healing is nowhere clearer than in the aftermath of 9/11, as American culture has not, as yet, consciously confronted the latent nuclear trauma embedded within its discourse.

It is fitting that the literary response to September 11 has been undertaken by writers whose earlier works took on related historical themes. Don DeLillo's *Underworld* (1997) (Cold War anxiety) begat *Falling Man* (2007), Ken Kalfus's *PU-239 and Other Russian Fantasies* (1999) (titular short story about selling uranium) begat *A Disorder Peculiar to the Country* (2006), and Jonathan Safran Foer's *Everything Is Illuminated* (2002) (the Holocaust) begat *Extremely Loud and Incredibly Close* (2005).[2] Even within their September 11 texts, these authors incorporate historical imagery to provide context for the contemporary condition: DeLillo and neo–Fascist terrorism, Kalfus and the invasion of Afghanistan, and Foer and the fire-bombing of Dresden. What I aim to show is that these texts extend the public discourse of atomic fear into the literary sphere, articulating the vision of the terrorist attacks as an *atomic* one. The effect of this has been to reconstruct post–9/11 America in terms recognizable as "Cold War culture," specifically employing the logic of containment and domesticity typical of the conformist 50s and the culture wars of the late 70s and early 80s.

PART II: LITERATURE

"America's first great air raid": Representations of the Bomb and 9/11

The origin of America's cultural obsession with nuclear imagery must inevitably return to its birth: August 6, 1945. Despite the fact that the United States perpetrated the atomic devastation on Hiroshima, American citizens could not help but feel victimized by its blast. That the Manhattan Project was a massive, secretive government venture only revealed to the public after the detonations in Japan contributed to the shocking nature of the event. In *By the Bomb's Early Light* (1985), Paul Boyer traces the "atomic neuroses" that developed in the aftermath of the bomb and persisted throughout the Cold War (317). Bomb shelters and dog tags, non-proliferation agreements and missile defense shields, and visions of mutant monsters, alien invasions, and nuclear holocaust in film and literature, the country girded itself for a destruction that never came. The bombardment of nuclear tales throughout the Cold War — Paul Brians' *Nuclear Holocaust* (1987) is a 1,400-entry bibliography of short stories, plays, and novels on the title topic (it omits literature that doesn't specifically refer to holocausts and novels where nuclear holocausts are never fully realized) — has made representations of the bomb commonplace.

Yet the ubiquity of these images has not fostered the working through that LaCapra's therapeutic model of trauma necessitates. In *Monsters, Mushroom Clouds, and the Cold War*, M. Keith Booker suggests that "in some ways, the predecessor of all of the post-holocaust works of the long 1950s" was John Hersey's *Hiroshima*. Hersey's 1946 New Journalist novel of six hibakusha (explosion-affected people) testimonials assumed an objective, distant position from the event. In one sense, it asked its readers to register the emotional charge of the bomb from their own perspective. However, it also received much criticism for painting the event with no emotional affect whatsoever. That is, for many, Hersey's novel asked only to be read and understood, not to be felt or processed. Such was the case in the post–9/11 cultural sphere where, according to Susan Faludi, films were designed to "replicate, not delve" into the meaning of the catastrophic event (3). Instead, these productions act out the trauma "as if one were back in the past," specifically the moment when Hiroshima was decimated by the first atomic bomb (21).

It is not surprising, then, that America's response to 9/11 has consistently fallen back on the rhetoric of bombings and nuclear devastation. Marshall Berman referred to the WTC as "bombed buildings," victims of "mainland America's first great air raid" (3; 5). Beverly Gage wrote an article titled "The First Wall Street Bomb," implicitly connecting the events of 9/11 with previous bombings. Nick Gillespie likened the War on Terror to the Cold War in that they both "restructured every aspect of American society, becoming the center around which every activity revolved" (72). Mark Wigley went so far as to claim the energy generated by the falling buildings was "comparable to nuclear blasts or volcanic activity" (73).

M. Christine Boyer draws our attention to the most intriguing connection, "that of Ground Zero itself, bringing to mind metaphors associated with the first atomic tests and all the paradoxes that entails" (117). "Ground Zero," the common appellation for the empty WTC plaza, was a spatial designator originally used to describe, as the *Oxford English Dictionary* puts it, "that part of the ground situated immediately under an exploding bomb, esp. an atomic one. [...] This naming connected the 9/11 attack through time and space to the World War II–era atomic testing sites in the Nevada desert, and to America's bombing of Hiroshima" (Melnick: 157). David Simpson extended this logic beyond the name, claiming that "one can see the connection of the 2001 event with the dropping of the bomb: there too, in Hiroshima and Nagasaki, hardly any bodies or body parts remained. There too most of the victims who died on those days were vaporized. There too no one had a clue what was coming out of a clear summer sky" (43).

John Mueller recently argued that

> there has been a particular fixation since the terrorist attacks of September 11, 2001, on the potential for a terrorist atomic bomb, and politicians of all stripes preach to an anxious, appreciative, and very numerous choir when they, like President Barack Obama, alarmingly proclaim it "the most immediate and extreme threat to global security" [x–xi].

This was evident in the United States' early emergency response to the attacks of September 11 when the country's nuclear power plants were immediately secured after learning of the attack. Logical to some degree — nuclear plants would seem to be reasonable targets — there were no comparable responses from the British government after the London Underground attacks in 2005. England's emergency response protocols, updated after the September 11 attacks, include no mention of increased security measures at nuclear power plants as part of the overall response. The same is true of Spain's response to the 2004 terrorist attacks in Madrid.[3]

These connections are borne out in the fictional representations as well. In *A Disorder Peculiar to the Country*, Ken Kalfus's tragicomedy of a bitter divorce punctuated by the September 11 attacks, one of the protagonists, Joyce Harriman, describes the Tower's collapse as "a rising mushroom-shaped column of smoke, dust, and perished life" (3). Despite having witnessed the airplane crash into the second tower, Joyce still draws on nuclear imagery to represent the witnessed event. That neither the physics nor the footage from 9/11 bears this out does not deter Joyce from the association.[4] The same applies to Florence Givens, one of DeLillo's WTC survivors in *Falling Man*, who heard the plane but grew convinced by the rumors that the buildings had been bombed. As she vacated the Tower she stated "it was dark wherever we were but then we came out and passed some windows and saw the plaza where it's *a bombed-out city*, things on fire, we saw bodies, we saw clothes, pieces of metal like metal parts, things just scattered" (58, emphasis added). And perhaps most tellingly, DeLillo's protagonist Keith Neudecker describes the event as "a shift in the basic arrangements of parts and elements" (240), articulating the tragedy as a reconfiguration on the atomic level.

The more refined details of Kalfus's and DeLillo's novels bear this nuclear association out as well, echoing Hersey's Ur-text of nuclear literature that defined the United States' vision of the bomb: a blinding flash, a thunderous rumble, a powerful shockwave, uncontrollable fires, radiation poisoning, and the severe burns of the survivors. Hersey's hibakusha described a "local column of dust" that filled the air in a "thick dreadful miasma" that prompted 10-year-old Myeko to ask at nine o'clock in the morning, "why is it night already?" (23, 24, 26). "Clumps of smoke, near and far, had begun to push up through the general dust" (24). Through the dust, the survivors glimpsed a decimated city described by psychiatrist Robert Jay Lifton as belonging to another world (431). Similarly, Kalfus's Marshall Harriman describes his escape from the South Tower as entering "another planet's landscape, lightning-charged, caustically lit, inimical [...] like a journey or transition to a new world" (13–14). The roar of the falling Tower "was like the break of the surf and it seemed to lift [Marshall] from the street. Debris rained down on his back and chalky dust filled his mouth and nose" (17).

DeLillo's opening line offers a similar assessment, claiming "it was not a street anymore but a world, a time and space of falling ash and near night" (3). DeLillo describes the "rumble of the fall" and the "seismic tides of smoke," the "smoke and ash [...] rolling down streets" and debris falling from the air, the "scorched objects trailing lines of fire" and the "steady rip of sirens in the air" (3–4). Keith is accosted by images of water—paper cups, broken sprinklers, a woman offering him a water bottle—recalling the desperate cries for "mizu," water, from the hibakusha whose "abnormal thirst" was one of the symptoms of radiation sickness (Schell 8). Similarly, the miscellaneous articles of clothing that float through the air and roll down the street echo the half-naked survivors of Hiroshima whose clothes were literally burned from their bodies.

One such miscellaneous object — the suitcase — appears in both DeLillo and Hersey to reinforce the latent nature of the traumas their characters experience. In Hersey, Father Kleinsorge notices that after the atomic detonation, "his desk was in splinters all over the room, but a mere papier-mâché suitcase, which he had hidden under the desk, stood handle-side up, without a scratch on it" (29). It contained important parish funds and documents and its survival, Kleinsorge claimed, had granted it "talismanic powers" (85). Later Kleinsorge travels downtown to deposit the suitcase in a bank only to return with radiation poisoning. The suitcase is thus responsible for his declining physical health, a detail reimagined in DeLillo's novel. Having rescued a mysterious briefcase from the Tower, Keith tracks down the owner, Florence, a co-survivor with whom Keith engages in a brief affair. Through their conversations she helps Keith to "find himself in the crowd" coming out of the North Tower (59), something Keith had been unable to do. While Hersey's briefcase manifests the physical symptoms of the nuclear blast, DeLillo's reinforces the psychological ramifications of the WTC attacks.

These impositions are even clearer in Foer's *Extremely Loud and Incredibly Close* where the atomic referent through which the reader interprets the events of 9/11 is directly provided. The novel is told from the perspective of the nine-year-old Oskar Schell whose father, Thomas, died in the attack. As such, the reader is not privileged with a first-hand account like those provided by Marshall, Keith, and Florence. Instead, the reader must make sense of the trauma through the eyes of those who were not present at Ground Zero. Although Oskar has listened intently to his father's frenzied messages on the home answering machine, the fear and pain his father experienced is still unknown to him. Oskar laments that the uncertainty forces him to "invent" stories about how his father died. One particularly revealing moment comes when Oskar presents the testimonial of a Hiroshima survivor named Tomoyasu to his class. The story details Tomoyasu's search for her daughter whom she finds on the verge of death, crying for her mother and repeating that she doesn't want to die (187). Later, when Oskar braves his way to the observation deck of the Empire State Building, he invents a 9/11 narrative whose language mirrors that of Tomoyasu's. Oskar envisions CEOs calling for their mothers and people shouting that they don't want to die; referencing the horrible burns Tomoyasu describes, Oskar declares "it would be getting so hot that my skin would start to get blisters" (244).

Published four to six years after the initial shock, these novels mirror and extend the public discourse surrounding 9/11 where the pervasiveness of nuclear imagery suggested that, far more than simply being the most significant attack on American soil, September 11 was perceived as an *atomic* attack. Obviously, the hard facts regarding 9/11—the highjackings of four airplanes, the demolition of two buildings, and the crippling of a third—make such linkages tenuous. But the large scale pervasiveness of nuclear concern after 9/11 suggests that this is far more than coincidental. And, as Jeffrey Melnick argues, one cannot simply attribute the concern to the fear-mongering of politicians, pundits, and capitalists. Rather it seems like a repetition of America's nuclear trauma. In her groundbreaking work in trauma theory, *Unclaimed Experience*, Cathy Caruth tells us that trauma includes "not only the reality of the violent event but also the reality of the way that its violence has not yet been fully known" (6). While America consistently forces the nuclear issue front and center, it has historically been resistant to conversations about its own nuclear past evident in the 1994 Smithsonian Controversy over the exhibition of the Enola Gay[5] or acknowledgment of the Downwinder population of Utah.[6] As such, America has never fully engaged the "trauma process" to negotiate the "the ideal and material consequences" of the event (Alexander 22). Instead, 9/11 operated in part as a traumatic acting out of America's nuclear fear whose conflation, LaCapra warns, may inhibit healing.

Cultural Trauma and Containment Culture

Significantly, acting out a cultural trauma can radically alter both the trajectory of social institutions (from national funding reprioritization to the type of art released in the marketplace) as well as individual psychology across generations. If we define culture as "information capable of affecting individuals' behavior that they acquire from other members of their species through teaching, imitation, and other forms of social transmission" (Richerson and Boyd: 5), then a cultural trauma is something inherited. I define a cultural trauma as an event that disrupts a population to the point where these transmissions become radically altered. While there are many ways in which these transmissions can become integrated into cultural information, narrative holds a privileged position in the field of trauma.[7] Jeffrey Alexander tells us that "trauma depends on constructing a compelling framework of cultural classification" (12). Alexander conceives of this framework of classification in terms of a cultural narrative.

The narrative built around 9/11 historicized the event through, among other things, its atomic imagery that promoted the reestablishment of Cold War culture, a culture whose beliefs and behaviors arose from the socio-cultural construction of a monolithic binary of "good" versus "evil" where the latter threatened the cultural annihilation of the former, either by means of nuclear holocaust, cultural and political insurgency, or both. Alan Nadel described this as a "containment culture" that extended the government's foreign policy to the domestic sphere. Where the foreign policy sought to limit the cultural, political, and geographical expansion of communism, the domestic policy was established to deal with America's cultural anxieties.[8] "Very shortly after the bomb initially exploded upon American consciousness," Nadel states, "a national narrative developed to control the fear and responsibility endemic to possessing atomic power" whose "central motif" was "containment" (14). America's domestic containment policy operated as a "rhetorical strategy that functioned to foreclose dissent, preempt dialogue, and preclude contradiction" (14). Gillespie identified the same impulse in Bush's Operation Enduring Freedom which "ushered in an age of explicit national purpose — an overarching political purpose to which everything else is subjugated" (71). For Nadel, this "national purpose" is evidence of what Jean Francois Lyotard called "metanarratives"— narratives that claim universal status and, in doing so, suppress dissent and enforce particular forms of knowledge — that led to the unprecedented conformity and rigid behavioral rules that would come to define the aftermath of World War II *and* September 11.

DeLillo's *Falling Man* employs this logic in Keith's poker games. Prior to September 11, Keith hosted a weekly game with friends and coworkers. The rules started off light, "but over time they began to reduce the dealer's options" to certain types of poker (96). They subsequently eliminated serving food, certain kinds of alcohol — only "scotch, bourbon, brandy, the manlier tones and deeper and more intense distillations. No gin, no vodka, no wan liquors" (98) — and banned talk of sports, movies, and television. "These free-flowing energies and gestures," DeLillo writes, "were posed against a single counterforce, the fact of self-imposed restriction, all the more unyielding for being ordered from within" (98). DeLillo is certainly self-conscious of this link, recognizing their betting strategy was grounded in "intuition and cold-war risk analysis" (97).

The weekly poker game and its unbending rules were abolished prior to the 9/11 attacks, but Keith seeks out these boundaries after the attacks by joining the tournament poker circuit. By engaging the official rules of the game, he found "he was fitting into something that was made to his shape" (225). Poker provides structure for Keith's post–9/11 life by imposing a set of rigid rules defined by an outside authority. As such, Keith "wondered if he was becoming a self-operating mechanism, like a humanoid robot that understands two hundred voice commands, far-seeing, touch-sensitive but totally, rigidly, controllable" (226). This is both desirable and necessary for Keith. When a former poker buddy, Terry Cheng, shows up at a tournament and offers Keith a spot at a private game like those they used to play, Keith is not interested; the public games provide him with the "crucial anonymity of these days and weeks, the mingling of countless lives that had no stories attached" (204). Keith's glorification of the "standard methods and routines" (197) and blind obedience to institutional power is in keeping with the American response to 9/11 where dissent was swiftly "handled" either by the government or the network news media.

The same can be said of the divorce proceedings between Marshall and Joyce Harriman in Kalfus's *Disorder*. Over the course of the multi-year debacle, they must cohabit their apartment and establish a certain code about handling the children, speaking to one another, and partitioning their time and space. "According to the precise, stringent, tacitly observed rules, Marshall and Joyce were prohibited from looking at each other directly, or from even recognizing the other's presence, even at home" (162). Each character conducts "border skirmishes," testing the limits of the system's stability without risking full-scale assault. The skirmishes are used to weaken the other's position after the divorce settlement which looms over their heads like a strategic arms negotiation: "Every once in a while an outside party would come up with a stratagem to break the deadlock—a simultaneous exchange of major concessions, a splitting of the differences—but Joyce and Marshall closed ranks against it. Their positions had shifted shape to exactly meet and oppose the contours of each other's interests" (188). Their willful prolonging of the process operates much like Keith's poker tournaments: a welcomed constraint that provides order for their lives in the wake of 9/11. When the settlement is finalized, both are relieved but directionless. Kalfus's clever vision of "domestic terrorism" is, of course, satiric, and the restrictions placed on Joyce and Marshall's behaviors border on ridiculous. But Kalfus is precisely pointing to the types of containment policies that establish order in the home, codify the bounds of personal relationships, and reaffirms institutional (legal) authority in the wake of a cultural trauma.[9]

Foer dramatizes this motif through Oskar's grandparents whose relationship juxtaposes the height of Cold War conformity in the 1950s (when Thomas Sr. and Oskar's grandmother are first reunited after the Dresden bombing) with the aftermath of 9/11 (when Thomas Sr. returns after forty years to help his estranged wife cope with the death of their son). Thomas Sr. describes their relationship: "everything between us has been a rule to govern our life together, everything a measurement, a marriage of millimeters, of rules" (109). One of these involved the demarcation of "Nothing Places" in the apartment where the occupying contents, animate or not, "temporarily cease to exist" (110). These spatial limits establish the dimensions of the apartment, the nature of their relationship, and their constructed memory.

Such is also the case for Oskar's main narrative arc. Prior to 9/11, Oskar's life is metaphorically encapsulated by his exploration of Central Park, a direction-less game his father created whose main task involves figuring out the rules. After 9/11, Oskar needs some kind of ordering principle and finds solace in the mysterious key marked "Black" in his father's closet. Oskar's subsequent search through all the Blacks in the New York City phonebook seems like the self-established boundaries of Keith's pre–9/11 poker games, but it is later revealed that his mother's curious lack of concern about his whereabouts is due to her careful orchestration of the quest. Oskar reflects that his "search was a play that Mom had written, and she knew the ending when I was at the beginning" (292). Oskar's freedom is merely an illusion, but rather than bucking these constraints, he finds comfort in them. It is through these constructed limitations that Oskar and his mother are able to reconcile their relationship, share their grief, and seemingly begin the healing process.

Interestingly, Foer's affirmation of traditional domestic authority rests in the family unit as opposed to the institutional authority of Kalfus and DeLillo. *Falling Man*'s Keith Neudecker has difficulty assimilating into family life. Although the WTC attacks first compel him back to his estranged wife and child and he attempts to rebuild their relationship, this reconciliation is complicated by the extramarital affair with Florence. In the end, Lianne is correct in her prediction that he will "drift away" (214). Kalfus's novel more clearly centers itself on the dissolution of the family bonds through the divorce of Joyce and Marshall. While 9/11 does not initiate the proceedings, it provides the structural matrix around which their relationship fails. By contrasting the political violence between the United States and the Middle East with domestic violence, Kalfus identifies the disorder peculiar to the country as one that has to do with America's construction of family identity in the aftermath of trauma.

Domesticity and the Next Generation

The heightened anxiety of Cold War culture was not envisioned simply as the physical threat of nuclear annihilation but also the socio-cultural threat of communism. Elaine Tyler May asserted that "although strategists and foreign policy experts feared that the Soviet Union might gain the military might and territorial expansion to achieve world domination, many leaders, pundits and observers worried that the real dangers to America were internal ones: racial strife, emancipated women, class conflict, and familial disruption" (22). Paranoia that American values would be corrupted from within by Soviet insurgents sowing social and political discontent became firmly entrenched in the United States. One of the defenses against this was domestication: "A home filled with children would create a feeling of warmth and security against the cold forces of disruption and alienation" (26). The pressure for men to settle into the role of financial supporter and women into housewife pervaded the country. May acknowledges that the fear of atomic devastation partly explains the Baby Boom, the lowered age of marriage, and increased conformity to the "American dream." In her own words:

> To alleviate these fears, Americans turned to the family as a bastion of safety in an insecure world, while experts, leaders and politicians promoted codes of conduct and enacted public policies that would bolster the American home. Like their leaders, most Americans agreed that family stability appeared to be the best bulwark against the dangers of the cold war [xviii].[10]

If domestic containment (both in the sense of national identity for Nadel and family life for May) reinforced United States foreign policy, depictions of its failure suggest more than just personal ennui; it suggested cultural weakness. In the 1950s, a failed family was indicative of successful Communist insurgency. The similar emphasis on broken homes in September 11 literature suggests the same of terrorists.

Acknowledging the post–9/11 affinity for Cold War imagery, Faludi asks the question: "What were we struggling to overcome with our 1950s fantasies?" (8). Faludi, like Nadel and May, suggests it has to do with the articulation of gender roles.[11] The traumatic, destabilizing nature of the bomb "revived the old fear of masculine insufficiency" (280). Men were asked to protect their women — militarily, financially, etc.— while women were forced once again to return to the home. Faludi traces this pressure in the post–9/11 narrative that suggested the "true" victims of the attacks were the widows; specifically, women who were not "ambitious careerists trading commodities on the eighty-fourth floor. They were at home that day tending to the hearth, models of all-American housewifery" (93). This tension is evident in the conflict between Oskar and his mother in *Extremely Loud*; Oskar is upset that his mother was not with him when he was sent home early from school on September 11. He develops an animosity towards her as she attempts to settle into a new life and takes comfort in the company of another man. Their relationship is repaired only when she affirms her role as mother. Oskar comments that their relationship was complicated but also incredibly simple: "In my only life, she was my mom, and I was her son" (324). Immediately after reinforcing this maternal bond, Oskar gives her permission to remarry. She refuses, but when she leaves the room, Oskar can hear her cry and he imagines her "wet sleeves. Her tired eyes" (325). Whether self-conscious or not, Oskar views his mother as a victim, another 9/11 widow "who accepted that their 'job' now was to devote themselves to their families and the memory of their dead husbands" (Faludi: 93).

The same victimization and maternal obligation is evident in Keith's wife Lianne who admits that Keith was "stronger than I was[...]. You were the one in the tower but I was berserk" (215). But as her shock wears off and Keith's traumatic symptoms set in, these roles reverse and her strength is required to keep the family together. When Keith joins the poker circuit, she sets the parameters of the relationship in accordance with the cult of domesticity by allowing him a certain emotional distance, but denying him total freedom: "This is the point I want to make, that we need to stay together, keep the family going" (214). Technically not a model housewife since she is estranged from Keith prior to the attacks, she makes up for it by being home when Keith arrives. She rushes him to the hospital, tends his wounds, and tries to return their lives to normal. Lianne is warned by her mother not to "let [her] sympathy and goodwill affect [her] judgment" but this is precisely her impulse (10). "Times like these," she later tells Keith, "the family is necessary" (214). Although Keith rejects this domestic life, DeLillo certainly paints it as the preferred alternative.

The domestic sphere is a crucial image for Faludi who compared the "nuclear insecurity and the securing of American domesticity" in the 1950s manifest "in the anointment of the era's symbolic bulwark and bunker: the nuclear family's suburban 'ranch' home" (Faludi: 282). This becomes refigured in the Manhattan apartments highlighted in DeLillo, Foer, and Kalfus's novels. While Foer's Oskar spends most of his time out of the apartment on his grand adventure through New York City, the novel ends with a literal return home where his relationship to his mother is mended. No such peace exists for Marshall and Joyce in *Disorder*. Their bitter fight is not a recapitulation of past wrongs but an effort to destabilize the other's position both within the apartment as well as in the legal process whose ultimate prize is ownership of said apartment. Just as communism posed a threat to the stability of the home, Kalfus's apartment is the "true" battleground of the war on terror. That Marshall and Joyce's actions mirror the contemporary issues of the day reinforces this connection. Marshall wiretaps Joyce's phone and Joyce uses sex as "a weapon" by sleeping with Marshall's best friend (on his bed) after interpreting a story she heard about how Afghani men view their women (63). And while the baby powder in the bathroom *incorrectly* leads to Joyce's suspicion that Marshall faked an anthrax scare in her building, Marshall *does* attempt a suicide bombing. When the divorce is finalized and Marshall is dispossessed, Joyce and the children watch Saddam Hussein's execution on television: the end of the war coincides with the purging of the home.

But purging the home does not seem to fix the ultimate crisis of domesticity in post–9/11 literature, in part because it fails to take into account the intergenerational nature of this trauma. Foer is certainly the most self-consciously aware of this. Told primarily from the perspective of a child, *Extremely Loud* depicts Oskar's invention of stories about his father's death on 9/11. Left to his own devices, Oskar's stories are emotionally crippling; his relationship with his mother is strained, he is increasingly isolated from his family and friends, he is afraid of answering machines, skyscrapers, bridges, and subways, and struggles to imagine the traumatic events of that day. His narratives act out rather than work through the event. While the final reconciliation with his mother alleviates some tension, Oskar still finds himself imagining time rewinding itself to a point when his father was still alive and the Towers had not fallen; that is, the trauma threatens to repeat itself.

The Harriman children in Kalfus's *Disorder* similarly struggle to make sense of 9/11 and what it has done to their family. Viola visits a psychologist who asks her to draw pictures of her family and "in each one she had placed her family near or around the burning World Trade Center" where they were depicted burning and screaming with amputated limbs (74): "In the last drawing the four of them had leaped from the towers and were falling hand in hand" (74). As Viola slowly realizes the animosity between her parents, she does so through parallels to September 11. In one scene, she and Victor hold hands while leaping from a back porch, playing "9/11." The game ends when Viola breaks her wrist because Victor let go, metaphorizing the failure of the family unit to provide protection.

But perhaps the most telling vision of the traumatic legacy of 9/11 is evident in Keith and Lianne's son Justin in *Falling Man*. Justin secretly gazes through a pair of binoculars with his friends, looking for the next attack by "Bill Lawton," the misheard name of Osama bin Laden. Justin and his friends are certain that they'll witness bin Laden's next attack when he will finally bring the Towers down. Neither Keith nor Lianne care to correct his misnaming the enemy, nor can they convince him that the Towers have already fallen. "He seemed to absorb" the fact that they had fallen, Lianne says, "but then, I don't know" (72). Lianne fears her child's "twisted powers of imagination" (72), but her condemnation falls flat under the broken skyline where twisted imagination has become reality. "They developed the myth of Bill Lawton," Keith concedes (74). Unable to work through the event, Justin and his friends stare through binoculars, "looking for more planes" and "searching the skies" (72, 73), waiting for a future in which "Lawton" will finish what he started, ominously echoing the unfinished business of the Hiroshima bombing that promised to be revisited upon America.

Conclusion

Justin's belief that the Towers did not fall demonstrates the ramifications of an inherited cultural trauma. His constructed myth echoes America's atomic legacy: the detonations whose traumatic impact was never fully processed, the terror of which haunts the country's cultural consciousness. The resulting socio-political discourse has trended towards paranoia and violence. In 2002, only months after the attacks, George Bush identified an "Axis of Evil" comprised of Iraq, Iran, and North Korea. What makes these countries distinct from Saudi Arabia and Afghanistan (where the terrorists were born and trained) is that they have pursued nuclear weapons programs. Thus the arguments that led America into invading Iraq on the principle of securing Saddam Hussein's stockpile of Weapons of Mass Destruction (WMD) are a tangible and bloody manifestation of this traumatic legacy. Most recently, the 2008 Presidential election that saw a revival of Cold War rhetoric — most directly, the questioned patriotism of liberals and the potential "socialism" (read: communism) of Barack Obama — demonstrated the pervasiveness of these fears even as communism loses steam in global politics. But socialism, in this context, seems to stand less for its standard definition than a fear of internal terrorist insurgency as seen in Justin's Americanization of bin Laden's name. This is similarly evident when Obama's opponents conflated his "socialist" political ideology with his affiliation to a "domestic terrorist," William Ayers of the Weather Underground. This logic establishes an equivalency between socialism, communism, and terrorism and joins representations of the WTC attacks with the bombing of Hiroshima.

Of course, to say that there is an equivalency drawn between the events of September 11 and the fear of the atomic bomb is not to denigrate the American response to its current trauma but to place our response in context. To be sure, there has been an earnest effort by each author to find new forms of representation after 9/11 from Kalfus's satire to Foer's visual manipulations. Perhaps the most moving and consistent image has been the falling man. At the heart of DeLillo's novel is the performance artist David Janiak who jumps from various public spaces before being caught by a harness attached to his leg. His body contorts into the form of the iconic image of Norberto Hernandez, the famous 9/11 jumper.[12] Where DeLillo emphasizes the isolating nature of fear and freedom, Kalfus focuses on the image of a jumping couple who held hands as they fell. As a metaphor for Marshall and Joyce's relationship, the jumpers also echo Viola and Victor's game of 9/11 where togetherness offers protection from harm. Foer diagrammatically represents the falling man, placing a series of photographs of a man falling from the towers in reverse so that when the reader flips through the images it seems as if the body is flying up through the air or backward in time until the sky is empty again.

Whether the body floats up or falls down, in 2001 DeLillo suggested that the emptiness of the sky after 9/11 forced writers "to give memory, tenderness, and meaning to all that howling space" ("Ruins" 39). Whether deliberately or not, DeLillo echoes Faulkner's obstinacy in 1950: "I decline to accept the end of man," he stated. "It is the poet's, the writer's duty to write about these things. [...] The poet's voice need not merely be the record of man, it can be one of the props, the pillars to help him endure and prevail" ("Banquet Speech"). In the same vein, DeLillo called for a "counter-narrative" to the Cold War memory that existed prior to the 9/11 events and it is this challenge that America must face if it is to work through them.

Notes

1. While numerous resources exist that detail nuclear paranoia in American culture, perhaps the most useful are Paul Boyer's *By the Bomb's Early Light*, Philip Jenkins' *Decade of Nightmares*, and Elaine Taylor May's *Homeward Bound: American Families in the Cold War*.

2. Paul Auster, John Updike, and Art Spiegelman also fit this mold in varying degrees.

3. This is not to suggest that the threat of terrorist attacks on nuclear reactors is inconceivable. In 2009 India placed their nuclear power plants on high alert in response to a terrorist threat, but in that case the threat was specifically directed toward those plants. Indeed, September 11 co-conspirator Moham-

mad Atta had considered targeting a nuclear reactor (Indian Point Energy Center is only forty miles north of Manhattan). But this information would take years to come to light and was certainly not available on the morning of September 11.

4. A mushroom cloud is formed when a sufficiently massive explosion creates a rising fireball that sucks colder air into itself creating a "stem" of debris and smoke while the toroidal vortices of circulating air form the "cap." But the WTC's collapse operated under different principles with smoke rising and debris falling.

5. In 1994 a bitter controversy erupted between the American Legion and the Smithsonian National Air and Space Museum over a new exhibit titled "The Crossroads: The End of World War II, the Atomic Bomb and the Cold War" whose central image was the Enola Gay, the B-29 bomber that dropped the first nuclear bomb over Japan. At its core, the debate raged over how to represent the tragedy at Hiroshima and Nagasaki and if it was the purview of the Smithsonian to do so. One side desired to suppress any suggestion that America's decision to drop the bomb was questionable while the other sought to faithfully record a historical moment. The Smithsonian ultimately backed down and established a heavily edited version of the original exhibit. See Kai Bird's *Hiroshima's Shadow* for more information.

6. The hundreds of nuclear tests in the "Atomic Southwest" created massive amounts of radioactive fallout that would travel downwind from the test site into western Utah. The "Downwinders," not officially recognized by the government until the Reagan Administration, were prone to increased cancer rates, particularly among women, as detailed in the epilogue to Terry Tempest Williams' *Refuge*, "The Clan of One-Breasted Women."

7. The importance of narrative for traumatic healing has been well-documented throughout the history of trauma studies and most recently in the work of narratologist Kitty Klein.

8. It should be noted that while this essay focuses largely on the domestic side of the containment narrative, the Bush Administration's foreign policy strategy (dubbed the "Bush Doctrine") of preemptive war was justified under the auspices of Cold War containment: contain the states that support terrorism and the regional terrorist networks will falter.

9. These rules are not, it should be noted, willfully constructed by some overarching power or grand governmental conspiracy. While politicians can certainly tap into these constructs, they are already evident within social interactions prior to their regimentation in governmental policy.

10. Novelists as diverse as Sloan Wilson and Jack Kerouac, Mickey Spillane and John Updike dealt with the institution of marriage — both its political and psychological importance — in the atomic age.

11. Nadel and May both track the resurrection of the "cult of domesticity" in 1950s America. In 2008, May revised her influential *Homeward Bound: American Families in the Cold War* and included an epilogue in which she begins to track the same threads in post–9/11 culture.

12. See Tom Junod's article in *Esquire*, "The Falling Man."

Works Cited

Allison, Graham T. *Nuclear Terrorism*. New York: Macmillan, 2005.
Berman, Marshall. "When Bad Buildings Happen to Good People." *In* Michael Sorkin and Sharon Zukin (Eds.). *After the World Trade Center: Rethinking New York City*. New York: Routledge, 2002: 1–12.
Booker, M. Keith. *Monsters, Mushroom Clouds, and the Cold War*. Westport, CT: Greenwood, 2001.
Boyer, M. Christine. "Meditations on a Wounded Skyline and Its Stratigraphies of Pain." *In* Michael Sorkin and Sharon Zukin (Eds.). *After the World Trade Center: Rethinking New York City*. New York: Routledge, 2002: 109–120.
Boyer, Paul. *By the Bomb's Early Light: American Thought and Culture at the Dawn of the Atomic Age*. New York: Pantheon Books, 1985.
Brians, Paul. *Nuclear Holocausts: Atomic War in Fiction, 1895–1984*. Kent, OH: Kent State University Press, 1987.
Caruth, Cathy. *Unclaimed Experience: Trauma, Narrative, and History*. Baltimore: The Johns Hopkins University Press, 1996.
DeLillo, Don. *Falling Man*. New York: Scribner, 2007.

_____. "In the Ruins of the Future." *Harper's* 303.1812 (2001): 33–40.
Erickson, Kai. *Everything in Its Path*. New York: Simon and Schuster, 1976.
Faludi, Susan. *The Terror Dream: Fear and Fantasy in Post–9/11 America*. New York: Metropolitan Books, 2007.
Faulkner, William. *Banquet Speech*. December 10, 1950. July 29, 2009. http://nobelprize.org/nobel_prizes/literature/laureates/1949/faulkner-speech.html.
Foer, Jonathan Safran. *Extremely Loud and Incredibly Close*. New York: Houghton Mifflin, 2005.
Gage, Beverly. "The First Wall Street Bomb." *In* Michael Sorkin and Sharon Zukin (Eds.). *After the World Trade Center: Rethinking New York City*. New York: Routledge, 2002: 45–56.
Gillespie, Nick. "The New Cold War." *Reason*, December 2001: 71.
Hersey, John. *Hiroshima*. New York: Bantam Pathfinder, 1968.
Kalfus, Ken. *A Disorder Peculiar to the Country*. New York: Harper Perennial, 2006.
Kristof, Nicholas D. *An American Hiroshima*. August 11, 2004. July, 29 2009. http://www.nytimes.com/2004/08/11/opinion/11kris.html.
LaCapra, Dominic. *Writing History, Writing Trauma*. Baltimore: The Johns Hopkins University Press, 2001.
Lifton, Robert Jay. *Death in Life: Survivors of Hiroshima*. Chapel Hill: University of North Carolina Press, 1991.
May, Elaine Tyler. *Homeward Bound: American Families in the Cold War Era*. New York: Basic Books, 2008.
Melnick, Jeffrey. *9/11 Culture*. West Sussex: Wiley-Blackwell, 2009.
Nadel, Alan. *Containment Culture*. Durham: Duke University Press, 1996.
Richerson, Peter J., and Robert Boyd. *Not by Genes Alone*. Chicago: University of Chicago Press, 2009.
Simpson, David. *9/11: The Culture of Commemoration*. Chicago: University of Chicago Press, 2006.
Sztompka, Piotr. "The Trauma of Social Change: A Case of Postcommunist Societies." *In* Jeffrey C. Alexander, et al. (Eds.). *Cultural Trauma and Collective Identity*. Berkeley: University of California Press, 2004: 155–195.
Wigley, Mark. "Insecurity by Design." *In* Michael Sorkin and Sharon Zukin (Eds.). *After the World Trade Center: Rethinking New York City*. New York: Routledge, 2002: 69–86.

DON DELILLO'S *FALLING MAN*
Countering Post–9/11 Narratives of Heroic Masculinity
Magali Cornier Michael

Published in June 2007, Don DeLillo's novel, *Falling Man*, opens with the figure of a man walking away from the first crumbling World Trade Center tower in New York City on the fateful morning of September 11, 2001, on a street that, as the novel's first line announces, "was not a street anymore but a world, a time and space of falling ash and near night."[1] This focus on the new or other "world" created by the seismic events of 9/11 is echoed in the next few paragraphs with the references "This was the world now" (3) and "The world was this" (4). *Falling Man* takes on the daunting task of attempting to represent the seemingly unrepresentable and traumatic 9/11 terrorist destruction with airplanes turned into bombs of the twin towers in Manhattan, events that remain relatively close in time, space, and memory to most Americans and thus make representing them all the more difficult.[2] Indeed, the personal shock and political ramifications of those events live on, front and center, in Americans' quotidian lives with daily news coverage of the wars in Afghanistan and Iraq that followed from the 9/11 attacks as well as the continued heightened attention to national security, especially at airports, that reminds citizens of the potential of another terrorist attack at any time. This continued centrality of 9/11 has produced a kind of "terror caused by the recognition of contingency" (Cohen: 374) or, in slightly different terms, trauma produced "by the threat of the worst *to come*" (Derrida: 96) that has so marked the present American cultural imagination that serious contemporary writers cannot choose *not* to engage the events of 9/11 and their repercussions. As DeLillo noted in a December 2001 essay published in *Harper's Magazine*, "The writer wants to understand what this day has done to us" in order to create a "counter-narrative" that "tries to give memory, tenderness, and meaning to all that howling space" ("In the Ruins": 39).[3] That *Falling Man* was not published until June 2007 (more than five years later) suggests that creating such a counter-narrative proved a difficult task for DeLillo, particularly given the proliferation of so many competing narratives immediately following 9/11 as well as his own proximity to the events since he lives in Manhattan.

Despite the difficulties of the task at hand, however, I argue that DeLillo's novel in subtle ways ultimately works to *counter* the reactionary bent of the dominant narratives created and disseminated by the media and the Bush administration following 9/11, which overtly reasserted and championed traditional notions of heroic, militarized masculinity that privilege physical strength and the power accorded by such strength.[4] Michael Kimmel goes so far as to describe the version of manhood championed and enacted by President George Bush in terms of "the compulsive masculinity of the school yard bully" (192), and Rebecca Carpenter argues that "the United States' increasingly hyper-masculine and bellicose posturing on the world stage" in response to the events of 9/11 highlights "the intersection (and, sometimes, conflation) of power on the world stage with [dominant] conceptions of masculinity" (144). In contrast to official narratives that "trumpeted the revival of traditional masculinity" (Kimmel: 249), *Falling Man* depicts a world in which the events of 9/11 so fully invalidate any notion of the self as whole, unified, powerful or as having any control or agency that the novel and its characters' task becomes one of finding alternative forms of order and stability as temporary grounds from which to salvage the shards of humanity and self to which they hang precariously.[5] Indeed, rather than paint a broad, large-scale picture of the 9/11 events, DeLillo's *Falling Man* focuses for the most part on the mundane day to day lives of one man and his wife as they attempt to find a way to live post–9/11 in Manhattan.

The novel simultaneously engages the personal trauma induced in its protagonist, Keith Neudecker, as a result of the shock of his material near death experience in one of the towers and the cultural trauma that Susannah Radstone argues arises not out of shock but rather when "an event's traumatic impact may be linked to its *puncturing* of a fantasy that has previously sustained a sense of identity — national, as well as individual"— in this case "*fantasies* of impregnability and invincibility" (458). Indeed, the novel undercuts the Bush administration and media's strategic "rehabilitation of heroic masculinity" in their depictions of "the firefighters, police, and other rescue workers" (Kimmel: 249), a strategy clearly aimed at shoring up a seriously punctured national "myth of invincibility" (Faludi: 14), by choosing *not* to use narrative genres typically associated with reinforcing such forms of masculinity. Instead, DeLillo's novel addresses and attempts to move past the trauma triggered by the recognition that neither the individual nor the nation is impregnable or invincible by creating a *counter-narrative*. To create this *counter-narrative*, the novel experiments with genre, using and molding for its own purposes a version of the domestic novel — a narrative form *not* usually associated with masculinity, with DeLillo's fiction, or with the telling of history and, in particular, that of large scale horrific historical events — as a means of representing the recent traumatic events of 9/11.

Scholars have often commented on the way many of DeLillo's past novels borrow, manipulate, and often subvert established narrative genres. According to John Johnston, for example, such borrowings have included the genres of "'artistic autobiography,' or *Bildungsroman*," "sports novel," "'pop' novel," "science fiction," "disaster novel," and "thriller" (261). In a more recent essay, Anne Longmuir further notes that DeLillo "has returned to the thriller more often than any other genre" (130). Moreover, she defines the thriller as a "masculine genre" that she argues is "predicated on the rejection of the feminine," in the sense that "women, and the domestic values that they represent, threaten the independence of the thriller hero, his supreme individualism" (130). In many ways the hero of the thriller functions much like a contemporary version of the "all guts and glory" cowboy hero of the American western novel and film—a hero that "was an anachronism, obsolete at the moment of his creation" but that nevertheless functioned as "the apotheosis of masculinist fantasy, a revolt not against women but against feminization" (Kimmel: 100–101). In the face of the cataclysmic events of 9/11, however, DeLillo's *Falling Man* makes clear that the genre of the thriller is no longer an option.[6] Indeed, the 2001 terrorist attacks on American soil shattered all of the values on which the thriller depends, revealing instantaneously, vividly, and definitively as myths ideals of macho masculinity, independence, and individualism. Although all of DeLillo's novels are "haunted," as Longmuir explains, by "the fear that in the culture of late capitalism, the autonomous, oppositional subject has become an impossibility" (144), that fear has been fully realized and instantiated in the world depicted by *Falling Man*.

Falling Man does not simply or simplistically present itself as a domestic novel, however. Instead, DeLillo's text engages in borrowings that allow the novel to use, subvert, and refashion a kind of narrative that might be termed domestic—although the term *domestic* has historically been fraught ideologically and has often suffered from oversimplification and derision because of its traditional association with women's writing.[7] Arguably, the novel creates a twenty-first century version of the domestic narrative that not only recognizes but assumes and moves past the artificiality and absurdity of any clear demarcation between the domestic and public sphere and their culturally constructed associations respectively with femininity and masculinity. As Keith's wife Lianne notes when she takes part with their son Justin alongside "five hundred thousand others" (181) in the February 15, 2003, march against the imminent American invasion of Iraq (on a day that saw parallel marches enacted in major cities across the globe), "since that day in September, all life had become public" (182). Indeed, that a mother and son participate in the march highlights the breakdown of a binary opposition between the public masculine realm and the domestic feminine realm.

Moreover, *Falling Man* both co-opts and moves beyond another aspect of the domestic that, as Amy Kaplan argues in her essay "Manifest Domesticity," "links the familial household to the nation" and "imagines both in opposition to everything outside the geographic and conceptual border of home" (581) so that "men and women become national allies against the alien" (582). Indeed, Susan Faludi points out such a linking of the family and nation within post–9/11 "media, entertainment, and advertising" that seemed to call for a kind of "neofifties nuclear family 'togetherness'" (3). Within the scope of DeLillo's novel, however, the domestic realm functions neither as a space separate from the public world nor as a space from which to oppose foreign elements—even though both would seem like viable, albeit overly predictable and potentially reactionary, options in the aftermath of the 9/11 terrorist attacks. Instead, the novel creates a narrative in which the communal ties of family accentuated by an ethics of care, the familiar physical spaces that create a conception of home, and the rituals of daily bodily existence provide a kind of psychological grounding for the shattered self and a means of beginning to recover a sense of shared humanity in the face of inhumanity.

The domestic sphere within *Falling Man* thus functions less as a space within which to escape the post–9/11 world and the traumatic effects of the terrorist attacks than as a space within which to engage that world and those traumas on a human scale, particularly given that personal and cultural trauma are so intertwined post–9/11. Indeed, as E. Ann Kaplan notes, the events of 9/11 produced such "complex interactions between individual and cultural trauma" that "where the 'self' begins and cultural reactions end may seem impossible to determine" (2). As a means of representing the effects of 9/11 and the post–9/11 world on the human psyche, the novel offers a new form of domestic narrative, one which brings the rituals of care into the public sphere at a historical juncture in which the domestic and public spheres overtly bleed into each other. On the morning of 9/11, Keith unconsciously makes the journey from ground-zero to the apartment of his wife Lianne, from whom he has been separated, which could be read as an escape to the domestic sphere. The narrative notes, however, that "he walked away from it [the chaos of the crumbling tower] and into it at the same time" (4), thus emphasizing the impossibility of escaping the traumatic events and their effects. Indeed, throughout its pages the novel insists that all illusions of an opposition between the public and private realms have been wiped away. Although Lianne initially believes that Keith chose to come home so as to be "outside the tide of voices and faces, God and country," the novel instead presents the domestic sphere as offering a nurturing space filled "with those nearby who mattered" (20) and a valuing of rituals that allow Keith to begin to cope with his traumatic near-death experience in the tower that remains marked as simultaneously public and private.

Moreover, the novel makes clear in its sharply detailed opening scene that the events of 9/11 sound the final note for any privileging of the public realm in its biting depiction of the "office paper flashing past, standard sheets with cutting edges" and of Keith, who incongruously "wore a suit and carried a briefcase," the standard costume of the public man within corporate America, at the same time as "there was glass in his hair and face, marbled bolls of blood and light" (3)—the "cutting edges" and "blood" highlighting the power and potentially lethal aspects of corporate America, this time turned back upon its own participants. While Keith's corporate attire points to the identity he had assumed as an American man at the turn of the twenty-first century, given that, "historically, work has often stood as the most fundamental foundation of masculine identity" within Western industrial nations (Edwards: 8), the glass and blood with which he is covered announces the shattering of that (constructed) identity and of any illusions about global capitalism as benign. Faith in the illusions of order, power, and individualism crumble along with the towers, symbols of the financial wealth undergirding American society; the towers' destruction removes the veil hiding from view the interconnections between the public and private realms as well as between American society, wealth, and global terrorism. Indeed, the recurring figure at intervals throughout the novel of "the performance artist known as Falling Man" (219), dangling from various structures around the city "always upside down, wearing a suit, a tie and dress shoes" (33) and thereby overtly miming the infamous photograph of a man falling from one of the towers taken by journalist Richard Drew, functions as a reminder of the link between the individualistic, properly costumed public corporate man who takes part in the global market and the events of 9/11.[8] As Jürgen Habermas, among others, has argued, "the globalization of markets, particularly the financial markets," has produced "a world society" that is "*split up* into winner, beneficiary, and loser countries" (32) and thus vastly imbalanced, with the United States positioned as a "winner" country and as such the target of terrorist attacks like the one against the World Trade Center — with the towers so clearly chosen as targets because of "their powerful embodiment of economic strength" (28).[9] Arguably, like the performances of the Falling Man within its pages, DeLillo's novel forces its readers to grapple with the ways in which Americans have been complicit with vast, complex, and arguably unjust global economic systems that cannot be totally divorced from the horrific events of 9/11.

As Keith walks away from the rubble after the attacks on 9/11, a scene that both opens and closes the novel and thus highlights the continuing traumatic presence of the event for both Keith and Americans in general, his sense of self has disintegrated much like the towers behind him: "He could not find himself in the things he saw and heard" (246). In what might be termed an instinctive or unconscious response to this state of existential nothingness, since no rational thought or planning seems to be involved, Keith makes a bee-line for his wife's apartment. Dazed and traumatized, Keith accepts a ride from a man in "an old panel truck" but asserts that "it wasn't until he got in the truck and shut the door that he understood where he'd been going all along" (6). Moreover, when Keith arrives at Lianne's door, "a man come out of an ash storm, all blood and slag," he heads specifically to the "kitchen" (87), demonstrating his need not simply for the general palliative effects of the domestic space and familial ties but also for the physical and psychic nourishment they provide. Lianne's apartment provides human proximity and contact — "She wanted him here, nearby[...]. She wanted contact and so did he" (35) — unlike his own apartment, which he describes as "two and a half rooms," "with nothing that mattered to him" (26). While he was separated from Lianne, Keith's own apartment functioned not so much as a home or domestic space but rather as a convenient "place [to live] close to the office" (26). After 9/11, however, Keith's traumatized state triggers a need for human connection that shifts his perspective when he returns to his apartment to collect a few belongings, to the extent that "he saw the place differently": a feeling of loneliness suffuses him as he looks around the rooms, which he now sees as "marked by the bloodguilt tracings of severed connections" (27). This recognition indicates the start of his critical examination of his life before 9/11 as a consequence of his life changing near death experience. The only memory associated with human connections that he situates in this apartment is that of his weekly poker games with his male buddies, as evidenced by his pinpointing "the poker table" as one of the few items in the apartment that "mattered." These games seemingly functioned as a kind of alternative domestic ritual among men with their camaraderie, clear moves, "call or fold" (27), and elaborate rules, including many "self-imposed restriction[s]" (98). Indeed, Keith's description of these pre–9/11 poker games in language that characterizes them as engaging in the domestic and in ritualistic behaviors unravels any clear association of the domestic with women and femininity, particularly since he describes these evenings of poker in terms of "men rolling their shoulders, hoisting their balls" (96)—a blatant caricature of masculinity that emphasizes the notion that masculinity is not only "socially constructed" but also "largely a homosocial enactment" (Kimmel: 5, 3).[10]

Once back in Lianne's apartment, Keith becomes "a hovering presence" (59), satisfying a primal need for human contact and connection. He sleeps next to Lianne in her bed and begins to spend increasing time with his son Justin, thus inserting himself into the daily rituals of their existence. As Lianne puts it, at some very basic level, "we need each other. Just people sharing the air that's all" (214). The narrative also makes clear that Keith consciously chooses to remain within his family's domestic space and to participate in its daily life, noting that "nothing seemed familiar, being here, in a family again [...] it was different now because he was watching" (65). The ordinary has become noteworthy as he struggles to recreate a new sense of self out of the shattered, traumatized self that walked away from the towers. Although the world has changed drastically and the characters reference time in terms of *before* and *after* the fateful day of 9/11, both Keith and Lianne find a sort of salve and salvation in the recognition that, within their quotidian lives, "things were ordinary in all the ways they were always ordinary" (67) and that sharing their ordinary existence makes it real and gives it validity in the sense that they are each other's witness. Through their taking responsibility for and mutual recognition of each other, they assure each other of their humanity in the face of the inhumanity of the terrorist attacks. The characters thus exemplify photo-editor Ruth Sergel's assertion that "the real reaction to 9/11 was to make everyone more *human*" (quoted in Faludi: 288). Indeed, Emanuel Levinas has argued that "love of the other, responsibility for one's fellowman" is the primary marker of being human (228). Moreover, Keith and Lianne learn to value the sheer wonder of being alive given their post–9/11 recognition of the precariousness and contingent quality of life. For instance, Keith feels "a contained elation" (66) in his new sharp awareness of the world around him and in the domestic tasks he now relishes, such as "the walks to and from school" with Justin and even the "breaking eggs for dinner" (66). Similarly, when Lianne spots Keith and Justin in the street coming to meet her as she is returning home, she sees them as "bright with urgent life [...] thirty-six days after the planes" (170), thus linking her valuing of the life they exude to a post–9/11 understanding and need to move into the future.

Ritual plays a vital role in the ordinary existence to which Keith and Lianne cling, in that it provides them with a sense of order and stability that they crave in the face of the chaos and potential for unimaginable violence that characterizes post–9/11 America.[11] Rituals entail sets of repeated culturally constructed and validated ordered actions or tasks that create a sense of soothing predictability as well as of agency for the person performing the rituals and, in most cultures, is often associated with the domestic sphere even though, in practice, rituals structure the public as well as domestic spheres of cultures. Arguably, the small steps Keith and Lianne take to move on after 9/11 are made possible by the rituals of everyday life that function as antidotes to paralysis.[12] Upon the sudden return of Keith into her life, Lianne's ability to function depends at least in part on her ability to keep focusing on the immediate needs of her family in terms of daily living: "She stepped into the street thinking ordinary thoughts, dinner, dry cleaning, cash machine, that's it, go home" (22). She also adheres to a regular exercise routine as a means of ordering her days and focusing on her bodily existence: "She ran early mornings and came home and stripped and showered" (235). Likewise, Keith finds a salve in the daily rehabilitation exercises for his injured wrist upon which he obsessively focuses, even after the pain has disappeared three years after 9/11. The ritualistic aspects of the exercise sessions — "the counting of seconds, the counting of repetitions, the times of day he reserved for the exercises, the ice he applied following each set of exercises" — are "restorative" for him and "brought him closer to well-being" (40) because they provide a shape to his days and force him to focus on a tangible material goal and on his physical existence. Similarly, the daily pattern he develops of "taking him [his son Justin] to school and picking him up, advising on homework" (59), creates a sense of order to his days that allows him to act and participate in his family's life at a time when, within the world at large, any sense of individual selfhood and agency has been stripped from him. Indeed, daily rituals keep at bay the existential nihilism that Keith's memories and dreams reinforce: "a thousand heaving dreams, the trapped men, the fixed limbs, the dream of paralysis, the gasping man, the dream of asphyxiation, the dream of helplessness" (230).

While the domestic sphere into which Keith actively inserts himself helps him begin to learn to live again and to rebuild a sense of self, he nevertheless continues to feel a kind of distance from his family in that their experience of the 9/11 attacks differs drastically from his and so he remains unable to talk to them about his. Unlike Lianne and Justin, Keith physically lived through the plane slamming into the tower in which he worked, which "sent" him "out of his chair and into a wall" as "the floor began to slide beneath him" (239); glimpsed a body falling from the tower, "an instant of something sideways, going past the window, white shirt, hand up" (242); witnessed his friend and colleague, Rumsey, die in his arms following "a noise in his throat, abrupt, a half second, half gasp, and then blood"; "walked down" the stairwell along with "thousands" of others "one step and then the next" (243); and miraculously came out of the burning building shortly before one tower after the other fell "diving into the smoke" (246). The trauma of those experiences is such that Keith represses his memories, does not talk about them, and thus cannot move past them. He and Lianne are brought "close" when they watch "the planes cross the sky" on T.V. and he even "reached" out and "took her hand," suggesting that sharing his experiences with her would help him deal with his near death experience, but he can only bear to watch "with her one time only" (134). Although for the most part he keeps silent about his experiences, bits of memories continue to intrude into his waking and sleeping life, especially of his friend Rumsey who died in the tower. Keith is able to face his traumatic memories only when he finds a fellow survivor, Florence Givens, with whom he begins to sort through the events of the morning of 9/11 by "crossing memories" (57). Keith initially meets Florence when he goes to her apartment to return her briefcase that he accidentally carried out of the burning tower; and he keeps returning for a period of two weeks, drawn by their mutual need to remember and thus face up to the traumatic ordeal they lived through on the morning of 9/11.

While Florence is essentially a stranger and the relationship Keith strikes up with her is temporary, the novel presents the scenes of their interactions as domestic in quality—again highlighting the key function of the domestic in the aftermath of the 9/11 attacks. On a literal level, these scenes take place in the domestic setting of her apartment, and during their first meeting she serves him "tea and a plate of sugar cookies" (54) as any good hostess would do. Moreover, the intimacy of the setting and their shared positions as survivors of the 9/11 attacks who managed to come out of the towers before they collapsed gives them a point of interconnection that allows them to begin to recall the events through which they lived. The socio-cultural differences between Keith, a white man, and Florence, "a light-skinned black woman" (52), make them "ill matched people" (107) and yet fade as their remembering reveals the striking similarity of their experiences on the morning of 9/11.[13]

Florence obsessively recounts in great detail her march down the tower stairwell, "often pausing to look into space, to see things again"; and Keith understands that "she wanted to tell him everything" about that morning "precisely" because he too had been "there, in the tower" (55) and "that they could talk about these things only with each other [...] because it was inside them now [...] the dazed reality they'd shared in the stairwells" (90–91). Each time she narrates her story, "he was ready to listen again [...] trying to find himself in the crowd" (59) of "spiraling men and women" she describes. Indeed, Keith believes he locates himself in her story when she recalls seeing "a maintenance man" with a "crowbar" going up the steps and he "thought he'd also seen the man, going up past him"—an example of "crossing memories" (57). In this verbal sharing of their seemingly unspeakable memories of their near death experiences in the tower, Keith and Florence in some sense authenticate for each other their respective traumatic memories that the novel posits as simultaneously personal and communal. Finding ways of verbalizing what they remember in order to tell each other their stories and establishing parallels and overlaps between their stories function as a validation of experiences that until then felt unreal and unrepresentable.

Such intimate sharing of experiences within the physical space of a private residence clearly contains a domestic resonance, in the sense that traditionally conversations within a home setting about individual experiences of emotional and psychic import remain associated with familial or friendship ties. Moreover, as the relationship between Keith and Florence moves to include a sexual component, it appears on the surface to replicate the typical extra-marital affair, complete with the stereotypic positioning of Florence as providing a kind of understanding of Keith that his wife lacks. Indeed, that Keith allows a sexual affair to develop makes clear that he has not completely moved past his pre–9/11 self, which the novel intimates included "lying" (105) to his wife, "looking at women" (120), and most likely having affairs. Lianne's mother asserts that Keith was a man "built for weekends," who "wanted a woman who'd regret what she did with him" (12). Given the post–9/11 context and Keith's traumatized state, however, I would argue that the novel presents the relationship between Keith and Florence as a means of depicting his tentative rebuilding of a sense of self. This process includes both a failure by Keith to completely step away from the masculine scripts he performed pre–9/11 and a movement toward the construction of a revised identity outside of those established scripts. Although Keith does not deny that he and Florence "took erotic pleasure from each other," he nevertheless insists that "what sent him back there" was "not rituals of anticipation" but rather "what they knew together, in the timeless drift of the long spiral down" the tower stairwell on the fateful morning of 9/11 (137). His insistence that the relationship included "sex, yes, but not romance" and that the "emotion" was "generated by external conditions" does not so much excuse his actions as define them as other than what "people refer to when they use the word *affair*" (166). While one could read Keith as self-deluded and disingenuous, his relationship with Florence needs to be read within the larger context of the novel and its presentation of Keith as a man working to construct a self in the face of the disintegration of his previous self in the aftermath of his traumatic 9/11 experiences.

Even though the sexual component of the relationship seems to be a throwback to his earlier self and the behaviors of that self, Keith nevertheless also exhibits a sense of critical distance from his relationship with Florence that seems to indicate a shift — particularly in terms of his increasingly self-conscious examination of his own behavior and the situation at hand. While Keith needs Florence in the sense that she functions as a means for him to work through his traumatic memories, given her position as a fellow survivor, he recognizes the banality of the conventional script they cannot seem to escape as an unmarried man and woman meeting in her apartment and engaging in intimate conversations in a culture that cannot imagine relationships between men and women outside of marriage or sexual conquest scripts. Indeed, he consciously notes the "resentment in her voice" (89), when he responds in the affirmative to her question about whether or not he is married, as part of that conventional script and anticipates that "later she would say what someone always says. 'Do you have to leave'" (137). Moreover, Keith's critical distance from the script in which he finds himself participating becomes further evident when Florence speaks of a future for their relationship and Keith "thought this kind of conversation was for other people" (108). Keith's sharp awareness of the scripted aspects of the relationship suggests a shift from his pre–9/11 self, when self-awareness seemed not to be one of his strengths, and is punctuated by his decision to break off the affair after two weeks.

Indeed, from the start, Keith understands that his brief secretive meetings with Florence on one level "contradicted what he'd lately taken to be the truth of his life, that it was meant to be lived seriously and responsibly, not snatched in clumsy fistfuls" (137) and that he could not ignore "the implications of one's conduct" (157), suggesting his development of a new ethics of living that marks a radical change from his pre–9/11 self. Not only does he follow through and go tell Florence that "it is ended now"— "Because what else finally was there to say?" (158) — and never see her again, but he also mulls over telling Lianne about the ended affair, again for ethical reasons: "It was the right thing to do" in the sense that "it was the kind of perilous truth that would lead to an understanding of clean and even proportions, long-lasting, with a feeling of reciprocal love and trust" (161). His rationale indicates that he is interested in developing a new kind of relationship with Lianne. Although, in the end, he does not tell Lianne about Florence, he chooses not to do so for Lianne's sake, recognizing that, while telling her would assuage his own conscience, it "would cause her to suffer enormously" (161), potentially drive her into "a period of long and tortured withdrawal" that might even require "medication and psychiatric counseling," and end all too predictably with her "call[ing] a lawyer" (162). Moreover, three years later, Keith's memories of Florence focus on her story about her "forced march down the stairwell" (228), thus validating his assertion that what drew him to her was their overlapping experiences that allowed him to glimpse his own experiences through her attempts to narrate hers and continue to do so as he recollects her story and sets it next to his own fractured memories. Florence thus remains tied to his ongoing struggle to cope with the psychic trauma he sustained from his experiences on 9/11, but his decision to stop seeing her after two weeks suggests that he has made an ethical choice to rebuild a relationship with Lianne.

The novel thus arguably presents Keith as actively choosing to work on constructing a relationship with Lianne that differs significantly from the one they had before their separation and before the events of 9/11. Keith attempts to embrace the domestic realm with its rituals and to view their relationship through an ethical lens rather than according to conventional scripts of marriage, masculinity, and femininity — which their failed marriage should have demonstrated were bankrupt but which he does not recognize until after his near-death experiences on 9/11 as needing to be re-imagined. However, given the magnitude of the shattering of Keith's sense of self post–9/11, DeLillo's novel does not provide a traditional happy ending or comforting closure; rather, *Falling Man* offers characters who are engaged in the difficult on-going process of reconstructing selves and lives — the process indicating a small ray of hope in its gesture toward an as yet unknown future. While the text depicts both Keith and Lianne as continuing to crave the routines and affective ties of family life, it also makes clear that they have to work to find ways of living in the world; they cannot simply hide within the cocoon of their familial existence since, as noted earlier, the events of 9/11 have made glaringly apparent how interwoven the domestic and public realms are. Indeed, as Keith and Lianne work to rebuild their lives over time, they continue to depend on the strategies they found to be effective within the domestic sphere and carry them outward into the world. They begin to engage in separate ritualistic behaviors outside their home and family as means of consolidating their precarious sense of self and not simply living for each other, working to balance a sense of an individual self and a self in community. Lianne begins to attend church services and to get back into her editing work, and Keith becomes a rather serious poker player; but they both manage to do so without completely reverting back to gender stereotypes.

Lianne's yearning for connection with others leads her to attend mass, not to allay her deep religious "doubts" but rather to feel a connection with others, a feeling that she associates with life. Within the physical space of the church, "it was not something godlike she felt but only a sense of others." Not only do the rituals of the church service connect her to others — "She followed others when they stood and knelt" — but she is also drawn to the connection she feels there with "the dead in the walls" that "she'd always felt in churches" and that provide her with "comfort, feeling their presence, the dead she'd loved and all the faceless others who'd filled a thousand churches." Attending mass becomes part of her daily routine outside her home and a means of connecting with others in the world in much the same way as her morning runs "along the river" (233), as DeLillo's text highlights by interspersing descriptions of Lianne in church and running on the same page. At the same time as Lianne reaches outside her domestic setting, however, she continues to view her family as providing stability and order in the face of chaos. As she tells Keith, "We need to stay together, keep the family going[...]. This is how we live through the things that scare us half to death" (214).

Although Keith tries to step back into his old life by taking a new job that "wasn't much different" from the one he held pre-9/11, he quickly recognizes that he cannot go back to "before" (215) and instead chooses to start anew and play poker for a living. On one level, Keith's participation in tournament poker functions as a kind of escape from the world in which terrorist attacks and crimes against humanity are a daily possibility and into an artificial and predictable world with clear rules of the game. Indeed, what Keith seems to most value when he plays poker is that "there was nothing outside the game but faded space" (189) and, in particular "no flash of history or memory" (225) to bring him back to his traumatic 9/11 experiences. Moreover, he finds the ritualistic aspects of the poker games and the ordered life he leads when engaged in a tournament soothing, deliberately organizing his days by "standard methods and routines," again highlighting the palliative effects of rituals. For example, he ordinarily took a "taxi to the casino, taxi back to his hotel" (197), and he "allowed himself five hours' sleep, barely aware of setting limits and restrictions" (198). Within this world, time seems to stand still and "the idea of later was elusive" (200) so that he need not worry about the future — including the possibility of future terrorist attacks. In addition, the world of the poker tournament differs drastically from the pre–9/11 weekly poker games in which he participated with a group of male friends. In contrast to the tone of masculine bravado and the domestic setting of those earlier games, the tournament arena (which includes both men and women) highlights a certain anonymity of both place and people that Keith finds soothing. He welcomes the "wordless din so deeply settled in the air and walls and furniture, in the moving bodies of men and women" (203), and "the crucial anonymity of these days and weeks, the mingling of countless lives that had no stories attached" (204). Much like Lianne's experience in church, Keith values a sense of being with others that remain anonymous while they all perform the rituals of the game. However, he also demonstrates an awareness of this tendency to seek an escape from the world at large, such as when he wonders if he is becoming "a self-operating mechanism, like a humanoid robot" (226), and when he acknowledges "how strange a life he was living" (227). These moments indicate that Keith has not simply retreated from reality.

On another crucial level, the novel highlights that Keith is drawn to playing poker as a means not simply of escape but of rebuilding a sense of self and of agency. For Keith, the world of tournament poker represents an arena in which "he remained the agent of free choice" and in which stability reigns since "the game had structure, guiding principles" (211). Within the parameters of the game, he has "the choice of yes or no. Call or raise, call or fold [...] the choice that reminds you who you are" (212), so that the game gives him a sense of control linked to his attempts to substantiate a sense of self after it is shattered by his near-death 9/11 experiences. After "months of mastering the game" (197), Keith begins to win more often and thus demonstrates to himself that "he had memory, judgment, the ability to decide what is true, what is alleged, when to strike, when to fade." He recognizes that "there was a certain logic he might draw on" (211), which provides a kind of grounding for him, even if limited, in a world in which he had believed that all logic had disintegrated alongside the towers. Although he is pleased to finally be "making money" (197), Keith's sense of satisfaction comes rather from his own ability to master the game itself and thus to prove to himself that he has reclaimed a least some level of agency: "The game mattered[...]. He wasn't playing for the money. He was playing for the chips" (228). While the long term value of playing poker tournaments remains tenuous at best — Lianne likens the game to "a séance in hell" and asks him, "What happens after months of this? Or years. Who do you become?" (216) — DeLillo's text indicates that, in the short term, it allows Keith to re-experience the possibility of individual agency, even if that agency remains severely limited given that poker remains at base level a game of chance.

The novel also makes clear that, even with his heavy involvement in the world of tournament poker, Keith cannot escape the trauma that continues to haunt him, as evidenced "every time he boarded a flight" when "he glanced at faces on both sides of the aisle, trying to spot the man or men who might be a danger to them all" (198). Moreover, the anonymity he so values within the tournament circuit is threatened when he runs into his old poker buddy Terry Cheng, who insists on talking about their common friend Rumsey and how he heard that Rumsey "went out a window" (205) and that "Rumsey's mother" became obsessed with collecting her son's personal items in order to find "traces of hair or skin" to take in "for a DNA match" (204). In response, Keith "looked into the [artificial] waterfall" as a means of steeling himself against unwanted memories that he knew would surface "if he closed his eyes" (205): "He didn't want to listen to Terry Cheng [...] three years after the planes" (229). World news also intrudes, such as when he hears radio reports about "terrorists taking hostages, the siege, the explosions" in Russia with "hundreds dead, many children," shifting him out of his safe, trance-like state and sparking into action his newly developed empathy and connection to Lianne in that he immediately "knew he had to call her" (206) and follows up on that knowledge.

At the same time as Lianne and Keith find different paths toward rebuilding their sense of self, they continue to crave the human connections and caring interactions that they find in their family domestic routines that provide them with vital human connections. Three years after 9/11, Keith spends weeks away from home playing in poker tournaments, which could be viewed as a cutting of ties to the domestic realm and certainly leaves unclear the future of his and Lianne's newly reformed and re-embraced marital relationship. Despite his geographical separation from his family, however, he continues to maintain his connection with his wife and son. Not only does he acknowledge that "he missed the kid" (207) and at one point wonder "what he might buy for the kid" (230), but he talks to Lianne regularly on the phone and goes "home periodically" for "love, sex, fatherhood, home-cooked-food" (197). Although Lianne argues for a more stable family life and "the idea that we're permanent" (214) to satisfy her need for human connection, by the end of the novel she feels "ready to be alone, in reliable calm" (236). As for Keith, he asks Lianne to "trust" him and embrace a kind of stable impermanence: "I go away a while, come back. I'm not about to disappear. Not about to do anything drastic. I'm here now and I'll be back" (215). While the relationship they have created does not fit established conventions of marriage, especially as developed and idealized in the United States after World War II, the novel seems to suggest that the times require the forging of new kinds of relationships that move beyond outmoded, binary conceptions of masculinity and femininity and of the domestic and public realms. *Falling Man* depicts Keith and Lianne as having begun to rebuild a sense of self that they know is precarious but that allows them to live, to act in the world. And both have had to accept the impermanence and lack of safety that the world offers at the same time as they mitigate the potential ensuing paralysis that this impermanence and lack of safety generates through rituals of care and affective ties as well as other ritualistic actions.

Although the novel's protagonist, Keith, does not fully recover from the traumatic events of 9/11 by the end of the text, as highlighted by the return to the chaotic 9/11 scene that opens the novel on its last pages, DeLillo's *Falling Man* nevertheless offers a *counter-narrative* in the sense that it explicitly depicts the process of attempting to live in the aftermath of the events of 9/11 and of recreating a sense of self that does not resort to a thoughtless reassertion of unquestioned notions of heroic (militaristic) masculinity tied to asserting power over others. Indeed, Keith no longer wishes to follow the accepted script of "corporate masculinity" (Kimmel: 249): "Keith used to want more of the world than there was time and means to acquire. He didn't want this anymore" (128). The novel depicts Keith as drifting away from and in time choosing to shift away from the "tough, power-oriented masculinity" he had previously performed, a masculinity deliberately "distanced from the feminized world of domesticity" that did "not valorize the family or the husband/father position for men" (Connell: 264, 257). By the end of the novel, set three years after 9/11, Keith ritually continues to perform "the full program" (235) of his wrist rehabilitation exercises even though he no longer needs to do so, to play in poker tournaments for the sake of playing rather than making money, and to return regularly to spend family time with Lianne and Justin.[14] Balancing these rituals allows Keith to live despite his traumatized state and to slowly recreate a self that moves toward — even if it never gets there — a new definition of masculinity that no longer depends on power over others and opens itself up to a more communal sense of living with others.

Notes

1. DeLillo, *Falling Man*, p. 3. All subsequent references to *Falling Man* will be noted parenthetically within the text of the essay.
2. As Keniston and Quinn note in their introduction to their edited collection of essays, *Literature after 9/11*, "literature has participated in the large cultural process of representing and interpreting the events of September 11, 2001, while also revealing the difficulties of doing so when cataclysmic events are still so recent" (2).
3. In his reading of DeLillo's essay, Heath argues that "the writer's words do not represent what happened" but rather "grow out of what happened" (352).
4. See the second edition of Kimmel's *Manhood in America: A Cultural History* and Faludi's *The Terror Dream: Fear and Fantasy in Post–9/11 America*, among many other scholarly books and essays that discuss this tendency to reassert traditional notions of masculinity in response to the events of 9/11 — a tendency, moreover, that echoes what happened following the Vietnam War as delineated by Jeffords in *The Remasculinization of America: Gender and the Vietnam War*.
5. In a less forgiving reading of the novel, Mary Parish argues in her as yet unpublished essay that *Falling Man*'s depiction of Keith reinforces the stereotype of the "strong, silent, 'man's man'" (4), including its "need for control and refusal of connection that reflect the internalization of the femiphobic anxieties implicit within the myth" (7). While Keith clearly remains caught within certain established scripts of masculinity, I view the novel's presentation of Keith after 9/11 as moving away from those scripts.
6. Stylistically, the novel not only rejects the (male-centered) unitary point of view of the thriller, sliding into the perspectives of multiple characters (including that of one of the highjackers), but also moves at a much slower pace than most popular thrillers and, indeed, has more in common with an existential novel (with the novel's references to Kierkegaard making that connection even more explicit).

7. See for example, Ann Douglas' *The Feminization of American Culture* and Anne McClintock's *Imperial Leather: Race, Gender, and Sexuality in the Colonial Context*.

8. Moreover, Junod argues that "the images of people jumping were the only images that became by consensus taboo" and that "the desire to face the most disturbing aspect of our most disturbing day was somehow ascribed to voyeurism, as though the jumpers' experience, instead of being central to the horror, was tangential to it, a sideshow best forgotten" (3). In DeLillo's novel, the Falling Man performances explicitly reject this erasure and force New Yorkers to face up to this aspect of the horror as well as to the link between terrorism and corporate America.

9. Clymer argues that "terrorist targets are generally chosen specifically for their symbolic value" (15).

10. Kauffman similarly notes that Keith's poker nights prior to 9/11 entail "a performance of masculinity" (368). In an essay written prior to the publication of *Falling Man*, Helyer argues that DeLillo's fiction in general often highlights "the performative nature of men's role" as well as "the insecurity of masculinity" (125).

11. Although Kauffman notes that "each character in the novel [*Falling Man*] adapts to the post–9/11 climate by adopting a set of rituals, superstitions, or obsessive-compulsive behaviors" (371), she does not explore this aspect of the novel in any detail.

12. Interestingly, the novel's brief depictions of the highjackers similarly highlight their ritualistic behaviors as they prepare for their mission — not only religious rituals but also what could be termed domestic rituals of everyday existence — as a means of keeping everything under control.

13. While some might object that by making Florence a black woman, DeLillo falls into a stereotypic portrayal of the white man attracted to the exotic other, I would argue that in this case the text highlights the ways in which their differences (in gender, race, and class) fade in the face of the terror attacks and their parallel experiences of them. Arguably, DeLillo takes a risk and opens himself to criticism; but, as Rothberg argues, "September 11 [...] demands a literature that takes risks" and "dares to move beyond near-sightedness" (141).

14. Unlike the highjackers who use rituals to enable their terrorist acts, which include their own deaths, Keith engages rituals as a means of survival in the face of the terror that the world offers.

Works Cited

Borradori, Giovanna. *Philosophy in a Time of Terror: Dialogues with Jürgen Habermas and Jacques Derrida.* Chicago: University of Chicago Press, 2003.

Carpenter, Rebecca. "'We're Not a Friggin' Girl Band': September 11, Masculinity, and the British-American Relationship in David Hare's *Stuff Happens* and Ian McEwan's *Saturday*.'" Keniston and Quinn: 143–160.

Clymer, Jeffory A. *America's Culture of Terrorism: Violence, Capitalism, and the Written Word.* Chapel Hill: University of North Carolina Press, 2003.

Cohen, Samuel. "The Novel in a Time of Terror: Middlesex, History, and Contemporary American Fiction." *Twentieth-Century Literature* 53.3 (2007): 371–393.

Connell, R.W. *Masculinities.* (2nd ed.). Berkeley: University of California Press, 2005.

DeLillo, Don. *Falling Man.* New York: Scribner, 2007.

_____. "In the Ruins of the Future: Reflections on Terror and Loss in the Shadow of September." *Harper's Magazine*, December 2001: 33–40.

Derrida, Jacques. "Autoimmunity: Real and Symbolic Suicides." *In* Pascale-Anne Brault and Michael Naas (Trans.). *Borradori*: 86–136.

Douglas, Ann. *The Feminization of American Culture.* New York: Knopf, 1977.

Edwards, Tim. *Cultures of Masculinity.* New York: Routledge, 2006.

Faludi, Susan. *The Terror Dream: Fear and Fantasy in Post–9/11 America.* New York: Metropolitan Books, 2007.

Habermas, Jürgen. "Fundamentalism and Terror." *In* Luis Guzman (Trans.). *Borradori*: 25–43.

Heath, Atchley J. "The Loss of Language, The Language of Loss: Thinking with DeLillo on Terror and Mourning." *Janus Head* 7.2 (2004): 333–354.

Helyer, Ruth. "DeLillo and Masculinity." *In* John Duval (Ed.). *In The Cambridge Companion to Don DeLillo*. New York: Cambridge University Press, 2008: 125–136.

Jeffords, Susan. *The Remasculinization of America: Gender and the Vietnam War*. Bloomington: Indiana University Press, 1989.

Johnston, John. "Generic Difficulties in the Novels of Don DeLillo." *Critique: Studies in Contemporary Fiction* 30.4 (1989): 261–275.

Junod, Tom. "The Falling Man." *Esquire* 140.3 (2003): 1–9.

Kaplan, Amy. "Manifest Domesticity." *American Literature* 70.3 (1998): 581–606.

Kaplan, E. Ann. *Trauma Culture: The Politics of Terror and Loss in Media and Literature*. New Brunswick, NJ: Rutgers University Press, 2005.

Kauffman, Linda S. "The Wake of Terror: Don DeLillo's 'In the Ruins of the Future,' 'Baader-Meinhof,' and *Falling Man*." *Modern Fiction Studies* 54.2 (2008): 353–377.

Keniston, Ann, and Jeanne Follansbee Quinn (Eds.). "Introduction: Representing 9/11: Literature and Resistance." *Keniston and Quinn*: 1–15.

_____. *Literature After 9/11*. New York: Routledge, 2008.

Kimmel, Michael. *Manhood in America: A Cultural History*. (2nd ed.). New York: Oxford University Press, 2006.

Levinas, Emmanuel, and Michael B. Smith, Barbara Harshaw (Trans.). *Entre Nous: On Thinking-of-the-Other*. New York: Columbia University Press, 1983.

Longmuir, Anne. "Genre and Gender in Don DeLillo's *Players* and *Running Dog*." *JNT: Journal of Narrative Theory* 37.1 (Winter 2007): 128–145.

McClintock, Anne. *Imperial Leather: Race, Gender, and Sexuality in the Colonial Context*. New York: Routledge, 1995.

Parish, Mary J. "9/11 and the Limitations of the 'Man's Man' Construction of Masculinity in Don DeLillo's *Falling Man*" (unpublished paper).

Radstone, Susannah. "The War of the Fathers: Trauma, Fantasy, and September 11." *Signs* 28.1 (2002): 457–459.

Rothberg, Michael. "Seeing Terror, Feeling Art: Public and Private in Post–9/11 Literature." Keniston and Quinn: 123–142.

MISPLACED ANXIETIES
Violence and Trauma in Ian McEwan's Saturday
Ulrike Tancke

A recently published essay on post–9/11 literature in the U.S., in the German literary studies journal *Amerikastudien*, opens with a brief reference to Ian McEwan's *Saturday* (2005). Summarizing the novel's theme and plot in a footnote, the author states that "this novel describes the violent intrusion of world politics in the domestic sphere after 9/11" (Däwes: 517). She uses *Saturday* as a way into her discussion of the cultural impact of 9/11 by discussing the one scene from the novel that reviewers and critics have most readily picked up on: the protagonist happens to observe a burning plane descending for an emergency landing at Heathrow airport, a scenario uncannily reminiscent of the events of September 11, 2001. Apparently taking their thematic cue from this scene, critics and reviewers have commonly read the novel as McEwan's timely commentary on the state of a post–9/11 world that fears the incalculable risks of new and daunting geopolitical alliances as well as ideological constellations, and is collectively traumatized by the possibility of large-scale destruction.[1]

In a similar way, the novel's publishers have obviously latched on to the 9/11 allusion. The Vintage paperback edition — the one with the largest print run, which could be seen on the bestsellers shelves at most bookshops for months and is the first and most frequently listed edition that appears when you search *Saturday* on Amazon — also draws on this element from the novel. Its cover shows London's Post Office Tower at night, with an indistinct object, looking like a flash of light rather than any identifiable entity, seemingly approaching the tower in mid-flight. A picture that, pre–9/11, we would simply have seen as something that looks like a comet against a dark city skyline now conjures up a host of related images of the attacks and their aftermath: planes crashing into the towers, clouds of smoke, bodies falling from the sky, and the devastation of "Ground Zero." At the same time, the very fact that this is the cover picture of a bestselling novel and hence geared towards attracting potential buyers' attention should give us pause. Is this a case of the commercialization of an assumed fear and collective trauma? As a consequence, is the idea of collective trauma that these pictures evoke the product of "media hype," rather than a genuine expression of widespread perceptions and feelings? After all, much of the titillating nature of these images stems from the fact that they ultimately keep the disaster and its genuine impact remote. That said, what is it that is being kept hidden behind immediately recognizable, easily categorizable associations like "9/11"?

It is these questions, I believe, that *Saturday* explores. True, the novel does use the events of 9/11 and their aftermath as a pivotal reference point. Yet, while 9/11 is one of its starting points, the event soon fades into the background as our attention is drawn to something quite different: the random eruption of violence into everyday lives, the destructive nature of coincidence, and the uncontrollability of human actions, biology and the human psyche. With this distinct shift of emphasis, the novel moves beyond post–9/11 discourse. It juxtaposes the idea of collective trauma with individual experience and hence problematizes the detachment that underpins such immediate identifications and visual associations as seen in the examples to which I have just referred. Its characters are not simply representatives of a traumatized generation, but capable of inflicting trauma themselves. With this decidedly individualist, small-scale perspective, *Saturday* transcends oft-met interpretations of 9/11 centering on collective experiences, precisely in order to foreground the mechanism by which collective explanations are drawn upon so as not to acknowledge individual responsibilities and personal decisions.

Saturday's emphasis on the individual is reflected in its very structure, as it exclusively centers on the perspective of its protagonist. The novel recounts the events of a single day in the life of Henry Perowne, a successful, middle-aged London neurosurgeon, married to journalist Rosalind and father of two (nearly) grown-up children. At the novel's outset is the scene that has attracted the strongest critical attention, the incident that is reminiscent — to both Henry and the reader — of the 9/11 scenario. Henry has woken up just before dawn and, as he stands at the window looking out at the night sky, he suddenly sees a plane on fire, presumably attempting to make an emergency landing at Heathrow airport. His perception of the scene is replete with allusions to 9/11 and expresses a repository of images that Henry (and we as readers) share in:

> [T]he spectacle has the familiarity of a recurrent dream. [...] It's already almost eighteen months since half the planet watched, and watched again the unseen captives driven through the sky to the slaughter, at which time there gathered round the innocent silhouette of any jet plane a novel association. Everyone agrees, airliners look different in the sky these days, predatory or doomed. [...] That is the other familiar element — the horror of what he can't see. Catastrophe observed from a safe distance. Watching death on a large scale, but seeing no one die [McEwan: 15–17].

Henry here reiterates a point that has often been made about 9/11, namely that the visual dimension of the attacks has ingrained itself in our collective unconscious because of its disturbingly alluring aesthetic qualities, and has thereby been instrumental in generating "the sense of monumental, irrevocable change that we, as a culture, feel we have experienced" (Hirsch: n. p.). The latter, however — the sense of fundamental change inaugurated by 9/11 — has also been questioned, most candidly by Slavoj Žižek. Žižek contextualizes the World Trade Center attacks as a moment that crystallizes what he calls the "passion for the Real" that permeates our culture (*Welcome*: 5–11). In a move to counter the postmodern fascination with semblance and simulacra, Žižek argues, we crave ever more intense, "real" experiences. The result is not, however, a more authentic and unmediated approach to reality, but rather the opposite: "we begin to experience 'real reality' itself as a virtual reality" (Žižek, *Welcome*: 11), that is, reality becomes its own imitation. The 9/11 attacks expose this trajectory in an exemplary fashion, reminiscent as they are "of spectacular shots in catastrophe movies, a special effect which outdid all others" (ibid.)—a special effect, that is, whose destructive impact is restricted to the virtual and hence remains remote.

Saturday alerts us to this mechanism and explores its workings on the level of narrative perspective and development. At the same time that we as readers are drawn into Henry's consciousness, the novel's powerful 9/11 allusions also mislead us, as they do him. After all, the parallels that the narrative voice draws to the events of 9/11 are not Henry's immediate associations, but only a secondary interpretation of the scene that is unfolding in front of his eyes. Initially, he mistakenly identifies the burning plane as a meteor and then as a comet: "In this first moment, in his eagerness and curiosity, he assumes proportions on a planetary scale" (McEwan: 13). Only when its noise becomes clearly audible is he reminded, initially, of a plane crash, and only when the burning plane comes in proximity to the Post Office tower does the narrative depiction of a repeat–9/11 incident emerge, creating an intensifying imaginative progression from "ordinary" plane crash to mirror terrorist attack, which culminates in the explicit alignment of the two scenarios in the passage quoted above. What this means, in effect, is that the immediate identification of the incident with 9/11 is a critical misconception that is undermined by a close reading of the text itself—just as much as the critical trajectory by which the 9/11 parallel becomes the focal point around which the novel revolves is based on a fundamental misunderstanding.

In fact, the narrative observation that "the spectacle has the familiarity of a recurrent dream" (15) refers, initially, not to the attacks on the World Trade Center, but to Henry's association of the rapidly descending plane with his—and, as he assumes, everyone's—half-suppressed nightmares dreamt on his frequent, largely work-related flights. Initially, the plane's descent is nothing out of the ordinary: "It's travelling along a route that he himself has taken many times in his life, and along which he's gone through the routines, adjusting his seat-back and his watch, putting away his papers, always curious to see if he can locate his own house down among the immense almost beautiful orange-grey sprawl" (McEwan: 14). The curious alignment of—and harsh contrast between—the globally identifiable paraphernalia of air travel (cabin-crew announcements and routine preparations prior to landing) and Henry's cozy domesticity (his child-like attempt to identify his own house while the plane descends) suggest that there might in itself be something amiss with a culture that has created and relies on an imaginary sense of security, bolstered by technology and upheld by schematic and familiar scenarios. The sense of anomaly that is attached to this recognizable everyday scenario is heightened when Henry goes on to muse about the frightful fantasies that occasionally take hold of him at that moment:

> Like most passengers, outwardly subdued by the monotony of air travel, he often lets his thoughts range across the possibilities while sitting, strapped down and docile, in front of a packaged meal. Outside, beyond a wall of thin steel and cheerful cracking plastic, it's minus sixteen degrees and forty thousand feet to the ground. Flung across the Atlantic at five hundred feet a second, you submit to the folly because everyone else does [McEwan: 15].

Viewed from this angle, a world in which thousands of people expose themselves to an absurd scenario of this kind, is perversely delusional. Adults are willingly reduced to and comply with a state of helpless, child-like dependence ("strapped down and docile") in a situation which epitomizes the virtual reality that pervades culture at large — a "reality without being so" (Žižek, *Welcome*: 11) whose artificiality is exemplified in the airline's pre-packed meals, designed to keep their consumers occupied rather than to respond to an actual physical need. A culture, in addition, which relies on instant accessibility and global connections has as its disturbing flip side such widely accepted, though, ironically, demeaning and undignified behaviors. What is more, apart from its absurd nature, the scenario is singularly fragile: "Your fellow passengers are reassured because you and the others around you appear calm. [...] Air travel is a stock market, a trick of mirrored perceptions, a fragile alliance of pooled belief; so long as nerves hold steady and no bombs or wreckers are on board, everybody prospers" (McEwan: 15). The scenario is held in balance as long as the fiction at its core is upheld and its behavioral codes are adhered to. Just as air travel is a commonplace cultural experience, so is the statistically unlikely scenario of a plane crash part of the collective imagination in which Henry shares and in which, so far, he has only indulged as a somewhat angst-inducing, yet ultimately inconsequential and trivializing fantasy ("Plastic fork in hand, he often wonders how it might go" [McEwan: 15]). It is these musings on the culture's built-in fragility and potential for destruction that prepare Henry's associative link of the burning plane with 9/11— significantly, the intellectual trajectory is not reversed. What this suggests, in effect, is that 9/11, far from marking a sea change in human perceptions of themselves and their understanding of their way of life, is the inevitable outcome of a diseased culture — a culture which, in Žižekian terms, indulges its "passion for the Real," but which for this very reason cannot but turn the "Real" into fiction. Henry's train of thought exemplifies the mechanism by which reality (the possibility of a plane crash) is mistaken for fiction (mind games or images), so that "the hard kernel of the Real" (Žižek, *Welcome*: 19) — the human capacity for violence and destruction and the fragility of human existence at the core of both — is overlooked. 9/11, then, is not the culmination of a world getting increasingly out of control, but one manifestation of the excesses of a thoroughly virtualized culture.

To argue along these lines is by no means to deny or undermine the scale of the destruction and human suffering inflicted by the attacks. What the novel does seem to question, however, by contextualizing the attacks with reference to globalized Western culture, is the legitimacy of the interpretive venture which elevates 9/11 to the level of a universal turning point. This caution ties in with Slavoj Žižek's hesitant judgment of the cultural impact of the event:

> So what about the phrase which reverberates everywhere: "Nothing will ever be the same after 9/11"? Significantly, this phrase is never further elaborated — it is just an empty gesture of saying something "deep" without really knowing what we want to say. So our first reaction to it should be: Really? What if, precisely, nothing epochal happened on September 11? [Žižek, *Welcome*: 46].

In what follows, Žižek reads the events of 9/11 and their aftermath in a large-scale, social and political context, observing that the ubiquitous displays of American patriotism and global hegemony through the military response in Afghanistan brought to the surface disturbing attitudes and a perception of self that had thus far been concealed. As we shall see, *Saturday* puts forward a similar argument as it plays with the reader's associations with 9/11 as a life-changing event, only to then point to underlying constants that are virulent independent of the terrorist attacks. The novel stages a move towards the "Real" as it explores disturbing human behaviors and inclinations and their material immediacy — unsettling dimensions of human nature that the momentousness and visual ubiquity of the 9/11 attacks serve to distract us from.[2] What is more, it traces these human inclinations on the level of individual actions and responsibilities — a narrowing of focus which highlights the way in which 9/11 functions as a projection screen to divert attention away from uncomfortable truths about human nature.

At a closer look, then, the 9/11 allusion early on in the novel is a red herring — an incident that seems significant, but turns out to be irrelevant to the plot. Henry later learns that the burning plane was indeed no terrorist attack, but a simple accident, and that the pilot succeeded in making an emergency landing. That is, the reality is much more mundane than the fiction — reality's imaginary representation — appeared to suggest. Again, the intellectual processes by which Henry arrives at this insight are highly complex. Unable to go back to sleep after the scene he has witnessed at the window, he goes to sit in the kitchen where his son Theo, an aspiring blues musician who keeps erratic hours by profession, is reading a magazine. As he turns on the radio, Henry is initially surprised by the fact that the plane has not yet made it on the news — for the moment, it remains "an unreliable subjective event" (McEwan: 29). As he tries to share his experience with Theo, he realizes "how little there is to tell" (ibid.). The factual dimension of the incident does not match the potential import that its powerful visual impression suggests. Henry's individual interpretation of the scene is, of course, in line with the latter, as signifying an event of potentially global impact. When, half an hour later, the plane does become a news item and is "made real at last" (McEwan: 34), the reality — a Russian cargo plane whose engine failed and caught fire was guided in to Heathrow, each step on the air traffic emergency plan kicking in smoothly and automatically — is much more sober and mundane than Henry's fantasies had caused him to fear. As he goes to bed, he reflects on his own propensity for falling prey to all too hasty chains of associations and the resulting misconceptions, which is in tune with the mood of the times:

> Sleepless in the early hours, you make a nest out of your own fears[...]. This past hour he has been in a state of wild unreason, in a folly of overinterpretation. It doesn't console him that anyone in these times, standing at the window in his place, might have leaped to the same conclusions. Misunderstanding is general all over the world. How can we trust ourselves? He sees now the details he half-ignored in order to nourish his fears: that the plane was not being driven into a public building, that it was making a regular, controlled descent, that it was on a well-used flight path — none of this fitted the general unease. He told himself there were two possible outcomes — the cat[3] dead or alive. But he'd already voted for the dead, when he should have sensed it straight away — a simple accident in the making. Not an attack on our whole way of life then [McEwan: 39].

What Henry clearly acknowledges here is his complicity in a cultural disposition, propelled by fear, in which certain stock images and phrases elicit stock responses — an oversimplifying mechanism that only serves to intensify the very fears that have generated it. In a sense, then, the passage prefigures my questioning of widespread responses to the novel which has opened this essay. Just as the protagonist is misled by the ubiquitous proclamations of impending terrorist follow-up attacks, so is the reader lured into mistakenly identifying 9/11 as the novel's key issue.

Clearly, Henry's train of thought on the incident with the burning plane that the novel traces puts in perspective the life-changing impact that the association with 9/11 seems to suggest. Obviously, this is no traumatizing event as such — for one thing, it is a scenario which, while it undeniably evokes a set of familiar associations, is observed from the sheltered space of Henry's home. To a large extent, its violently disruptive effect in the novel stems from the fact that it contrasts harshly with the vision of human perfection that Henry's preceding contemplation of his life has created. In a city which he sees as "a success, a brilliant invention, a biological masterpiece," his life as a whole is "a triumph of congruent proportion" (McEwan: 5), revolving around his work, his wife and his children. Of course, Henry's profession as a neurosurgeon itself epitomizes the fantasy of control that he lives by; he derives pleasure from performing "fast and accurate" operations and is fascinated by the "delicate trick[s]" of modern medicine — "all done in fifteen minutes; three years' misery, of sharp, stabbing pain, ended" (McEwan: 7). His superior power over the world and his insight into the most complicated and essential part of the human body makes him construct around himself an aura of exclusiveness and untouchability. His professional life is instrumental for maintaining his self-image as orderly and in control: "Operating never wearies him — once busy within the enclosed world of his firm, the theatre and its ordered procedures, [...] he experiences a superhuman capacity, more like a craving, for work. [...] He's too experienced to be touched by the varieties of distress he encounters — his obligation is to be useful" (McEwan: 11). While there is a disturbing note to Henry's apparent lack of empathy and detachment from individual fates, there are more complex mechanisms that put his singular fascination with control in perspective. Ironically, the very vision of orderliness and contentment that marks Henry's professional life is constantly, if subtly, being undercut. As Henry joins Theo in the kitchen, the narrative expresses a train of Henry's thoughts on the biological implications of having children that are voiced as general statements, but unmistakably reflect Henry's outlook and are clearly focalized through him: "It's a commonplace of parenting and modern genetics that parents have little or no influence on the characters of their children. You never know who you are going to get. [...] It can be quite an affront to parental self-regard, just how much of the work has already been done. On the other hand, it can let you off the hook" (McEwan: 25). Henry's penchant for (self-)control has its limit when it comes to the random and unpredictable mutations of the gene pool to which human beings are inevitably subject, to favorable or detrimental effect. These ruminations on the impact of biology on human relations are a mere prologue to the exploration of a much larger threat to Henry's ideal of perfection that the novel subsequently explores: his vision of control is most forcibly undercut by the threat of unpredictable violence.

At first glance, this is related to the fact that *Saturday* is clearly situated in the wake of the War on Terror and, more specifically, in the immediate build-up to the Iraq war. A climate of ubiquitous fear pervades ordinary lives and everyday activities, generating hastily conceived preventative measures. For instance, Henry has to review the hospital's emergency procedures: "There's to be a new look — there's always a new look — at the hospital's Emergency Plan. Simple train crashes are no longer all that are envisaged, and words like 'catastrophe' and 'mass fatalities,' 'chemical and biological warfare' and 'major attack' have recently become bland through repetition" (McEwan, 11–12). The ubiquitous representation of collective fears and possible global disasters reduces their existential violence to bureaucratic trivia. This is only one indication that the novel's chief concern is not, I believe, with the atmosphere of collective fear that is evoked by these political circumstances. Rather, it explores the unexpected and hence all the more destructive intrusion of violence into personal lives, independent of world historical events — a violence that is intrinsic to and perpetrated by individuals and that has the potential to be traumatic.

As the day progresses, other events unfold that immediately affect Henry and carry much more profound significance. On his way to his weekly game of squash with a colleague, he is involved in a minor car accident as he is waved across a road officially closed for the demonstrations against the war on Saddam Hussein's Iraq. In a sense, of course, this scenario offers another red herring: the setting of the accident suggests that it is implicated in the generally shared sense of upheaval and uneasiness of the time, whereas the accident itself could have happened anywhere, any time and does not bear any global significance. The reader immediately and inevitably notices and presumably identifies with Henry's notion that "the world has changed beyond recall, that harmless streets like this and the tolerant life they embody can be destroyed by the new enemy — well-organised, tentacular, full of hatred and focused zeal" (McEwan: 76). Taking careful note of the context of this passage reveals, however, that these are thoughts that Henry denounces and feels "a vague sense of shame and embarrassment" (ibid.) about. Looked at rationally — as is Henry's scientific default mode — he has been all too readily persuaded by "foolishly apocalyptic" (ibid.) visions that are both inappropriate and self-indulgent.[4]

And yet, Henry falls prey to a similarly self-congratulatory, but equally flawed self-indulgence. His first thought is of the accident as an intrusion into his Saturday routine and a taint on his self-image of perfection: "Something original and pristine has been stolen from his car, and can never be restored, however good the repair. [...] His car will never be the same again. It's ruinously altered, and so is his Saturday" (McEwan: 82). Yet the implications of the accident quickly move beyond the petty annoyances of paperwork and insurance claims, as the driver of the other car, a young man called Baxter, becomes increasingly aggressive. With his neurosurgical training, however, Henry is able to make an off-the-cuff diagnosis of Baxter's mood swings and muscular spasms as probable indications of Huntington's disease. Henry automatically gives a biological explanation of Baxter's behavior; and because he approaches Baxter's aggression on an abstract level, it does not really affect him. In spite of Baxter's mounting aggression, Henry is able to approach him with professional superiority and to subdue him with his objective doctor's gaze, diagnosing Baxter with "reduced levels of GABA among the appropriate binding sites on striatal neurons" (McEwan: 91). Of course, the medical jargon that characterizes Henry's attitude distances him from the physical immediacy of Baxter's aggression, and Henry is clearly aware of the power that accrues to his position. What his narrative voice observes about kicks as opposed to punches in a fight — "[t]he foot [...] [is] liberated by distance from responsibility" (McEwan: 92–93) — is even more true with respect to Henry's medical knowledge and choice of register. It is this superiority of insight, based on reason and scientific objectification, that triumphs over the physical violence with which Baxter threatens him.

Admittedly, Henry acts in self-defense; and yet, he is forced to acknowledge shortly after the confrontation has ended and he has resumed his Saturday morning routine that his behavior also expressed a desire to dominate and exert power over Baxter. The animalistic urge to assert superiority sheds an ironic light on Henry's earlier allusion to the Hobbesian notion of Leviathan that he made in anticipation of Baxter and his friends' aggression at the site of the accident: "the stock of Thomas Hobbes keeps on rising [...] drug dealers and pimps, among others who live beyond the law, are not inclined to dial nine-nine-nine for Leviathan; they settle their quarrels in their own way" (McEwan: 88). Henry, too, settles his quarrels in his own way — a way that is not all that far removed from the unrestrained violence of Baxter and his companions. While Henry's own potential for violence is, at this point, restricted to the merely verbal and, in a sense, the ideological, his squash game shortly after the accident brings to the surface the implicit violence that lies dormant in him: feeling himself to have "been in some form of combat" (McEwan: 112) all morning, he is now free to act out "the irreducible urge to win, as biological as thirst" (McEwan: 113).

These questions of power, which have thus far only been addressed indirectly, are exposed in their true significance when Baxter and one of his companions turn up at the Perownes' house later that Saturday and the violence that has so far been subdued and repressed comes to a head. Baxter and his friend Nigel take the Perowne family, who have gathered for a long-awaited reunion, hostage in their living room; Baxter threatens them with a knife, beats Rosalind's father and attempts to rape their daughter Daisy.

This violent attack can be read as Henry's figurative violence turning back on him. It is at this point that Henry becomes fully aware of the complex way in which he is implicated in Baxter's aggression and recognizes the shortcomings of his earlier attitude:

> Perowne can't convince himself that molecules and faulty genes alone are terrorising his family and have broken his father-in-law's nose. Perowne himself is also responsible. He humiliated Baxter in the street[...], and did so when he'd already guessed at his condition. [...] He used or misused his authority to avoid one crisis, and his actions have steered him into another, far worse. The responsibility is his [McEwan: 210–11].

In spite of the very real threat of Baxter's unpredictable violence, the balance of power never tips in his direction completely. Although Baxter is violent, the family withstands his onslaught because of their cultural, social and intellectual superiority. In a somewhat unlikely plot twist, Daisy, held at knifepoint, manages to enchant him by reciting Matthew Arnold's poem "Dover Beach." Baxter assumes she has written it herself; it leaves him spellbound and makes him release his violent grip on the family. He then recalls Henry's promise of drugs that he made that morning. Ironically, taking a somewhat dazed Baxter upstairs to his office gives Henry the chance to overwhelm him and, with the help of Theo, to push him down the stairs so that he loses consciousness. In essence, then, it is not Henry's professional or social superiority that allows him to defeat Baxter, but the same kind of primeval violence that Baxter resorted to, combined with chance — sheer good luck — and biological accident (Baxter is terminally ill, Henry is not). In a sense, then, biology wins in more ways than one, as a human reality and as a discursive category. Henry capitalizes on Baxter's mental and physical fragility to achieve his victory; and by extension, the plot thereby affirms the power of Henry's professional control and scientific detachment whose terminology pervades the novel.

As Henry is clearly aware, his triumph over the intruders is a thoroughly ambiguous one. Henry's victory is based on socio-economic advantage, but even more on sheer coincidence. Even more significantly, it has unleashed the same violent impulse in him that he considered himself superior to when confronted by Baxter — his actions are reduced to a primeval act of defense, the primitive impulse of protecting your own kind. In a sense, Henry's earlier allusion to Leviathan comes back to haunt him. Henry, too, is momentarily reduced to the pre-civilized state "where every man is enemy to every man" (Hobbes: 84) that the ordered society which he considers himself a part of deems to have long overcome. When all is said and done, the surrender to an overarching authority of the power to exert violence only thinly veils the inclination to engage in "such a war, as is of every man, against every man," which inheres in human nature (ibid.).

Even more disturbingly, the violence that Henry resorts to cannot neatly be pitted against the civilized middle-class society of which he considers himself to be a part. Based as it is on Henry's desire to defend the very cornerstones of his self-image — his perfectly balanced and controlled professional and family life — his violent impulse must be read as a dimension intrinsic to his sense of self. Violence is not the remote and hence controllable antithesis of a cultured personality and civilization, but its obverse, the dark underbelly which it cannot shed.[5]

The novel's ending is fraught with ambivalence, as it explores — and has its protagonist explore — the disturbing implications of this insight. Ironically, as the most experienced neurosurgeon, Henry is called in to the hospital to operate on Baxter, who has been brought in with the head injuries that result from his fall down the stairs. Familiar certainties and a new awareness of responsibility and loss of control oscillate in Henry's thoughts. On the one hand, in his doctor's role, he is, once again, in his usual position of power towards Baxter. At the same time, however, Baxter's under-researched and as yet incurable illness exposes the limitations of Henry's own discipline: "faced with these unknown codes, this dense and brilliant circuitry, he and his colleagues offer only brilliant plumbing" (McEwan: 255). What is more, the events of the day have made Henry aware of his own potential for causing suffering and inflicting violence and destruction:

> All he feels now is fear. He's weak and ignorant, scared of the way consequences of an action leap away from your control and breed new events, new consequences, until you're led to a place you never dreamed of and would never choose — a knife at the throat. [...] He's responsible, after all; twenty hours ago he drove across a road officially closed, and set in train a sequence of events [McEwan: 277–78].

What Henry comes to acknowledge is that human acts of violence point to a capacity that we all share. The kind of violent incident he experienced can happen to anyone, anytime; to some extent, it is banal and every-day. While Baxter's intrusion is potentially traumatizing, the true significance of the plot lies elsewhere. Awaking his awareness of his capacity for primitive violence, the events expose the inadequacy of Henry's sense of self and hint at the trivializing and delusional mechanisms by which we make sense of the world.

This focus on individual human behaviors is also the reason why I take issue with the prevailing critical tendency to read *Saturday* as an allegory of the Western response to 9/11.[6] Such readings take Perowne to be the symbolic equivalent of the West and Baxter the prototypical terrorist who breaks into and wreaks havoc in the latter's sheltered space of security and prosperity. Just as Henry uses violence to overwhelm Baxter, such is the logical conclusion to this argument, "the West" is not above the terrorists in resorting to violence, as happened in Afghanistan and Iraq. While the parallel may seem evident, reading the novel in this allegorical fashion is precisely the kind of projection that the text itself works against. It entails the same dangers as identifying the terrorists as the embodiment of evil; after all, it is much easier to say that "the West"— vaguely and collectively—has used violence on a par with the terrorists, or has even brought terrorist violence upon itself because of its neo-imperialist ventures, than to acknowledge that individuals in their everyday lives resort to violence and are motivated by self-interest, the urge for power, the desire for dominance and the capacity to pursue these ends by violent means — which is what the novel does, especially by focalizing the narrative exclusively through Henry Perowne.

Hence the traumatic potential of the events of the novel lies in the insight that Henry has gained into his own psyche and reactions. As his exclusive reliance on scientific evidence and accuracy receives a fatal blow, the belief in logic and reason that we as a culture like to subscribe to is also thwarted. Henry's rejection of and distaste for fiction, or "stories"— expressed in his initial claim that "[t]his notion of Daisy's, that people can't 'live' without stories, is simply not true. He is living proof" (McEwan: 68)— is thereby revealed to be equally fictitious. It is not just that "[h]e is living a fiction to the extent that he considers himself apart from the violence of the streets, which he spies from his bedroom window, or the horrors of the world, about which he reads in the papers" (Childs: 147). Throughout the novel, the narrative voice consistently suggests Henry's unacknowledged reliance on stories to make sense of and impose overarching meaning on his biography. For instance, Henry recounts his and Rosalind's love story as a modern-day, neurology-ward version of the damsel in distress rescued by a knight in shining amour (Henry himself as a junior doctor) whose life is changed for the better by what started as a chance encounter under tragic circumstances. In a more subtle, but all the more powerful fashion, Henry's self-image as a rational, self-controlled doctor is guaranteed by the presence of his daughter Daisy, his "other" who believes in the powers of art, creativity and the imagination to shape human lives. What this means, in effect, is that Henry's sense of self is upheld by a profound narrativizing impulse, as he subscribes to the fiction of (self-)mastery. By extension, as the novel's violent denouement reveals, the belief in rational control, too, is nothing more than a story all too easily proven fictitious in the face of the brutal realities of sheer coincidence, random biology and the human propensity for violent deeds.

Curiously enough, reviewers of *Saturday*, while acknowledging the centrality of the question of violence in the novel, consistently shy away from drawing this final connection. Tim Adams, for instance, comments that "the accident [in the closed road] eventually hardens into something much darker and involves questions of how humane and civilised men might confront terror to protect things they hold dear" (n.p.). Obviously, to "confront terror" is a rather vague and ambiguous choice of phrase that glosses over the fact that the protagonist actually uses violence himself and thereby *perpetrates* terror.

This is where the novel's disturbing statements on the human potential for violence dovetail with its exploration of 9/11 and its associative linkages. The cultural preoccupation with 9/11 and its allegedly traumatizing effects is a prime example of how we tend to turn our lives — and history more generally — into narrative, into a convincing story boasting turning points and life-changing events. While this is an all too human tendency, it also entails the danger of shaping the narrative according to preconceived ideas and ideals and thereby ignoring the potentially violent and destructive impact inherent in the attempt.[7] *Saturday*'s perspective on 9/11 suggests that the cultural repercussions of 9/11 and its aftermath feed into a self-protective and ultimately self-congratulatory strategy. The very ubiquity of the images of the attack in our collective unconscious facilitates upholding "the distance which separates Us from Them[8][...]: the real horror happens *there*, not *here*" (Žižek, *Welcome*: 13; emphasis in the original).

The novel seduces us with seemingly easy associations, only to then gradually turn our gaze to where we really should look: at ourselves. With its unmasking of the traumatizing potentials of everyday violence and guilt, *Saturday* makes us aware of where the real threat lies. A culture obsessively preoccupied with global, large-scale risks and threats all too easily loses sight of the seemingly banal manifestations of violence and the individual human predisposition to harm and inflict hurt on others.

Notes

1. For instance, in his review of *Saturday*, David Sexton classifies *Saturday* as "by far the most deeply considered imaginative response in British fiction to the changes in our lives, in our sense of security and the possibility of simple happiness, imposed by 9/11 and the resulting wars" (n. p.).

2. This is a similar mechanism to the conservative and politically affirmative reaction that Žižek traces in American culture: "What if [...] the shattering experience of September 11 ultimately served as a device which enabled the hegemonic American ideology to 'go back to its basics,' to reassert its basic ideological co-ordinates against the antiglobalist and other critical temptations? [...] [The USA] opted to reassert its traditional ideological commitments: out with feelings of responsibility and guilt towards the impoverished Third World, *we* are the victims now!" (Žižek, *Welcome*: 46–47; emphasis in the original).

3. This is an allusion to Henry's previous thoughts on "Schrödinger's Cat," a theory used in physics, which Henry is reminded of as he wonders about the fate of the airplane passengers: "A cat, Schrödinger's Cat, hidden from view in a covered box, is either still alive, or has just been killed by a randomly activated hammer hitting a vial of poison. Until the observer lifts the cover from the box, both possibilities, alive cat and dead cat, exist side by side, in parallel universes, equally real. At the point at which the lid is lifted from the box and the cat is examined, a quantum wave of probability collapses. None of this has ever made any sense to him at all. [...] He's heard that even the physicists are abandoning it. To Henry it seems beyond the requirements of proof: a result, a consequence, exists separately in the world, independent of himself, known to others, awaiting his discovery. What then collapses will be his own ignorance. Whatever the score, it is already chalked up. And whatever the passengers' destination, whether they are frightened and safe, or dead, they will have arrived by now" (McEwan: 18–19).

4. As Henry muses: "Talk of a hundred-year crisis is indulgence. There are always crises, and Islamic terrorism will settle into place, alongside recent wars, climate change, the politics of international trade, land and fresh water shortages, hunger, poverty and the rest" (McEwan: 77).

5. My argument parallels Slavoj Žižek's analysis of the violence unleashed in New Orleans in the

wake of hurricane Katrina in August 2005: "what if the tension that led to the explosion in New Orleans was not the tension between 'human nature' and the force of civilisation that keeps it in check, but the tension between the two aspects of our civilisation itself? What if, in endeavouring to control explosions like the one in New Orleans, the forces of law and order were confronted with the very nature of capitalism at its purest, the logic of individualist competition, of ruthless self-assertion, generated by capitalist dynamics, a 'nature' much more threatening and violent than all the hurricanes and earthquakes?" (Žižek, *Violence*: 81–82).

6. For examples of these allegorical readings, see Head: 181–82, Carpenter: 150–52.

7. My argument here draws on Galen Strawson's critique of narrativity, which argues that the "tendency to look for story or narrative coherence in one's life is, in general, a gross hindrance to self-understanding: to a just, general, practically real sense, implicit or explicit, of one's nature" (Strawson: 4).

8. Žižek's "Them" refers to "Somalis dying of hunger, raped Bosnian women, men with their throats cut" (Žižek, *Welcome*: 13) — i.e., signifiers of evil that are easily recognizable precisely because they are remote from our own lives.

Works Cited

Adams, Tim. "When Saturday Comes." *The Observer*, 30 January 2005.
Carpenter, Rebecca. "'We're Not a Friggin' Girl Band': September 11, Masculinity, and the British-American Relationship in David Hare's *Stuff Happens* and Ian McEwan's *Saturday*." *In* Ann Keniston and Jeanne Follansbee Quinn (Eds.). *Literature After 9/11*. London and New York: Routledge, 2008: 143–60.
Childs, Peter. *The Fiction of Ian McEwan: A Reader's Guide to Essential Criticism*. Houndmills: Palgrave Macmillan, 2006.
Däwes, Birgit. "On Contested Ground (Zero): Literature and the Transnational Challenge of Remembering 9/11." *Amerikastudien/American Studies* 52:4 (2007): 517–544.
Head, Dominic. *Ian McEwan*. Manchester and New York: Manchester University Press, 2007.
Hirsch, Marianne. "The Day Time Stopped." *The Chronicle Review*, January 25, 2002. July 15, 2009. http://chronicle.com/free/v48/i20/20b01101.htm.
Hobbes, Thomas. *In* J.C.A. Gaskin (Ed.). *Leviathan* (1651). Oxford: Oxford University Press, 1996.
McEwan, Ian. *Saturday*. London: Vintage, 2006.
Sexton, David. "The Pick of the Summer Reads." *Evening Standard*, July 4, 2005.
Strawson, Galen. "Against Narrativity." *Ratio (New Series)* 17:4 (2004): 428–452.
Žižek, Slavoj. *Violence: Six Sideways Reflections*. London: Profile Books, 2008
_____. *Welcome to the Desert of the Real! Five Essays on September 11 and Related Dates*. London and New York: Verso, 2002.

The Mediated Trauma of September 11, 2001, in William Gibson's *Pattern Recognition* and David Foster Wallace's "The Suffering Channel"

Marc Oxoby

Introduction

We saw the first tower burning. Then we saw the second plane collide with the building, erupting into a fireball. We heard various officials discussing the emergency response to an unprecedented crisis, and we saw the Pentagon in flames. Then we heard the thunderous rumble, swelling to a roar as the towers came cascading to the ground. We saw the faces of onlookers filled with horror, then with panic as mountains of dust, of powdered concrete, billowed through the downtown streets, darkening the sky, and rendering sightless the *cameras* that took it all in.

And there's the rub. Most Americans did not actually see the events of September 11, 2001, so much as they saw what those cameras saw, images recorded on film and video, processed and disseminated electronically, shrunken to the size of the most readily available TV screen. At best, what most of us saw was a reproduction, a simulation of what was happening in New York City and Washington, D.C. And this has posed a problem for postmodern thinkers, who have traditionally invested significant interest in how mass media shapes our perspectives of the world, often in a less than commendable way. At question is the authenticity of experience conveyed by mass media, and especially by television. That the media shaped public perception of the events remains unquestioned. Consider, for example, TV's use of specialized graphics and various editing techniques, and most importantly its near-constant re-playing of the video footage in the days that followed the attacks. Certainly, mass media tends to avoid the complexity of the situations it depicts, as well. The attacks become about the moment, rather than about the complex historical, political, and personal stories underlying them. But it is difficult to deny the authenticity of the visceral emotions felt upon seeing these images, heavily media-crafted though they might be.

William Gibson and David Foster Wallace were among the first fiction writers to address 9/11 beyond simply narrating the events themselves. Additionally, both writers had long exhibited an interest, an obsession, even, with the nature of mass media, and the way it shapes experiences and perceptions. For these writers, the mediated presentation of the September 11th attacks posed a problem of how to maintain the appropriate critical distance from the media, despite the deeply felt emotions evoked by that very media. On the one hand, who could deny the power of those images of the attacks? Who could deny the heart-sickness so many felt on that day, regardless of whether they were in New York, or Washington, D.C., or Reno, Nevada, or even overseas? On the other hand, what of the healthy skepticism towards the mass media, fostered in the writing of, say, Walter Benjamin, Guy Debord, and Jean Baudrillard, and in the earlier fiction by Gibson and Wallace? Where is the post-modern novelist to posit him- or herself in light of this?

Gibson's novel *Pattern Recognition* (2003) and David Foster Wallace's novella "The Suffering Channel" (2004) both represent careful reevaluations of media in light of September 11. For Gibson and Wallace, both of whom are known for their particularly keen insights into media culture, this issue of how we were affected by the indirect experience of the attacks is key to understanding 9/11 as both personal trauma and as cultural construct, notions which, in this particular case, are not mutually exclusive. In *Pattern Recognition* and "The Suffering Channel," Gibson and Wallace have created works of fiction that are not "about" 9/11, but use it as an important backdrop. In treating the attacks indirectly, they address the question of how an indirect experience of September 11 affects the characters and by extension the popular audience for broadcasts that covered the attacks. Their complex, nuanced readings of 9/11 acknowledge the role of media in "fictionalizing" the attacks, but reject the notion that 9/11 was merely a simulacrum, as Jean Baudrillard might have it. Instead, *Pattern Recognition* and "The Suffering Channel" problematize easy answers about the mediated experience(s) of 9/11 and suggest that literature, in contrast to mass media which canvas and frame images, is capable of rendering more nuanced perspectives about traumatic events. Both works distance themselves from televised images and mass productions, while paradoxically developing personal narratives around them. As such, the works under discussion depart from the "spectacle" and "incompleteness" of mass media artifacts and illustrate that fiction and language may offer a deeper understanding of 9/11.

Mass Media and Postmodernism

Jean Baudrillard famously, or perhaps infamously, cast into question the reality of American operations in the Persian Gulf with his 1991 book *The Gulf War Did Not Take Place*. In typical form, Baudrillard overstates in order to make his point about the conflict, which certainly did happen, but was experienced by most of us as something less than the reality actually experienced by those on the ground, for instance, in Kuwait City. We saw a simulation, a simulacra of what occurred. We saw "a masquerade of information: branded faces delivered over to the prostitution of the image, the image of an unintelligible distress" (40). And as such, questions arise about the authenticity not of the events themselves, but of our mediated perception thereof, a perception shaped by commentators and endless repetition of the images, in addition to the very distanciation created by the media itself.

But when it came to the September 11th attacks, even that distance seemed reduced by the magnitude of the event, which was felt with a different kind of immediacy than was experienced by most Americans faced with the comparatively abstract images of the Gulf War. For those of us who were rattled watching the twenty-four hour broadcasts of 9/11 the authenticity of our emotions is not in question, despite the intellectual realization that what we saw was but a fragment of the entire story. As A. Michael Noll has pointed out, "Television bombarded the world with continuous coverage for days after the tragedy, even though there frequently was little new to report" (Noll: xii). There is, of course, no question that the images we saw on that day were crafted ones. Deliberate shaping of experience by the media certainly merits attention in understanding its impact on September 11th and the days that followed. An excellent examination of this can be found in *Framing Terrorism: The News Media, the Government, and the Public* (2003), which is representative of a considerable output of books addressing not only 9/11 but specifically the role of mass media in relation to these events.[1] According to the editors, "terrorist events are commonly understood through news 'frames' that simplify, prioritize, and structure the narrative flow of events" (10). In addition, "News frames bundle key concepts, stock phrases, and iconic images to reinforce certain common ways of interpreting developments." They "prioritize some facts, images, or developments over others, thereby unconsciously promoting one particular interpretation of events" (Norris: 11).

However, this deliberate shaping of data does not represent the only issue at hand in discussing the nature of mediated experience. Even the rawest of data, of imagery, is still conveyed through the varying apparatuses of the media. Marshall McLuhan's famous proclamation that "the medium is the message" is appropriate here, though it is not, strictly speaking, a new concept. Consider, for instance, Walter Benjamin, who, in examining "The Work of Art in the Age of Mechanical Reproduction," accurately suggested that "even the most perfect reproduction of a work of art is lacking in one element: its presence in time and space, its unique existence at the place where it happens to be" (220). Although Benjamin's concern here was obviously with the importance of the immediate, direct effects of an artistic creation, the idea can easily be expanded to a consideration of how any reproduction becomes something less, or at least something different from the initial object or event being reproduced. Jerry Mander, coming at the subject with a definite socio-political axe to grind, uses this as one of his arguments for the elimination of television, claiming that

> [t]elevision is no open window through which all perception may pass. Quite the opposite. There are many technological factors that conspire to limit what the medium can

transmit. Some information fits and some doesn't. Some information can pass through, but only after being reshaped, redefined, repackaged and made duller and coarser than before [266].

He further suggests that television (and, one could argue, much of mass media in general) places viewers "looking at today's world from the outside in" (88), and that it gives viewers a mere illusion of reality, emphasizing images in the place of real objects, "plac(ing) in our minds images of reality which are outside our experience" (111).

Naturally, postmodern philosophy has taken these ideas into account. Postmodernism is informed, at least in part, by the rise of mass media in the latter half of the twentieth-century. While the definition of postmodernism is notoriously slippery, and can differ from text to text, it is rare to find a study of postmodernism that does not address mass media. Fredric Jameson, for example, cites the emergence of "television and media generally to a hitherto unparalleled degree throughout society" as one of the primary influences on postmodernism. Jameson also argues that this expansion of media has resulted in the loss to society of "its capacity to retain its own past," and its inclination "to live in a perpetual present and in a perpetual change that obliterates traditions" (205). This treatment of a "derealized" sense of presence and history reveals the typical skepticism and wariness with which postmodern thought approaches media. Consider, too, Jean Baudrillard's examination of how mass media calls into question "the distinction between cause and effect, between active and passive, between subject and object." He writes, "Television [...] is no longer a spectacular medium[...]. The medium itself is no longer identifiable as such, and the confusion of the medium and the message [...] is the first great formula of this new era. There is no longer a medium in the literal sense: it is now intangible, diffused, and diffracted in the real" (30). Or consider John Docker, who builds upon the ideas of Jameson and Baudrillard:

> In the new space of postmodernism, then, bodily and critical distance have been abolished. We can see this disaster in other postmodern cultural phenomena. People now are immersed in "image addiction," especially in the way television images transform "older realities" into the logic of the simulacrum (the ideal copy for which no original exists) [118].

As postmodern philosophy has adopted this attitude towards mass media, it is hardly surprising that postmodern fiction should do so as well. As Kathleen Fitzpatrick writes, "In the postmodern novel, for instance, one repeatedly finds film and television characterized as mind-numbing, individual-crushing, potentially fascistic forms that are largely responsible for the deterioration of the American reading public" (34). Through the "castigation of television for the mechanicity, the deceit, and the surveillance that have seemingly destroyed the novel's cultural position" (37), the writer of postmodern fiction is a writer who uses his or her work to paint TV as an insidious force, corrupting viewers, polluting their ability to grasp reality. Moreover, doubting the media's ability to capture the actuality, the authenticity of reality, has become something of a staple of postmodern fiction. Consider as an example when the protagonist of Kurt Vonnegut's *Hocus Pocus* (1990) remarks on the contrast between the scripted and news television broadcasts as they depict combat: "Oddly enough, the actors always turned out to be a lot more believable on the little screen than we (the real combatants) were. Real people in real trouble don't come across, somehow" (63). Like John Docker, Vonnegut laments the "loss of the real." If the characters embodied by mere actors feel more "real," it stands to reason, then the actual people involved in combat and other traumatic situations are somehow diminished, their miseries reduced in comparison, at least for the removed viewer. Docker implies that these circumstances, rather than any events depicted in the media, seem to constitute the true "disaster."

But who could possibly say of September 11 that the "real people in real trouble don't come across"? The real people, the real trouble obviously came across, even as people commonly remarked that the visuals of the attacks, particularly the crashing of the second plane into World Trade Center's South Tower, looked like something out of an action movie.[2] David Foster Wallace's essay "The View from Mrs. Thompson's" (2006) clearly makes a counter claim to the notion that the real people and real trouble of 9/11 didn't come across. The title of the work alone is telling. The view in question is that of Mrs. Thompson watching the attacks on the World Trade Center by way of TV in Bloomington, Illinois. Wallace's fiction has always treated TV and media rather skeptically. However, his conflicting emotions about mass media come through nowhere so strongly as in "The View of Mrs. Thompson's." In this essay, he discusses victims jumping from the towers and notes: "It seems grotesque to talk about being traumatized by a piece of video when the people in the video were dying" (136). Fundamentally, however, Wallace's essay is about exactly this: the undeniable emotional disturbance he felt as he watched the video.

William Gibson's Pattern Recognition

By his own admission, William Gibson began writing *Pattern Recognition* before the events of September 11, 2001. Returning to the one-hundred page manuscript about three weeks after the attacks, he found "that my protagonist's back story, that I'd been sort of interrogating and looking for and starting to find, was taking place right then — her memories were of *that autumn*" (Leonard: 3). As a result, Gibson concluded "that my world no longer existed and that the meaning of everything — I felt that just as strongly as I've ever felt anything in my life — the meaning of everything, *ever* that had gone before had to be reconsidered in light of something that had happened" (3). As a consequence, *Pattern Recognition* became one of the first "9/11 novels," despite the fact that it was initially conceived otherwise.

The plot of *Pattern Recognition* follows Cayce Pollard, described as a "coolhunter" (2), with an uncanny sensitivity to commercial iconography which allows her to predict trends for her employer, marketing firm Blue Ant. She has been commissioned to find the source of mysterious video footage that has begun to appear online, and has developed a rabid cult following, dubbed "footageheads." Her employer is, of course, interested in the potential commercial possibilities of this footage, with which even Cayce is obsessed. But Gibson posits the footage as something outside of the realm of mass media. He writes of this footage, "Whenever the media do try to pick it up, it slides like a long noodle from their chopsticks. It comes in mothlike, under the radar evolved to detect things with massive airframes" and because lifestyles and popular culture shows that have run stories on the footage have "elicited no viewer response whatever" (52–53).

The primary storyline, then, has little to do directly with 9/11. However, *Pattern Recognition* uses the attacks as its historical backdrop, and the author also gives them a very personal significance for Cayce. Her father, Win Pollard, was one of the many who went missing on this morning, though he is never definitely identified as one of the attacks' victims. Cayce herself, as a New Yorker, is a kind of eyewitness to the events, but she does not at first acknowledge them for what they are. She hears and possibly sees one of the airplanes passing by, "incredibly loud and, she'd assumed, low. She thought she'd glimpsed something, over West Broadway, but then it had been gone. They must be making a film" (135). Her easy dismissal of reality as cinema-work is followed up by more examples of her explaining away what she experiences. She hears the crash, dismissed as "some impact of large trucks," and she hears sirens, "but there are always sirens in New York" (135–136). She even sees the smoke from the towers, a simple fire in her mind, and is told of a plane, which she mishears as "a plan." But it is only upon seeing the images on TV that the reality of the attacks sinks in. Finally catching the news coverage on CNN, she watches the second plane crash into the North Tower of the WTC, and then turns to look out the nearby window, which frames very much the same image. Cayce has apparently come to distrust her own sensory experiences, yet immediately believes in the image shown on the TV. The reason for this, however, may lie in how Cayce's perceptions have come to be defined by television and media, which is what appears to occur when Cayce watches the towers burn and fall, and Gibson writes that "[i]t will be like watching one of her own dreams on television. Some vast and deeply personal insult to any ordinary notion of interiority" (137).

The event is perhaps even more insulting to Cayce because of how it undercuts her sense of certainty in her own abilities. She has professionally prospered by her ability to anticipate events and trends, particularly in the realm of iconography and media. But the attacks are unprecedented; they fail to fit into any recognizable pattern, and therefore confound Cayce's ability to fully understand them, to make sense of them. It is for this reason that she readily dismisses the evidence of the attacks as something else: "making a film," "impact of large trucks," "told of a plan." Notably this chapter of the novel is entitled "Singularity," which implies its uniqueness as an event unlike any others, before or after. Gibson describes Cayce's efforts to find her missing father in such a way that amplifies this notion: "She had, while producing her own posters, watched the faces of other people's dead, emerging from adjacent copiers at Kinko's, to be mounted in the yearbook of the city's loss. She had never, while putting hers up, seen one face pasted over another, and that fact, finally, had allowed her to cry, hunched on a bench in Union Square, candles burning at the base of a statue of George Washington" (186). In this passage, images lose their traditional ephemerality; new posters are never used to obscure previous postings. So, too, do the images of 9/11 become indelible, the novel seems to suggest. There will never be a story that will displace this one. And as a singular event, understanding of it cannot be predicated on previous knowledge.[3] As Andrew Leonard has suggested, the novel is "obsessed with finding meaning and connection in the most significant event thus far in the 21st century — the terrorist attacks of Sept. 11," but complicates the matter by asking, "how are we to impose meaning on it? [...] It is, by definition, overpowering, and any reference to it is inescapably heavy-handed." Appropriately, Leonard applauds Gibson's ability to keep the event from overwhelming his characters, "even though it informs nearly every page" (2).

The idea of "singularity" can also be applied to the mysterious footage. As it is unlike anything else, it evades Cayce's ability to easily categorize it. In this case, she finds this comforting, bombarded as she typically is by commercial, iconographic trends, sometimes to the point of physical discomfort — her sensitivity is also described as "closer to allergy, a morbid and sometime violent reactivity to the semiotics of the marketplace" (2). It's likely that the "singularity" of the footage also accounts for its ultimate lack of commercial value. Despite attempts to use it in political campaigns, 9/11 imagery has also been decidedly resistant to commercial exploitation. And this is hardly the only similarity between the online footage and the pictures of 9/11.

In discussion with Boone Chu, a security expert hired to assist Cayce on her quest for the source of the footage, Cayce asks what he feels when he watches it, to which he responds "Lonely?" Cayce, who has watched the footage a great deal more than Boone has, responds, "Most people find that that deepens. Becomes sort of polyphonic. Then there's a sense that it's going somewhere, that something will happen. Will change ... It's impossible to describe, but if you live with it for a while, it starts to get to you. It's just a powerful effect, induced by so little actual screen time" (109). The application of this description to the footage of the twin towers falling is certainly viable, as many TV viewers did live with the footage, repeated seemingly endlessly over the course of several days following the attacks. In light of this, the continuation of the conversation is also revealing:

> Or maybe it's the repetition. Maybe you've been looking at this stuff for so long that you've read all this into it. And talking with other people who've been doing the same thing.
> I've tried to convince myself of that. I've wanted to believe it, simply in order to let the thing go. But then I go back and look at it again, and there's that sense of ... I don't know. Of an opening into something. Universe. Narrative [109].

The implied question is: where does our understanding of the footage come from, and how much of that understanding, intellectual or emotional, is shaped by the process of viewing, the technological phenomenon of repetition?

Several critics have recognized the important doubling of Cayce's quest, with Phillip E. Wegner going so far as to note a parallel between Cayce's quest and the aims of the book itself: "Cayce's quest as well as that of the novel as a whole [is] a double one: as Cayce struggles to find both the maker of the footage and to learn the fate of her father, the novel itself attempts at once to map out the parameters of a newly emergent global order, *and* to come to grips with the consequences of 9/11 for this new world" (196). This double-questing that Cayce engages in must be recognized not as two discrete quests, but rather as operating under a single thematic framework. It is true that the disappearance of Cayce's father and the creation of the mysterious footage have nothing directly to do with one another. However, the fact that Cayce is seeking a kind of truth behind the created footage necessarily resonates with the desire of not only Cayce, but of many Americans to understand the truth behind the 9/11 attacks which seem to baffle comprehension. The average American's experience of the attacks was also, of course, heavily mediated, so that quest to understand how and why this could happen is also an attempt to venture beyond the images, behind the necessary packaging of mass media, to understanding the source and reason behind these images. This undertaking, then, is not much different than what Cayce is trying to do with the mysterious footage. It is also, largely, what Gibson is trying to do with the novel. The lack of context for the footage is part of its allure to Cayce and other "footageheads," and drives many of Cayce's actions. Likewise, the images of 9/11 were in many ways contextless. In *Pattern Recognition*, Gibson seems to realize that the abstracted footage of the attacks on the World Trade Center is as powerful and as alluring (albeit in a horrific way) as the online footage, but is also as bereft of meaning and of depth.

As a result, virtually everything that Gibson's writes about the online footage must be read with the imagery of 9/11 in mind. Moreover, given that most of Gibson's previous novels employ virtual reality as a plot device, often complicating the distinctions between virtual and actual realities, it is not surprising that *Pattern Recognition*, despite its lack of virtual reality, should also explore how we take what we see as authentic, often regardless of how heavily mediated. There are two important examples of media manipulation in *Pattern Recognition*. First, the footage is revealed by the novel's end to be old surveillance footage, heavily manipulated by a catatonic woman living in Moscow named Nora, who does little else but assemble and reassemble these pieces of film.[4] Secondly, Parkaboy and Mushashi, two of Cayce's "footagehead" associates, create an image designed to get Cayce closer to an individual Taki, who is suspected to have information about a watermark discovered on the footage. This image is of a semi-fictional girl, a falsified persona used as an online tease/seduction. Parkaboy describes the process involved:

Judy Tsuzuki, five-foot-eleven and about as Japanese as you are, aside from the DNA. Texas. Twenty-seven…. What we did to up the wattage for Taki, aiming to maximize libidinal disturbance, we shot this long tall Judy then reduced her by at least a third, in Photoshop. Cut'n'pasted her into Musashi's kid sister's dorm room at Cal. Darryl did the costuming himself, and then we decided to try enlarging her eyes a few clicks. That made all the difference ... the resulting big round eyes are pure Anime Magic. This is the girl Taki's been looking for all his life, even though nature's never made one, and he'll know that as soon as he lays eyes on this image [129].

The ruse proves largely successful, though it is clear that it "makes (Cayce) extremely uncomfortable" (145). The creation of "Keiko" is nothing if not a crass attempt to sell an idea, to manipulate its intended target. It is, then, consistent with typical postmodern disdain for the corrupting influence of mass media. It is certainly indicative of exactly what Blue Ant is in business for. Yet as shallow as an image like "Keiko" may be — and it most certainly is shallow — within the context of this novel it cannot be read as a blanket condemnation of media and the shaping of imagery. Nora's manipulation of the footage operates in a very different way, in a way that touches Cayce. She finds herself identifying with the footage as she doesn't with any of the other images that she experiences and works with, so that as a human parallel to the footage, "Eyes closed, she finds herself imagining a symbol, something watermarking the lower right-hand corner of her existence" (78). For Nora, the footage appears to have become the only outlet that she has, after experiencing a debilitating injury, and because of this, the footage can be read as an honest, personal expression, whereas the creation of "Keiko" is an act of deception. The footage can also be seen as a symbolic way of making sense out of a chaotic world. As Alex Link writes, "In this reappropriation of surveillance images, the footage becomes a way of recycling and/or organizing historical traces, of creating historical narratives, of (personally) processing (collective) trauma, and of engaging in tactical productions of localized communities that are at the same time spatially dispersed via the web" (211). But Link also points out the problems with reading the footage as pure artistic expression. That the footage as assembled by Nora is then processed in a prison suggests something exploitative about the product, which according to Link "sours the mystique of the footage for Cayce" (220). Further, Link asks, "can the footage truly redeem pain? The novel's answer is pragmatic, provisional, imperfect, and necessarily without mass appeal. In the narrative, the footage finishes, fading into the obscurity of cultural junk" (223).

Does the footage then offer anything, or is it mere illusion? And if we are to read it as analogous to the images of 9/11, then how are we to read those? Clearly, the novel is deeply ambivalent about this. Obviously, the footage has meaning to Cayce and the select group of "footageheads." The mechanisms of its processing may be disillusioning, but there is something profoundly moving in the efforts of Nora to work and rework the footage, permutating it into something new, something artistic, that may lose its touch with the reality or its original subject matter, but may also be an honest way of coping with the trauma that she has experienced, perhaps even as *Pattern Recognition* is likewise an attempt to find a new way of living when the old world no longer exists. Pictures usually can't tell the entire story, and they can even be misleading. But *Pattern Recognition*, while acknowledging this, also suggests that there is something nevertheless authentic in our responses to these pictures. But, of course, in the case of the novel, there is much more to the story than simply what appears on the screen. There is Nora, the person behind the footage, whose own life story, whose own traumas are far more than just shocking; they are resonant, they are complex, and they are *human*. Gibson describes Nora at work, her eyes "only truly present when focused on this screen.... Only a wound, speaking wordlessly in the dark" (305). This cryptic line seems a reference to the footage itself, comparable perhaps to the 9/11 footage, likewise only a wound. It is not the whole story, but is a sign of the injury sustained. It is from the visible wound that we are able to realize something is wrong, it is the starting point, we might hope, of diagnosis, the recognition of a pattern, if you will, which may bring people on the way to healing.

David Foster Wallace's "The Suffering Channel"

At first, there is little to suggest that "The Suffering Channel," the concluding story of David Foster Wallace's collection, *Oblivion*, has anything to do with September 11, 2001. Its opening premise seems little more than a juvenile scatological joke. It begins with a discussion between reporter Skip Atwater and his editor, about a prospective story in the lifestyles magazine *Style*. The topic of their conversation is the viability of a proposed article about a new artist, whose unfortunate medium is his own excrement. The artworks emerge fully formed through mysterious means by the bodily processes of the artist, Brint Moltke. Although Atwater proclaims the works to be "literally incredible," his editor is naturally hesitant about running such a story, with accompanying photos no less, arguing, "I don't want to look at shit. Nobody wants to look at shit. Skip, this is the point: people do not want to look at shit" (238). In Wallace's hands, however, the toilet humor of this opening is weaved into an elaborate 92-page exploration of how media disseminates information, and the profound effect it can have on viewers. The editor's words, plain spoken as they are, take on deeper significance as Wallace forges ahead into an examination of presenter and spectator, of how the latter becomes spectator of even the most horrible images, despite the initial proclamation that "nobody wants to look at shit."

This idea is central to the object of the novella's title. The Suffering Channel offers another possible topic for Atwater's regular *Style* column, and one that the editor finds almost equally as dubious. Atwater's column, after all, is meant to focus on light, breezy stories. As a writer, Atwater is defined by his tendency toward shallowness, described as his "fatal flaw": "He had no innate sense of tragedy or preterition or complex binds or any of the things that made human beings' misfortunes significant to one another. He was all upbeat angle" (270). So how can his column deal with something like this? The Suffering Channel, "a puzzling marginal entry," Wallace writes, was begun in New York, as a simple televised montage of well known photos involving anguish or pain: a caved in Jackie next to LBJ as he's sworn in on the plane, that agonized Vietcong with the pistol to his head, the naked kids running from napalm. There's something about seeing them one right after another. A woman trying to bathe her thalidomide baby, faces through the wire at Belsen, Oswald crumpled around Ruby's fist, a noosed man as the mob begins to hoist, Brazilians on the ledge of a burning highrise. A loop of 1,200 of these, four seconds per, running 5:00 P.M.–1:00 A.M. EST; no sound; no evident ads [288–289].

The still photos are gradually replaced by video footage, constituting "phase two," and then by the autumn '01 Sweeps unveiling of phase three's live broadcasts. Phase three brings together the stories of Brint Moltke and of the Suffering Channel. Molke, largely as a result of being pushed by his celebrity-obsessed wife, is scheduled to appear and produce his art on the Suffering Channel, the art being less of the draw than the excessively timid Moltke's mortification at being displayed on such intimate terms.

The significance of the Suffering Channel in this story is consistent with Wallace's career-length obsession with media and particularly television. As Lance Olsen explains, "In Wallace's work, the simulacra-producing media becomes as pervasive as planetary background radiation. Televisions seem like they're *always* on. Which turns out to be not so much a critique of the media on Wallace's part as it is just a video recording the way things really are for a couple of generations raised on airwaves" (211). We see this in Wallace's novel *Infinite Jest* (1996), which features a video cartridge so addictive as to result in the wasting away of its viewers. We see it, too, in his story "Little Expressionless Animals" (1989), which uses the TV show *Jeopardy!* as its primary set piece, and in which one character muses about

> disturbed people who've had only the TV all their lives, their parents or whomever started them right off by plunking them down in front of the set, and as they get older the TV comes to be their whole emotional world, it's all they have, and it becomes in a way their whole way of defining themselves as existents, with a distinct identity, that they're outside the set, and everything else is inside the set [31].

Wallace has also addressed the power of media, especially as it affects a younger generation, *his* generation of writers, in several essays. According to Wallace, in the 1990 piece, "E Unibus Pluram," "the most dangerous thing about television for U.S. fiction writers is that we don't take it seriously enough as both a disseminator and a definer of the cultural atmosphere we breathe and process" (27). This essay builds on his 1988 essay "Fictional Futures," which describes how television and popular entertainments have "imposed themselves on our generation's psyches for so long and with such power that they have entered into complicated relations with our very ideas of the world and the self" (40). He further argues that

> raised on an activity at least partly passive, we experience a degree of manipulation as neutral, a fact of life. However, wooed artfully as we are for not just our loyalty but our very *attention*, we reserve for that attention the status of a commodity, a measure of power; and our choices to bestow or withhold it carry for us great weight. So does what

we regard as our God-given right to be entertained — or, if not entertained, at least stimulated: the unpleasant is perfectly OK, just so long as it *rivets* [40–41].

This description is clearly a perfect fit for the Suffering Channel, which is most certainly repugnant. Yet it is also wildly successful, a media phenomenon, not because people necessarily like the "anguish or pain" that it reveals, but because they cannot simply look away. Undoubtedly, many felt the same way watching the terror of September 11 unfold. An even sharper parallel can be found in the commercial-free days that followed, as little new information was reported, and the images continued to roll, over and over, not unlike the looped imagery of the Suffering Channel. Indeed, Tamar Liebes and Anat First, in discussing the competition between image reproduction and more in-depth, contextualized reportage, might well be describing the Suffering Channel of Wallace's story:

> In the case of television news ... the compatibility of images of suffering with the visual medium wins[...]. [T]he need for effective, minimalist, touching visual footage brings about the selection of dramatic images, transmitting emotional, empathy-arousing images, that can be simultaneously absorbed everywhere. These pictures are removed from the relevant sequence of events, as well as their political and historical context [62].[5]

Wallace's story never actually mentions the date, September 11, 2001, but underlying the action of "The Suffering Channel" is the memory of the attacks on the World Trade Center towers. The events of that day play little direct part in the narrative itself, and are mentioned but briefly in the course of the story, but they nevertheless serve to evoke strong emotions in the reader. The main offices of *Style* magazine are located on the sixteenth floor of the South Tower of the World Trade Center, and the events narrated take place just a few months before the towers' collapse. The excremental art story is actually pitched by Atwater for the September 10 issue of *Style*. Moreover, lest the importance of these dates be forgotten (if, indeed, it could be), Wallace places a few reminders that these are no ordinary days in New York. We are told, for instance, that Atwater's intern, Laurel Manderley, "was herself destined to survive, through either coincidence or premonition, the tragedy by which *Style* would enter history two months hence" (245). But this tragedy is never reached within the story itself, which concludes just before Moltke's Fourth of July "performance" on the Suffering Channel. As such, 9/11 is less of a plot point and more of a thematic signifier. It must be remembered that for most Americans, the terrorist attacks were not a first-hand experience, but were, in fact, a mediated one. On that day, many, even most, Americans, and much of the international world, sat glued to the television screen as the horror unfolded. And while TV has often been seen as a potentially divisive force for fragmentation of experience, it could be argued that in this case, people from coast to coast were exposed to the same mediated experience, united in the similarity of their exposure to the attacks and their aftermath. In reading Wallace's novella, one can't help but draw the comparison between those days and the programming of the Suffering Channel. In short, all TV broadcasting of 9/11 and the events that followed were manifestations of the Suffering Channel. One could argue that by their mediated nature these events lost something, that they were watered down, that they lost a sense of "life," as Jerry Mander would have it. Yet even if the attacks were experienced in a distinctly different way for TV viewers than they were for on-scene witnesses, they nevertheless provoked sharp emotional reaction from people in what has typically been regarded as an archetypal position of passivity, sacked out in front of the television.

Brint Moltke's appearance on the Suffering Channel is never depicted in the story. Instead, Wallace concludes immediately before it begins. This climactic moment is avoided, just as the narrative of the story never catches up to the events of 9/11 which inform it so strongly. It could be argued that these scenarios have greater impact because of the omission. Their absence forces readers to construct on their own what is about to happen on the Suffering Channel, or reconstruct what happened on 9/11, based on the information already received by way of the television and other media. The video images may be less than the truth, but there is a kind of truthful impact to seeing the horrors unfold. Certainly, we feel the anguish that Brint Moltke, cripplingly introverted in the best of circumstances, feels without our having to experience the actual moment of his greatest mortification directly. The story, then, also raises the question of how much we really need to see things like Moltke's suffering, how much we really needed to see the images of the twin towers' collapse. To understand what happened, perhaps, we needed no images. But both "The Suffering Channel" and "The View from Mrs. Thompson's" seem to acknowledge a certain need to *feel* something that can only be felt when faced with those images.

Wallace thus uses this story to raise significant issues about how we react to the televised world. Are Suffering Channel images real? Do they have the impact that those events depicted properly should? Or is the image of the thalidomide baby as removed from the actual afflicted child as the celebrity image of Phillip Spaulding is from the actual man from whom it is created? Does the Vietcong with gun to temple become a mere symbol of himself, once pixilated and distributed via TV? And what of those trapped in the Twin Towers on September 11? Does their imagistic distribution maintain the tragedy of their situation, or turn it into grotesque spectacle, like the Moltke Suffering Channel appearance? Do we risk having, like Skip Atwater, "an insufficient sense of the tragic" (245)? The answers to these questions remain profoundly ambiguous in Wallace's fiction. But "The Suffering Channel" certainly serves as a kind of warning about what may come if we submit too fully to the life of images. Wallace writes, "When anything painful or unpleasant happened to his body, Skip Atwater often got the queer sense that he was in fact not a body that occupied space but rather just a body-shaped area of space itself, impenetrable but empty" (313). Television, and mass media as a whole, the story suggests, runs the risk of providing an all too convenient tool for people to divorce themselves from the pain of others in the society, when they ought to be seeking unification by means far more intimate than the act of spectating. Late in the novella, the overwhelmed Brint Moltke, using his unique talents, leaves a message for Atwater. The impact of the message is diluted, however, because, even though the writing is "ornate and calligraphic," it still is written in excrement. Echoing McLuhan's claims, Wallace writes that "the content of the message was obliterated by the overwhelming fact of its medium" (315). Were it not for this medium (whatever medium that might be), Atwater (and we consumers) might more readily see the import of the message itself: "HELP ME."

This image, ridiculously profane as it may be, speaks to what both "The Suffering Channel" and *Pattern Recognition* are attempting to bring to the field of 9/11 representation. Moltke's fecal medium is one that invites attention because it is so unusual, because it is a spectacle. It is remarkable, in its way, and it certainly provokes a powerful reaction on the part of the viewers. But it is also one that does not lend itself to readings of nuance and subtlety (even if Moltke were to attempt to create such work). Instead, the attention is to the shock of the surface value of the art. The September 11th attacks may have had a similar effect. The images were powerful, certainly, but they represent a kind of surface spectacle. Nuance and subtlety are not the stuff of spectacle. But they are the stuff of fiction. Both Gibson and Wallace, in their close examination of mass media, and their notably circuitous, indirect treatment of 9/11 itself, delve beneath the surface images associated with that date. If anything, the written word, as a device that requires deciphering on the part of the reader, demands that we make our own images. An image, even one as powerful as that of a man falling from the one of the twin towers, fails to uncover the human truths that live behind it, such as the examination of the interior lives of Cayce and Atwater in *Pattern Recognition* and "The Suffering Channel."

Coda

At the time of this writing, a similarly traumatic, though smaller scale, piece of video has been circulating on the internet. The video, evidently filmed with a cell phone, of a young woman named Neda dying from a gunshot wound in the streets of Tehran has stirred discussions much like the ones addressed in this essay through the works of Gibson and Wallace, and also to varying extent by other writers, Jonathan Safran Foer's *Extremely Loud & Incredibly Close* (2005), Paul Auster in *Man in the Dark* (2008), and perhaps most notably Don DeLillo in *Falling Man* (2007). This "Neda video" has come to be used as a symbol for the protests against a repressive regime, in reaction to a disputed election. Yet the details, the actuality of the circumstances surrounding Neda's death, have been slippery. Writing for *Newsweek*, Jennie Yabroff raised the question of whether this "endless dissemination (of the video) is doing us good, or harm." Noting that "[l]ooking at the screen is a passive experience, not a political act," she rightly explains how "[i]mages can be as deceptive as words — in some ways, even more so, in the ease with which a part can come to stand for a not entirely related whole."

Clearly, Yabroff's claims, her insistence that answers to any situation "can only be found beyond the edges of the frames," are applicable to more than just this immediate situation in Iran. Stripped of their context, we can easily imagine these words being said of those "endlessly disseminated" images of the doomed towers of the World Trade Center. Yet in acknowledging the incompleteness of these images, we need to take care not to ignore the particular qualities of them. A detailed, rational, linguistic analysis of September 11 will certainly yield more in the way of intellectual understanding, at least so far as we will ever be able to understand such a disaster. But that analysis will never equal the visceral impact that images can carry. And it is because of this, perhaps, that fiction is so well suited to addressing the role of media on 9/11. Fiction does not deal in purely rational thought, but gives itself over to emotional responses. It embraces the visceral reactions we have to what happens around us. As such, fiction offers a fuller representation of singular events than televised images and mass media productions in general. More specifically, Wallace and Gibson's works, while acknowledging the visceral power of media images, suggest that literature can instill a capacity for (re)action into readers, and offer a deeper understanding of trauma in contrast to the "incompleteness" of media images and their attendant inclination to communicate passivity to viewers.

Notes

1. Whereas fiction writers were rather slow to begin addressing September 11, let alone the role of media (see Wyatt), non-fiction on the subject filled the shelves rapidly. In addition to Norris, Kern and Just, a list of books consulted before commencing this project provides but a minute sampling of the non-fiction addressing September 11 and mass media: *Media Representations of September 11* (2003), Steven Chermak, Frankie Y. Bailey and Michelle Brown, Eds.; *Communication and Terroris*m (2002), Bradley S. Greenberg, Ed.; *Media in an American Crisis* (2005), Elinor Kelley Grusin and Sandra H. Utt, Eds.; *Crisis Communication* (2003), A. Michael Noll, Ed.; *Media and Political Violence* (2007), Hillel Nossek, Annabelle Sreberny and Prasun Sonwalkar, Eds.
2. For an examination of this phenomenon, see Bill Schaffer's "Just Like a Movie: September 11 and the Terror of Moving Images."
3. The issue of how fiction has dealt with singular, traumatic events has, of course, been addressed before. See, for example, Whitehead's *Trauma Fiction*. But September 11 represents something new, partly because of the fact that it was so thoroughly documented by mass media, and that specific images were repeated *ad infinitum*.
4. For an excellent comparison of Nora and her twin sister Stella, who distributes the footage, to the twin towers of the World Trade Center, see Link.
5. This, of course, is not to say that such imagery, divorced from original contexts cannot be recontextualized for political purposes.

Works Cited

Auster, Paul. *Man in the Dark*. New York: Holt, 2008.
Baudrillard, Jean, and Paul Patton (Trans.). *The Gulf War Did Not Take Place*. Bloomington: Indiana University Press, 1995.
Baudrillard, Jean, and Sheila Faria Glaser (Trans.). *Simulacra and Simulation*. Ann Arbor: University of Michigan Press, 1994.

Benjamin, Walter, and Harry Zohn (Trans.). "The Work of Art in the Age of Mechanical Reproduction." *Illuminations*. New York: Schocken, 1969: 217–251.

Chermak, Steven, Frankie Y. Bailey, and Michelle Brown (Eds.). *Media Representations of September 11*. Westport, CT: Praeger, 2003.

DeLillo, Don. *Falling Man*. New York: Scribner, 2007.

Docker, John. *Postmodernism and Popular Culture: A Cultural History*. Cambridge: Cambridge University Press, 1994.

Fitzpatrick, Kathleen. "Network: The Other Cold War." *Film & History* 31.2 (2001): 33–39.

Gibson, William. *Pattern Recognition*. New York: Berkley, 2004.

Greenberg, Bradley S. (Ed.). *Communication and Terrorism*. Cresskill, NJ: Hampton, 2002.

Grusin, Elinor Kelley, and Sandra H. Utt (Eds.). *Media in an American Crisis*. Lanham, MD: University Press of America, 2005.

Jameson, Fredric. "Postmodernism and Consumer Society." *In* Ann Gray and Jim McGuigan (Eds.). *Studying Culture: An Introductory Reader*. London: Arnold, 1996: 192–205.

Leonard, Andrew. "Nodal Point." *Salon*. February 13, 2003. June 6, 2009. http://www.salon.com/tech/books/2003/02/13/gibson/index.html.

Liebes, Tamar, and Anat First. "Framing the Palestinian-Israeli Conflict." *In* Pippa Norris, Marion Just and Montague Kern (Eds.). *Framing Terrorism: The News Media, the Government and the Public*. New York: Taylor and Francis, 2003.

Link, Alex. "Global War, Global Capital, and the Work of Art in William Gibson's *Pattern Recognition*." *Contemporary Literature* 49.2 (Summer 2008): 209–231.

Mander, Jerry. *Four Arguments for the Elimination of Television*. New York: Quill, 1978.

McInerney, Jay. *The Good Life*. New York: Knopf, 2006.

McLuhan, Marshall. *Understanding Media: The Extensions of Man*. (2nd ed.). New York: Signet, 1966.

Minzesheimer, Bob. "Novels About 9/11 Can't Stack Up to Non-Fiction." *USA Today*. September 11, 2007. June 17, 2009. http://www.usatoday.com/life/books/news/2007-09-10-911-novels_N.htm.

Noll, A. Michael. *Crisis Communications: Lessons from September 11*. Lanham, MD: Rowman & Littlefield, 2003.

Norris, Pippa, Marion Just, and Montague Kern (Eds.). *Framing Terrorism: The News Media, the Government and the Public*. New York: Taylor and Francis, 2003.

Nossek, Hillel, Annabelle Sreberny, and Prasun Sonwalkar (Eds.). *Media and Political Violence*. Cresskill, NJ: Hampton, 2007.

Olsen, Lance. "Termite Art, or Wallace's Wittgenstein." *The Review of Contemporary Fiction* 13.2 (Summer 1993): 199–215.

Schaffer, Bill. "Just Like a Movie: September 11 and the Terror of Moving Images." *Senses of the Cinema* 17 (Dec. 2001). June 8, 2009. http://archive.sensesofcinema.com/contents/01/17/symposium/schaffer.html.

Vonnegut, Kurt. *Hocus Pocus*. New York: Putnam, 1990.

Wallace, David Foster. "E Unibus Pluram: Television and U.S. Fiction." *A Supposedly Fun Thing I'll Never Do Again*. Boston: Little, Brown, 1997: 21–82.

_____. "Fictional Futures and the Conspicuously Young." *The Review of Contemporary Fiction* 8.3 (1988): 36–53.

_____. *Infinite Jest*. Boston: Little, Brown, 1996.

_____. "Little Expressionless Animals." *Girl With Curious Hair*. New York: Avon, 1989.

_____. "The Suffering Channel." *Oblivion*. Boston: Little, Brown, 2004: 238–329.

_____. "The View from Mrs. Thompson's." *Consider the Lobster*. New York: Little, Brown, 2006: 128–140.

Whitehead, Anne. *Trauma Fiction*. Edinburgh: Edinburgh University Press, 2004.

Wyatt, Edward. "Literary Novelists Address 9/11, Finally." *New York Times*. March 7, 2005. June 17, 2009. http://www.nytimes.com/2005/03/07/books/ 07novel.html?_r=1&scp=1&sq=literary%209/11&st=cse.

Yabroff, Jennie. "The Woman in the Picture." Newsweek.com. June 24, 2009. http://www.newsweek.com/id/203446

PART III: PERFORMANCE

TERROR AND MISMEMORY
Resignifying September 11 in World Trade Center *and* United 93

Gerry Canavan

In theoretical physics we find the concept of a "singularity," an infinitesimal concentration of matter into a single point with zero volume and infinite density in the face of which the laws of physics break down.[1] Singularities are locations of radical isolation in the cosmos; because our physical laws cannot describe such a space, nothing that happened before the collapse into singularity can be scientifically described, much less conceived, from a perspective inside it — nor can anything that happens inside the singularity after the moment of its creation be modeled from outside its event horizon. In a very real sense, then, the singularity exists, but it does not exist in time; there is no possibility of temporal continuity either with what came before or with what comes after, and therefore no possibility for history itself. Singularities are said to lurk in the unknowable, unreachable centers of black holes; it is believed the universe itself sprang out of a singularity in the instant of the Big Bang, and that it may die in the future cosmological contraction called the Big Crunch — both liminal boundaries that neither scientific experimentation nor mathematical models can ever reach past, the beginning and end of time.

I believe the concept of singularity, with its overlapping connotations of hermetic isolation, radical discontinuity, and gravitational inescapability, can help us think about the non-linearity of the memory of September 11, 2001, both in terms of individual memory — which I will argue becomes a kind of perverse nostalgia — and collective memory, which I will characterize in terms of national myth-making. Singularity provides the missing metaphor we need to understand what the violent shock of that morning did to the American psyche, how it initiated an ongoing and eternally recurring nightmare that the nation has only just started to wake from.

September 11 functions first as a singularity in the political rhetoric of American politics, with its constant evocation of "pre–9/11 mindsets" and "post–9/11 worldviews." In this sense the events of September 11 quickly became coded as "9/11," the moment of singularity from which all politically relevant consequences spring and the barrier to a prelapsarian past which collective memory and political praxis can no longer reach. In other words, "9/11" functions as a buzzword, denoting a type of imagined Big Bang. But I hope to go beyond this first cognitive erasure of the actual memory of September

11 to a second and even more pernicious one; I will argue that in the years following September 11, 2001, the attack on the Twin Towers became for Americans the endlessly prolonged and inescapable figuration of the present, an event to which we imagined ourselves to be permanently bound and to which we, even now, somehow feel at risk of return. My discussion will follow this phenomenon from the initial event itself through its various mass media reformulations, culminating in readings of *World Trade Center* (Stone, 2006) and *United 93* (Greengrass, 2006) that show how the relentless gravitational pull of the 9/11 singularity has distorted cultural memory by resignifying the disaster as a permanent state of emergency from which there is no possible relief or escape.

Debord, Baudrillard, Žižek

During the Bush years, it was commonplace to note that September 11, 2001, exemplified a radically new form of terror attack, one carried out primarily on the level of the image. It is almost impossible to attempt to theorize the day without first recalling Karlheinz Stockhausen's memorable claim that the attack on the Twin Towers was "the greatest work of art there has ever been" (qtd. in Hilferty). In his 2002 book on September 11, *Welcome to the Desert of the Real*, Slavoj Žižek notes the importance of Stockhausen's claim when he writes "we can perceive the collapse of the World Trade Center towers as the climactic conclusion of twentieth-century art's 'passion for the Real' — the 'terrorists' themselves did not do it primarily to provoke real material damage, but for *the spectacular effect of it*" (11).

Though the Twin Towers were undoubtedly important centers of finance capital, and their destruction extracted great cost not only in lives and trauma but also in infrastructure and ultimately in GDP, they were not infrastructural targets in any traditional military sense. The Pentagon might be understood as such, and arguably the White House and Capitol believed to be possible targets of the fourth, thwarted plane attack as well — but not the towers. Nor did the Twin Towers occupy an especially central place in America's historical self-conception before September 11, 2001. Neither monuments nor memorials, but rather a pair of visually striking office buildings, it seems unlikely that the Twin Towers would have made most Americans' shortlists of defining national structures prior to their collapse. As would have been the case with most people worldwide, before September 11 most Americans' visual memory of the Twin Towers would have been confined to establishing shots from popular New York–based television programs like *Sex and the City* and *Friends*.

But despite their lack of military importance, monumental symbolism, or particular iconic prominence, it is certainly the fall of the Twin Towers that has come to represent September 11, the Twin Towers whose collapse turned a horror into a day that, famously, "changed everything."[2] That the two towers collapsed may not, by itself, have even been enough to accomplish this immediate total reordering of national priorities — because they did not merely collapse, they collapsed "unexpectedly," on live TV, on every channel, with everybody watching.

"Of course the martyr-pilots knew that bringing down the Twin Towers would do nothing, or next to nothing, to stop the actual circuits of capital," write the members of the leftist protest group Retort in their 2005 September 11 manifesto, *Afflicted Powers* (26). But — borrowing from Guy Debord's concept of the spectacle society — Retort goes on to argue that the life of capitalism is entirely bound up in the social imaginary, in "patterns of belief and desire" that manifest themselves in commodities and are regulated in large part by "perpetual emotion machines," i.e., television, the Internet, and other forms of mass media (26). "Supposing those machines could be captured for a moment, and on them appeared the perfect image of capitalism's negation," they go on, beginning to ventriloquize a possible thought process of the terrorists

> would that not be enough? Enough truly to destabilize the state and society, and produce a sequence of vauntings and paranoia whose long-term political consequences for the capitalist world order would, at the very least, be unpredictable? [26].

This motivation, they add, drove the selection of the Twin Towers themselves as the primary target:

> If, to trot out Debord's over-famous aphorism again, "the spectacle is capital accumulated to the point where it becomes image," then what more adequate encapsulation of the process could there be but the World Trade Center (with its multiplication of the terminally gigantic by two)? [27].

Jean Baudrillard, too, locates the unparalleled imagistic power of the attacks in the Towers' twinness (43). And certainly the attacks could not have had the same overwhelming impact had the first impact on the North Tower not given the television networks sufficient time (eighteen minutes) to set up a live feed at the site and thereby catch the second impact live in front of a huge (inter)national audience. We must recognize the attacks as the carefully stage-managed spectacle they were, a spectacle generated neither by Hollywood nor the state but by an independent force outside both, a spectacle which we watched not with the confident safety of the moviegoer but with the panicked terror of one who realizes, "this time the disaster is really happening."

Debord defines the spectacle as "a social relationship between people that is mediated by images," which is "the very heart of society's real unreality":

> In all its specific manifestations — news or propaganda, advertising or the actual consumption of entertainment — the spectacle epitomizes the prevailing mode of a social life. It is the omnipresent celebration of a choice *already made* in the sphere of production, and the consummate result of that choice. In form as in content the spectacle serves as total justification for the conditions and aims of the existing system. It further ensures the *permanent presence* of that justification, for it governs almost all time spent outside the production process itself [12–13, *italics in the original*].

To say that September 11 occurred first and foremost as spectacle is simply to recognize not only the central importance of the television newscast in both the experience and the memory of the event but also the communal nature of this viewing, the ways in which global capitalist society (especially American society) suddenly and immediately ground to an unprecedented, days-long halt in the wake of the attacks, leaving the bulk of the populace free to watch the same televised images all at the same time, over and over again. In this way we must correct Stockhausen: September 11 is surely not the greatest work of art there has ever been, but it is the greatest (and worst) spectacle. No other media event has so thoroughly dominated social relations; for no other stretch of time do so many people share, in quite the same way, exactly the same memories.

In spectacle, too, we find a possible motive for Baudrillard's otherwise strange insistence on the willful suicide of the towers and the displacement of agency from the terrorists back onto the West itself. Baudrillard writes that the West's fantasies of its own destruction were made concrete on September 11, that "they *did* it, but we *wished for* it" (5). He even makes the startling claim, repeated throughout *The Spirit of Terrorism*, that the Towers somehow committed suicide, that "you had the impression that they were responding to the suicide of the suicide-planes with their own suicide" and that "the West, in the position of God (divine omnipotence and absolute moral legitimacy) has become suicidal, and declared war on itself" (7).[3] Žižek, too, is drawn to the psychoanalytic possibilities of the "disaster movie" made real: "[...] the impossible which happened was the object of fantasy, so that, in a way, America got what it fantasized about, and that was the biggest surprise" (16). Nor can we forget here the 9/11 Truth Movement, which seeks to expose September 11 as an "inside job."[4]

What are we to make of this desire to relocate agency for the terror attacks, to see Al Qaeda as the concrete manifestation of the West's own death drive? I find the answer in Debord's enunciation of the spectacle's "enormous positivity":

> The spectacle manifests itself as an enormous positivity, out of reach and beyond dispute. All it says is: "Everything that appears is good; whatever is good will appear." The attitude that it demands in principle is the same passive acceptance that it has already secured by means of its seeming incontrovertibility, and indeed by its monopolization of the realm of appearances [15].

The collapse of the World Trade Center was and is an unimaginable shock, and yet we find it difficult to process it as anything but an historical inevitability — as a "necessity" rather than as pure contingency. This is the logic of the spectacle. The immediate visual force of September 11 presents itself to us as originating outside human intervention, the culmination of a historical trajectory that began in 1973 with the first construction of the Towers — almost as if (as Baudrillard suggests) it had always been the very *telos* of the Twin Towers to someday fall, as if *Independence Day* (1996) and a thousand other imagined apocalyptic disaster movies were simply prophetic prefigurations of the event that must someday follow. Art Spiegelman goes even further than this in his 2004 graphic memoir of September 11, *In the Shadow of No Towers*. He finds strange precursors to the terror attacks in turn-of-the-twentieth-century newspaper cartoons, which once had innocent readings but whose apparent prescience now seems entirely sinister.

Žižek writes that September 11 was the day "the image entered and shattered our reality" (16). What a Debordian reading of September 11 highlights is that this "image" is no less a spectacle than the "reality" it seems to shatter. What September 11 shatters is the system's monopolization not of violence, as Retort would have it,[5] but rather of "the realm of appearances itself." The collapse of the towers is a terror precisely because it is an outsized, radical contingency caught on film, which the spectacle-making powers-that-be did not cause, could not prevent, and cannot undo. The collapse of the Towers is "out of reach and beyond dispute," not as the enormous positivity of a system that produces value in the form of spectacle, but as the terrible (but equally enormous) "negativity" of that system's annihilation, a very different sort of return of the repressed than the one Žižek foregrounds in *Welcome to the Desert of the Real*. Those harmless establishing shots from *Friends* suddenly possess, when viewed today, a wholly unexpected valence of tragedy and threat; even post–2001 establishing shots, as in the altered title sequence of seasons four through seven of *The Sopranos*, speak volumes through the Towers' glaring "absence." Familiar images have been co-opted and used against us; our television sets are in bed with the enemy.

One local, often overlooked effect of the collapse of the Towers may now seem to take on transcendent metaphorical importance: the sudden cessation, concurrent with the collapse, of some broadcast television signals in the New York Metropolitan Area, due to the loss of the transmitting antenna housed at the towers' top. Worldwide, September 11 disrupted the invisible networks of shared spectacle that grease our mediated, tightly controlled social relations and left us instead with spectacle's opposite number: contingency, or terror.

In this way, I argue, September 11 is best understood as the spectacle's rebirth as an anti-spectacle. What September 11 tells us is this: "Everything that appears is bad; whatever is bad will appear."

The Initial Disaster

> *What happens but once might as well not have happened at all.*
> — MILAN KUNDERA

At 8:49 A.M. on the morning of September 11, 2001, CNN cut from a Dietech commercial to live coverage of a fire at the North Tower of the World Trade Center, approximately three minutes after it was struck by American Airlines flight 11. As of August 2009, this footage, the first television broadcast of the attacks, is not only available on YouTube but is replayed (almost ritualistically) every September during 9/11 retrospectives, as well as in both *World Trade Center* (2006) and *United 93* (2006), the first two major Hollywood releases concerning September 11. These are the first images anyone outside of lower Manhattan saw of the World Trade Center disaster, and provide a starting point for what viewers in living rooms, schools, and workplaces saw next. The repetition and confusion of that day is already in evidence; with nothing to say and no information to report, no narrative or structure or cognitive framing can be provided for us, and so indeed there is nothing to be "said" at all.[6] Soon afterwards, many other broadcast channels began to switch to live coverage of the disaster; as a consequence, eighteen minutes later, the crash of the second plane into the South Tower is broadcast to millions of people over live TV — often unbeknownst to the anchors themselves, who see an explosion but, unlike their audience, do not understand at first where it came from.[7]

At 9:59 the South Tower collapses. Although this is recorded on live TV, that the tower collapsed is not immediately evident — rewatching CNN's live coverage of that moment, we find again the anchors lost in confusion, not sure how to describe what they are seeing but at the same time unable to do anything but talk.[8] The definitive image of the collapse, the one burned in most people's memory, is again the "second" collapse, at 10:28 A.M.[9] — not only because the wind is now blowing in a different direction, offering a better view, and not only because a better camera angle now catches the collapse directly, but also simply because we now know that this sort of thing can happen, and thus we know what we are seeing when we see it. Again, doubling, the fact that the Towers were twinned, allowed the attack to reproduce itself, to produce multiple takes.

This moment is the initial trauma, one that manifests itself first as pure confusion, as a complete breakdown in the signifying power of our "perpetual emotion machines," a moment of terror in the discovery that no one is in charge — and it is this trauma that the spectacle culture sought to rewrite, in the days and years that followed, through the careful inundation and repetition of particular sorts of images and not others. As the initial experience of the attack faded, it was replaced instead by a new experience that had been deliberately sanitized and was much more carefully controlled: an effort on the part of spectacle culture to reassert its authority and regain the sense of total control that had been lost.

"Floaters"

Between the initial impact and the collapse of the towers — a period of approximately ninety minutes — between 100 and 200 people without hope of rescue leapt out of the upper floors, mostly out of the North Tower (Cauchon). These people jumped alone, in pairs, in small groups, and in at least one famous case, holding hands; in many cases images of these jumpers went out over live TV.

It is these victims of September 11 that Alejandro González Iñárritu memorializes in his segment of the multinational, multi-director September 11 documentary *11'9"01* (2002). Audio captured at the site of the World Trade Center attack is played against an all-black screen. Periodically, for just seconds at a time, extremely brief images of the World Trade Center jumpers are flashed. One particularly evocative image, "The Falling Man," was also the subject of a 2007 retrospective in *Esquire* magazine and ultimately provided the title for Don DeLillo's post–September 11 novel. The photo depicts a single individual in the upper third of an otherwise empty foreground, one knee tilted and arms crossed behind his back, falling towards the unseen ground against the backdrop of the doomed World Trade Center. The piece's author, Tom Junod, describes the effect of this photograph on those who saw it, the scant times it appeared in newspapers:

> In most American newspapers, the photograph that Richard Drew took of the Falling Man ran once and never again. Papers all over the country, from the *Fort Worth Star-Telegram* to the *Memphis Commercial Appeal* to *The Denver Post*, were forced to defend themselves against charges that they exploited a man's death, stripped him of his dignity, invaded his privacy, turned tragedy into leering pornography [Junod].

Footage of the jumpers, despite their striking visual qualities, have been rare or non-existent in the major cultural reproductions of September 11. They do not appear in either *Fahrenheit 9/11* or in *United 93*, and are referenced in only a single shot of *World Trade Center*. The video footage, seen on live TV at the time, is generally not played during annual September 11 retrospectives; most newspapers ran one or two photos of jumpers, if that, and then never ran the images again (Cauchon).[10] This silent self-censorship is all the more startling given the undeniable vividness of the memory of the jumpers for those who saw the coverage live on September 11, 2001— the elimination of the jumpers has become something like mandatory cultural amnesia, a refusal on the part of the spectacle-makers to acknowledge a powerful image they now wish they had never showed us.

The excision of the jumpers—sometimes called "floaters" because of how they seemed, briefly, to hang in the air, and because for people watching on TV they were never seen to land—is but the most visceral example of what Žižek calls the "'derealization' of the horror" of September 11:

> [...] while the number of victims—3,000—is repeated all the time, it is surprising how little of the actual carnage we see—no dismembered bodies, no blood, no desperate faces of dying people ... in clear contrast to reporting on Third World catastrophes, where the whole point is to produce a scoop of some gruesome detail: Somalis dying of hunger, raped Bosnian women, men with their throats cut [13].

Žižek believes that the sanitized, antiseptic nature of edited September 11 news coverage— those images which were repeated again and again, in contrast to the raw, uncontrolled contingency of the live images that aired only during the event itself—are part of an ideological effort to make the attacks unreal, and thus unthreatening. The September 11 we consume, then — the September 11 whose endless repetition Žižek says we experience with a kind of strange *jouissance* (12) — can therefore be seen as an attempt to stave off the psychic consequences of our national trauma.

Retort, for its part, notes:

> It is a confirmation of the terrorists' hopes that after the first few days, in the U.S., the fall of the Towers became exactly the event image that *had not to be shown*. The taboo only made the afterimage more palpable and effective. Everything in the culture went on, and still goes on, in relation to that past image-event; nothing in the culture can address the event directly [28].

Retort likewise locates the U.S.'s seeming inability to escape the haunting of September 11 in its persistent inability to craft a successful counter-image, a search for a sort of totemic counterspell that might once and for all dispel the unchecked power of the collapse (34–35).[11] Though both Žižek's repression model and Retort's taboo model are both intriguing in their own ways, I'm not convinced that either alone fully describes the self-censoring surrounding images of September 11. I suggest instead we consider not just repression, or just taboo, but perhaps the two at the same time: "repressive desublimation."[12] The calculated response of the media-state apparatus has been the attempt to rechannel the raw, unpredictable trauma of September 11, 2001, into a prepackaged and premythologized "9/11"— a sign I have avoided using until now because I will use it to refer self-reflexively not to the attacks themselves but to the after-the-fact "resignification" of the attacks as spectacular narrative. This is the only means spectacle society has at its disposal to reestablish control over anti-spectacle — to tame it, and to especially tame its more contingent, uncontrolled elements, in order to bring them back into the logic of recognizable, controlled spectacle and make September 11 as safe as *Independence Day*. That initial, unmistakable recognition of contingency — not merely the system's own loss of control but also the confrontation with death itself, both the possibility of our individual deaths and the specter of death on a mass scale — has been carefully desublimated into images which have deathlike *auras* but in which no one can actually be seen to be dying, images in which, though the world seems to be ending, someone is always still in control.

While the towers fell for us, over and over, in the immediate aftermath of September 11, they now no longer do so; the iconic image for 9/11 today is surely a tower smoking but "always still standing." If the collapse of the towers must be acknowledged, it is always a *fait accompli*: an image of Ground Zero, so named to suggest the site of an atomic explosion, which is to say a violent flash at the end of history, a boundary point past which history cannot progress. It is between these two moments, impact and collapse, that the 9/11 singularity traps us. Can it be coincidence, after all, that both Hollywood dramatizations of September 11 are centered around plots which conveniently make the actual, physical collapse of the World Trade Center impossible to directly confront?

PART III: PERFORMANCE

World Trade Center *and* United 93

Oliver Stone's *World Trade Center* opens silently on a black screen as the words "These events are based on the accounts of the surviving participants" gradually fade away. After five minutes of establishing shots that focus on scenes of domestic mundanity, mostly male police officers leaving for work in the early morning, the Twin Towers suddenly appear on a highway's distant horizon, followed by the appearance of a date onscreen: "September 11, 2001"—as if we didn't already know.

Because the first plane crash was not broadcast live—and therefore was not spectacle—it cannot be reproduced for the film. Instead, the initial impact is depicted as an eruption of narrative discontinuity through a brief montage. A plane-shaped shadow on a skyscraper is followed by a lingering pause on an all-black visual screen, which is in its turn followed by a very quick shot of the World Trade Center. This almost visually void image, as we have already seen with *11'9"01*, is a popular choice for directors attempting to evoke the gravity of September 11. Michael Moore uses a similar strategy in his anti–Bush polemic movie *Fahrenheit 9/11* (2004). We hear sounds of the explosion and of people screaming, but the visual field is left empty. In short, one attempt to grapple with September 11's radical contingency is the refusal to depict it at all.

Inside the station for the Port Authority police, the collective experience of 9/11 as a communally mediated event is established. The police officers gather around a television set playing CNN's initial coverage. Staring at the screen, with Carol Lin's words interspersed throughout the conversation, several characters have a conversation that will be repeated, almost word for word, in *United 93*:

> KASSIMATIS: "Holy shit."
> POLNICKI: "Can you believe this? What schmuck would fly a plane into the Trade Center?"
> COLOVITO: "Maybe he just ran out of gas or something?"
> POLNICKI: (*skeptical*) "Yeah, Colovito, right."
> PEZZULO: "Just some jerkoff who forgot which lever to pull on his twin-engine."
> RODRIGUES: "That's not a small plane."
> POLNICKI: (*resolute*) "Hell no."

Compare this to the identical dialogue in FAA headquarters at the same moment in *United 93*:

> "Holy cow."
> "That's a huge...."
> SLINEY: "I don't know. I'll tell you what, that is not a small plane. No way."
> "A Cessna would have bounced off that thing."
> "Look at that hole."
> SLINEY: "I've got a bad feeling about this. I'll tell you right now."

Although several of their younger compatriots attempt to find innocent explanations for what they are seeing, Sliney and Polnicki (both the oldest men in their respective rooms) seem to recognize instantly that this has been a deliberate attack. Likewise, both, especially Polnicki, are already ready to "do what must be done"; we can find here evidence for Susan Faludi's memorable claim that September 11 ushers in a public celebration of the virtues of manliness and the patriarchy, which I would suggest is best understood as another failed attempt to shoehorn September 11 into a safe, pre-scripted narrative.[13]

What we see here, in short, is nothing less than an erasure of the confusion and uncertainty that actually permeated the historical 9/11. We are assured now that we knew— we "always" knew—exactly what was happening, why it was happening, and what was going to have to be done about it. *Contra* Baudrillard, our myths now assert that the attack on the second tower "wasn't" necessary, after all, to mark this as a terror attack— the wise and sufficiently grizzled among us always knew what we were facing, and were always ready.

Likewise, note the way that the TVs in both movies are able to catch the entire initial report, aired only on CNN less than three minutes after the planes hit. Again, this is a crucially important erasure—unlike the real-life flurry of phone calls and panicked notifications that followed the first and second impacts, no one in the film versions of September 11 ever needs to be told "Turn on CNN." It's almost as if the TVs "turn themselves on'" at the very moment they are needed—as if in our hypermediated culture we can never suffer from a lack of information or reassurance because the media will always be there for us. This is a stunning admission of the spectacle's omnipresence in culture, made all the more remarkable insofar as these films have set out in the first place to depict the day of all days in which the media was most clearly unable to fulfill this role it claims for itself. Nonetheless, we are assured, we must not panic. Someone is in charge. Someone, somewhere, knows what's going on.

The Collapse of the Collapse

It should come as no surprise that the plots of both *World Trade Center* and *United 93* conspire to hide the collapse of the towers. In *World Trade Center*, the principal storyline is the real-life experience of two Port Authority police officers (Will Jimeno and John McLoughlin, played by Michael Peña and Nicholas Cage) who were eventually dug out of the rubble, the eighteenth and nineteenth of only twenty survivors. Upon hearing the roar of the South Tower beginning to collapse, these characters run to an elevator shaft and then black out; shortly after they awake, the second tower collapses, an event they can hear and feel but obviously cannot see.

The focus in *World Trade Center*, both before and after the towers' collapse, is always on survivors, especially on their faces: a long parade of bruised, bloody, teary, shocked, ash-covered, screaming, but nonetheless *alive* faces. Such images of faces, especially when accompanied by the famous makeshift memorials and photos of missing persons in New York City, appear to be a central part of any mainstream repro-duction of September 11—they are even alluded to in such disparate works of translation as the movie adaptation of *War of the Worlds* (Spielberg, 2005) and 2003's reimagining of the 1970s TV series *Battlestar Galactica*, both science fictions in which the disaster of September 11 is hyperbolically allegorized as the near-total extinction of the entire human race, at the hands of alien outsiders (*War of the Worlds*) or their own rebelling robotic servants (*BSG*).

In most instances, as is the case in *World Trade Center*, significantly more attention is paid to the response of survivors to the attack than to the attack itself or its victims. There is a brief image of a single jumper in *World Trade Center*, who like the rest of the floaters never lands, even though these characters are *at* the World Trade Center site and would be able to *see* the final fate of the jumpers we never see on TV. In fact, despite the carnage of the real-life atrocity, there are never any corpses in *World Trade Center*; the few bodies lying on the sidewalk are depicted as still being worked on by EMTs, and thus always as potential survivors. The only person who is directly shown on-screen to have died is a third trapped Port Authority police officer, Dominick Pezzulo (Jay Hernandez), who escapes injury in the first collapse but is fatally injured by rubble from the second. After his death, this character is largely forgotten; he is rarely mentioned, and unlike our two married-with-children principal protagonists there is no narrative attention paid to those who will mourn him. It is noteworthy that the death of Pezzulo — the film's most direct and unflinching confrontation with death's aura — is shot in almost total darkness; nothing can be made out.

What *World Trade Center* presents us with, then, is the impossible promise that we can all somehow survive *even this*, bolstered further by its claims to factual veracity, by the fact that it "all really happened." The film works in this way to place death itself under erasure, to shift the anti-spectacle of September 11 safely back into the realm of the spectacle as "9/11."

This Utopian promise of survival is made even more explicit in the early scenes of *United 93*, about the flight that crashed outside Shanksville, Pennsylvania, after what is believed to have been a passenger revolt. The fetishization (for lack of a better word) of the United 93 attack is itself perhaps the most pointed example of the attempted rebranding of September 11 from a site of trauma and defeat to one of resolve and victory — of pure positivity. "Let's roll," the final recorded words of one of the passengers, Todd Beamer, became a national catchphrase, used in a number of presidential speeches and extensively in the media, especially in coverage of the war in Afghanistan. There have been no less than four documentaries and reenactments of this single aspect of the day, with such titles as *Flight 93*, *I Missed Flight 93*, *The Flight That Fought Back*, and the big-budget adaptation, *United 93*.

If *World Trade Center* seeks to put the collapse of the towers and the casualty counts under erasure, from its earliest moments *United 93* primes us for an even more impossible fantasy: that the crash of Flight 93 *itself* might somehow, ahistorically, be avoided altogether. The focus in the first half of the movie is on the improbable accident of the flight's late departure — air traffic control realizes that American 11 has been highjacked mere minutes too late to save United 93 (with the implication being that such a mistake would never happen again). Likewise, in the film almost ten minutes separate the pilots' hearing about the World Trade Center attacks and the terrorists taking control of the cockpit; in reality, it was approximately five minutes, and probably less. The suspense generated in this long temporal disjuncture only further primes the fantasy that the crash might somehow be avoidable despite having already happened.

The highjackers in the film are disorganized and cowardly, completely unsure of their mission and how to accomplish it. The pilot and "lead terrorist" in particular seem unwilling to go through with the highjacking at all, and at times seems as though he might even switch sides, like a reluctant fictional terrorist in some summer blockbuster. The Americans, in contrast — especially men — are immediately resolute and completely united, with nary a moment of doubt. Only one passenger resists the idea of retaking the plane — a German, Christian Adams, for whom there is no real-life evidence of cowardice or opposition to the plan but who in the jingoistic with-us-or-against-us logic of post–Iraq America can only be "against us." Perhaps not surprisingly, in early screenings the film ended with a title card reading "America's war on terror had begun," illustrating just how thin the line between entertainment and propaganda can be when it comes to the subject of September 11 (Lim).

As noted above, *United 93* keeps the sheer uncontrolled spectacle of the attacks at bay in much the same way as Stone's *World Trade Center*. The aftermath of the first plane impact is briefly shown (though once again not depicted directly), but after this the movie avoids showing subsequent images of the towers or acknowledging their collapse at all, going so far as to completely abandon subplots involving FAA air traffic control and the U.S. army that would necessitate acknowledging the fate of the Twin Towers and the attack on the Pentagon. Once the plane is highjacked, these locations are never returned to; the movie instead focuses entirely on the drama in the air, which had already been reconfigured culture-wide as September 11's primary site of heroic victory. That the plane ultimately crashes, despite the passenger revolt, is tellingly acknowledged in the way the movie ends: a spiraling look through the cockpit as the ground rushes upward, following by a quick cut to black and silence, a point of view shot that positions the audience *in the plane itself*. If, in *World Trade Center*, no one died on 9/11, in *United 93* we all did.

Nostalgia and Myth

These two trajectories — universal salvation in *WTC* and universal death in *U93* — work together in the respectaclization of September 11 to create a new, mythologized "9/11" that replaces both the actual event and the original mediated experience of it by the TV-watching population.¹⁴ The spectacle of "9/11" works to reassert September 11, in Debordian terms, as an enormous positivity, not merely in the obscuring of the carnage but also in the assertion of collective experience; we are told over and over again that 9/11 happened to all of us, that the shock and horror of that day opened the door to a better, safer, freer world — for Americans, at least. The closing monologue of Nicholas Cage's character in *World Trade Center* makes this Utopianism explicit:

> 9/11 showed us what humans are capable of, the evil, yeah sure, but it also brought out a goodness we forgot could exist. People taking care of each other, for no other reason than it was the right thing to do. It's important for us to talk about that good, to remember, because I saw a lot of it that day.¹⁵

As time has passed, and as the governmental response to the 9/11 myth (especially the military response) has grown more and more unpopular — as the old political feuds have reasserted themselves and the old pessimism has proven more resilient than the spectacle-makers might have hoped — the Utopian feelings of shared threat and collective survival now inscribed into the myth 9/11 increasingly become something to be nostalgic for. For many, 9/11 is something to be mourned, yes, but something also to be welcomed when it comes again, after the long-predicted, "inevitable" next attack. The widely criticized Stu Bykofsky of the *Philadelphia Daily News* is only one of many political commentators to be caught uttering this unspeakable wish out loud. Especially in the free-flowing, editorless world of the right-wing blogosphere, ruminations about the resurgence of the Republican Party and the grand neo-con vision of American empire after we are "hit again" have been common since at least 2003 and especially as the popularity of the Bush administration began to plummet. So, too, have disturbingly macabre speculative blog posts about the destruction of whole cities to dirty bombs and mass death on even grander scales, which sometimes seem to read less like warnings, predictions, or fears and more like deranged wishes or even revenge fantasies, with San Francisco and Seattle particularly common targets for destruction. As late as 2009, Michael Scheuer, a guest on Fox News Channel's *Glenn Beck*, was still remarking that "the only chance we have as a country right now is for Osama bin Laden to deploy and detonate a major weapon in the United States."¹⁶ And Glenn Beck himself has branded a "9/12 Project" in explicit evocation of this sort of nostalgia.

Like the Normandy Invasion, like World War II, as time passes 9/11 is increasingly figured as a lost, Utopian past, a perverse sort of Golden Age which in the same singular instant is both forever lost and always just around the corner.

Waiting for the Other Shoe to Drop

Although I grew up forty miles from New York City, I was in Cleveland, Ohio, on September 11, 2001, finishing my senior year of college. From the time my father called to wake me and let me know about the first attack, I watched the news coverage nearly continuously. I remember, vividly, the chaos, the violence, and the uncertainty, but I also remember events which are no longer referenced, the phantom attacks: false reports of car bombs on New York City bridges and outside the State Department, threats and evacuations across the country reported once and then never mentioned again. In Cleveland, at least, it was initially reported that United 93 had crashed into Camp David; the anchor also told us that there were as many as 20 planes out of contact with the FAA still in the air and that any number of them — possibly all — could have been highjacked. One of the planes forced to land at Cleveland Hopkins airport was raided (on live TV), believed to have terrorists aboard; this was later revealed to have been a false alarm.

In the face of so many reports, only four attacks becomes something like a relief — the violence of that day might have been so much *worse*. It might have never ended. And yet the deluge of phantom attacks — attacks which "seemed" to have happened but never actually did, which like the collapse of the Towers themselves have erased — left us for a long time with the foreboding sense that another attack is always just around the corner, that at any moment the world could again be shattered by terrible violence. Nightly news reports have regaled us for years with wild possibilities of where the terrorists might strike next, anything from blowing up the Hoover Dam to poisoning local gumball machines (Fahim).[17] The Department of Homeland Security's threat level, prominently visible at every airport in the country, remains perpetually "High." We were waiting, still, for the other shoe to drop, for the last planes to fall out of the sky.[18]

This feeling of permanent, unmitigated existential threat has begun at last to dissipate, but it has never really left us — a temporal loop caused by that day's repeated reconsumption as a spectacle. Though the attacks lasted only a few hours on one very devastating morning, on the level of spectacle they remain ongoing and unending. This is perhaps one reason why Freedom Tower, the new office complex and memorial long scheduled to be built on the ruins of Ground Zero, has for so long remained unbuilt and perhaps in some real sense *unbuildable*. We have been frozen in time, unable to move on. Whatever else might be said about the rewritten ending of the 2009 film adaptation of Alan Moore's *Watchmen*, we might find some comfort in the brief shot near the end of the film of construction crews already at work at the film's own Ground Zero. Perhaps the infinite temporal looping of the 9/11 era is finally over; perhaps, at last, we have reached September 12.

Notes

1. A good popular introduction to the concept of gravitational singularity can be found, among other places, in the latest edition of Stephen Hawking's popular science text *A Brief History of Time* (2008), particularly Chapter 3.

2. There are over one million Google hits for this phrase, including usages originating with George W. Bush, Dick Cheney, Rudy Giuliani, and others.

PART III: PERFORMANCE

3. Also repeated word for word 43–44 and paraphrased elsewhere.

4. The 9/11 Truth Movement is the umbrella term for a number of groups that have sprung up following September 11 which seek to prove using video evidence that the attacks were undertaken by intelligence agencies rather than al Qaeda for the purposes of justifying American military intervention in the Middle East. They typically spread their ideas through online discussion forums and viral videos, most notably the ninety-minute Internet film *Loose Change*.

5. See, for instance, Retort 31: "What [the attacks] point to, far beyond the specific atrocity and its grisly religious fuel, is a new structural feature of the international state system: that *the historical monopoly of the means of destruction by the state is now at risk.*"

6. Carol Lin begins the CNN coverage with this commentary: "(*speaking to her producer*) Yeah. (*to the audience*) This just in: You are looking at obviously a very disturbing live shot there. That is the World Trade Center, and we have unconfirmed reports this morning that a plane has crashed into one of the towers of the World Trade Center. CNN Center right now is just beginning to work on this story, obviously calling our sources and trying to figure out exactly what happened, but clearly something relatively devastating happening this morning there on the south end of the island of Manhattan. That is once again, a picture of one of the towers of the World Trade Center." The picture on the screen can only be described, over and over — the power of the uncontrolled image already crowding out any potential narratization.

7. See, for instance, "CNN Second Plane Collides" on YouTube.

8. See "CNN — 9/11 South Tower collapses." The utter chaos of the moment is again reflected in the loss of composure of CNN's Aaron Brown as he watches the South Tower collapse: "And there as you can see perhaps the second tower, the front tower, the top portion of which is collapsing — good lord. (pause) There are no words. You can see large pieces of the building falling, you can see the smoke rising, you can see a portion of the side of the building now just being covered on the right side, as I look at it, covered in smoke. This is just a horrific scene and a horrific moment." Again, there is nothing for the anchor to do but simply narrate what he sees, no pre-scripted frame available to him through which these images can be processed or contained.

9. See "9/11: North Tower 'collapse' live on CNN."

10. The nation's highest-circulation newspaper, *USA Today*, for example, ran only a single image of a jumper, on November 16, 2001.

11. Retort addresses the same point in a different way on page 25: "The state was wounded in September in its heart of hearts, and we see it still, almost four years later, flailing blindly in the face of an image it cannot exorcize, and trying desperately to convert the defeat back into terms it can respond to."

12. I am of course indebted here to Herbert Marcuse's treatment of repressive desublimation in *One-Dimensional Man*.

13. Faludi finds this selfsame patriarchal confidence, wisdom, and determination poured into no less august a personage than George W. Bush himself, whose blustering and awkward real-life performance on September 11, 2001, is replaced in the hagiographic *DC 9/11: Time of Crisis* (2003) with competence and razorlike resolve: "The film features a Kryptonite-proof commander in chief (played by Timothy Bottoms) who, when he is not hefting barbells, pumping iron at the butterfly press, and running 'three hard miles,' is barking out lines like 'Rummy, high alert status! Delta. Military. CIA. FBI. Everything! And if you haven't gone to Def Con 3, you oughta!'" The comparison to *Fahrenheit 9/11*'s documentary portrayal of Bush's *real-life* panic after being notified of the attacks, and his palpable reluctance to leave a classroom of second-graders to deal with the national security threat, is simply unavoidable. The book is filled with examples like this; there is even more to say about the Über-Bush of *DC 9/11*.

14. This effect, while hegemonic in America, is by no means limited to it; consider the Japanese film *Peep "TV" Show* (2004), which is focused on the relationship between voyeurism, violence, and 9/11. The characters in that movie, having made a little bit of money on a Web site catering to the voyeuristic impulse unleashed by modernity in general and September 11 in particular, consider leaving Tokyo to visit Ground Zero as a kind of pilgrimage. But they ultimately reject the plan, concluding, "This is where the plane hit us; we can't escape it.... This [Tokyo] is our Ground Zero."

15. This speech is quoted in Kathryn Jean Lopez's glowing July 21, 2006, review of *World Trade*

Center at *National Review Online*, itself a veritable hotbed of propagandistic mythmaking and neo-con 9/11 nostalgia.

16. This video of this appearance was widely circulated on left-leaning blogs, including popular video site Crooks & Liars.

17. I'm partial to this story because it concerns the town next door to the one in which I grew up, and because it involves the most ludicrous potential terror attack I've heard of. Stories like this one have aired across the country since September 11—perhaps, somewhere or another, every single night.

18. This cliché is driven powerfully home in a Spiegelman comics in *In the Shadow of No Towers*, in which a man whose sleep has been disturbed by his neighbor's loudly dropped shoe waits angrily for the other to finally fall so he can go back to sleep in peace.

Works Cited

Baudrillard, Jean, and C. Turner (Trans.). *The Spirit of Terrorism*. 2002. London and New York: Verso, 2003.
Bykofsky, Stu. "To Save America, We Need Another 9/11." *Philadelphia Daily News*. August 9, 2007. December 1, 2007. http://www.philly.com/.
Cauchon, Dennis, and Martah Moore. "Desperation Forced a Horrific Decision." *USAToday.com*. September 2, 2002. August 3, 2009. http://www.usatoday.com/news/sept11/2002-09-02-jumper_x.htm.
"CNN — 9/11 South Tower collapses." YouTube. October 29, 2006. August 3, 2009.
"CNN Second Plane Collides." YouTube. July 9, 2007. August 3, 2009.
Debord, Guy. *The Society of the Spectacle*. New York: Zone Books, 1994.
Fahim, Kareem. "Where Candy Machines Are Viewed with Suspicion." *New York Times*. October 12, 2007. August 3, 2009. http://www.nytimes.com/2007/10/12/nyregion/12gumballs.html.
Faludi, Susan. *The Terror Dream: Fear and Fantasy in Post–9/11 America*. New York: Metropolitan Books, 2007.
González Iñárritu, Alejandro et al. (Dir.). *11'9"01 September 11*. CIH Shorts, 2002.
Greengrass, Paul (Dir.). *United 93*. Universal Pictures, 2006.
Hawking, Stephen. *A Brief History of Time: From the Big Bang to Black Holes*. New York: Bantam Books, 1988.
Hilferty, Robert. "The Greatest Work of Art in the Entire Cosmos." *Andante*. September 2001.
Junod, Tom. "The Falling Man." *Esquire.com*. September 11, 2007. August 3, 2009.
Lim, Dennis. "A Flight to Remember." *VillageVoice.com*. April 18, 2006. August 3, 2009.
Lopez, Kathryn Jean. "Get Stoned: *World Trade Center* Is Good." *National Review Online*. 21 July 2006. 3 August 2009.
Marcuse, Herbet. *One-Dimensional Man*. Boston: Beacon Press, 1964.
Moore, Michael (Dir.). *Fahrenheit 9/11*. Lion's Gate Films, 2004.
Moore, Ronald D. (Created by). *Battlestar Galactica*. R&D TV, 2003.
Neiwert, David. "Michael Scheuer on Fox: America's Only Hope Is for Another Terrorist Attack." *Crooksandliars.com*. July 1, 2009. August 3, 2009.
The 9/11 Commission Report: Final Report of the National Commission on Terrorist Attacks Upon the United States. U.S. Government Printing Office, 2004. August 3, 2009. http://9-11commission.gov/.
"9/11: North Tower 'collapse' live on CNN." YouTube. December 4, 2007.
"9/11/01— CNN News Coverage 1st 5 Minutes." YouTube. July 9, 2007. August 3, 2009.
Retort (Iain Boal, T.J. Clark, Joseph Matthews, and Michael Watts). *Afflicted Powers: Capital and Spectacle in a New Age of War*. Verso: New York, 2005.
Snyder, Zack (Dir.). *Watchmen*. Warner Brothers, 2009.
Spiegelman, Art. *In the Shadow of No Towers*. New York: Pantheon Books, 2004.
Spielberg, Steven (Dir.). *War of the Worlds*. Paramount Pictures, 2005.
Stone, Oliver (Dir.). *World Trade Center*. Paramount Pictures, 2006.
Tsuchiya, Yutaka (Dir.). *Peep "TV" Show*. W-TV Office, 2004.
Žižek, Slavoj. *Welcome to the Desert of the Real*. New York: Verso, 2002.

FROM FLYING MAN TO FALLING MAN
9/11 Discourse in Superman Returns *and* Batman Begins
Dan Hassler-Forest

From their first appearance in the comics of the 1930s, superheroes have always served overtly political causes. Since their breakthrough as champions of the working man, they have battled exploitative employers, irresponsible mine owners, and other unsavory capitalist figures. Yet, if characters like Superman and Batman have retained their familiar iconic appearance, they nevertheless have shifted ideological positions several times over the course of their seventy-odd year existence. Given the fact that the most radical redefinitions of superheroes always took place during periods of ideological conflict between the United States and its political enemies, it would make sense to investigate whether the attacks of 9/11 and the resulting War on Terror have had a similar repositioning effect.

This question may be considered even more relevant when one considers that the superhero has become an increasingly dominant figure in popular culture over the past decade. With examples ranging from Golden and Silver Age comic book heroes like Spider-Man, the Incredible Hulk, the Fantastic Four and Iron Man to more recent, even alternative creations like Hancock, Hellboy, and the characters from the multimedia phenomenon engendered by the TV show *Heroes*, superheroes now make up a larger part of our popular media landscape than ever before. Nor does these characters' connection to political rhetoric form a one-way street. In the political speeches of the Bush administration, we have witnessed the return of comic book terminology associated with the binary opposition between good and evil that dates back to World War II, e.g., the rehabilitation of the bizarrely chosen misnomer "Axis of Evil" to describe whichever nation states are currently singled out as "our" enemies:

> Bush's term "Axis of Evil" itself employs unique rhetoric. First, it creates [...] a "condensation symbol" for the complex web of anti-American governments and networks. Hence, one does not need to analyze the complex structures or causalities of separate nations and/or groups[...]. Second, it associates these regimes and groups with one of the United States' greatest enemies, the Axis Powers of World War II. [...] And third, by equating these countries with the "Axis"—as well as the biblical notion of "evil"—Bush defines the regimes as inherently our enemies [Maggio: 830].

But while comic books clearly served as a form of government propaganda during the "Long War" against fascism and communism and therefore fulfilled a clear-cut hegemonic purpose (in the Gramscian sense), we have so far failed to see our contemporary superhero figures join the fight explicitly and sock Osama in the jaw, as Captain America famously did to Hitler on the cover of his very first issue. In fact, overt references to 9/11 and the War on Terror have been relatively rare in superhero comics.

Similarly, most superhero films have steered clear of any specific mention of the 9/11 attacks and their social and political aftermath, even in films that take place in post–9/11 New York City, such as the Spider-Man and Fantastic Four films. But although explicit references to this decade's most politically and culturally defining events and their after-effects have been absent on the surface of new superhero films, we find metaphoric and symbolic representations aplenty. Significantly, the debate surrounding the blockbuster phenomenon *The Dark Knight* (Christopher Nolan, 2008) dealt not with the question of whether it was in fact about the War on Terror, but on what it was saying about it. Whether films such as these actually offer a coherent critical or political perspective on current events or simply "pluck out bits of cultural flotsam opportunistically" (25), as David Bordwell has maintained, it seems evident that these narratives also serve as vehicles for metaphorical representations of contemporary conflicts and debates. This roundabout way of dealing with national trauma conforms in fact with Cathy Caruth's use of trauma theory to explain the indirect ways in which trauma victims use narrative to engage with personal trauma, like sexual abuse, or historical trauma, such as the Holocaust.

Following this line of thought, this paper offers an investigation and analysis of how the events of 9/11 have been transfigured and re-visualized in recent superhero films. My main case studies in this essay are *Superman Returns* (Bryan Singer, 2006) and *Batman Begins* (Christopher Nolan, 2005), two reboots of major superhero franchises that are notable not only for the fact that they feature the two most iconic and enduring superhero figures, but also because they mark a transition in the superhero film genre. For unlike earlier superhero blockbusters that spearheaded franchises of diminishing returns, such as *Superman: The Movie* (Richard Donner, 1978) and *Batman* (Tim Burton, 1989), these 21st-century revisions managed to draw in new audiences by attracting directors who brought their independent auteur credentials to bear on the project. On top of this, these films are also the first to draw heavily on Frank Miller and Alan Moore's celebrated wave of graphic novels that are most famous for deconstructing the classical superhero archetypes in the late 1980s.

Those highly influential comics, which have been generally recognized as a critical response to the neo-conservative policies of the Reagan-Thatcher era, were the first to draw critical and academic attention to superhero comics. The major themes in *Batman: The Dark Knight Returns* (1986), *Batman: Year One* (1987) and *Watchmen* (1986–1987) include issues such as the problematic morality and legality of superhero figures, the manipulative role of the mass media in contemporary society, and an ambiguous investigation of how real-world superheroes would most probably adversely affect the flow of world history. But although the popularity of these comics was certainly a factor in

Warner Brothers' decision to launch a Batman film franchise, the themes from these books somehow failed to appear in superhero film adaptations until after 9/11.

In this essay I aim to demonstrate how the above themes are addressed in different but related ways in the two recent superhero pictures *Superman Returns* and *Batman Begins*. More specifically, I argue that both films draw explicitly on imagery and motifs associated with 9/11 in order to imbue familiar icons and narrative tropes with new relevance. I will show how both films display ambivalent attitudes towards the narrative traditions of the superhero genre from which they are derived, simultaneously reaffirming the essential genre tropes and traditions and introducing new elements that establish connections to a contemporary, specifically post–9/11 American context.

The Superhero Trope

In their extensive work on the subject of twentieth-century popular mythology embodied by American superheroes, John Shelton Lawrence and Robert Jewett have established how these modern myths are clearly distinguishable from the classical heroic archetypes as defined by Joseph Campbell. Unlike the hero of classical Campbellian mythology and Propp's structuralist analysis of folk tales, a figure who sets out to venture into a world of supernatural wonder to become a man and ultimately return to his community, the myth of the American superhero always seems to revolve around an invincible figure saving a helpless community from danger. According to Lawrence and Jewett, one of the most problematic aspects of this quintessentially American narrative paradigm is its implication for democratic ideals and institutions: without exception, the superhero figure, embodied by a diversity of characters ranging from cowboys like the Virginian to supermen like John Rambo, is forced into action by the ineffectual nature of democratic institutions. With only incidental exceptions, police officers, lawyers, judges, and politicians are portrayed as irredeemably corrupt, bureaucratic and incompetent. The superhero figure is called upon to cleanse this helpless community of sin through his use of redemptive violence. His task accomplished, the savior ultimately rides into the proverbial sunset, leaving the community to its own means once order has been restored, at least until the next crisis appears on the horizon.

This narrative formula has obvious advantages within the comic book culture industry. Indeed, hero archetypes such as these can come to the rescue of an infinite number of communities in crisis. And because there are no clear ideological elements contained within the formula, it makes the superhero figure extremely adaptable to changing political and social values. In other words, the superhero figure is a free-floating signifier ready to be mobilized and take up arms against whichever kind of threat its age presents. In *Comic Book Nation* (2001), a book-length study of American comics, Bradford Wright clearly demonstrates how adaptable these figures have proved themselves to be throughout nearly a century of their history as icons of popular culture.

The final defining characteristic for Lawrence and Jewett's superhero figure is the fact that he is never rewarded for his deeds. The superhero must remain celibate, unlike the classical heroic archetype, who is rewarded with a bride, both as an indicator of the community's normative heterosexuality and of implied maturity. For not only would any kind of romantic or sexual commitment conflict with the superhero's ability to operate independently, any reward might also imply that his actions were not entirely motivated by altruism. And it is precisely this altruistic nature that has allowed superhero figures to function as metaphorical embodiments of American national policy and identity. The fact that they use superior physical force only to defend an imagined "greater good" made the superhero a convenient symbol for post-war American interventionist policy. These flag-waving figures range from the most literal embodiments of nationalist iconography like Captain America and Uncle Sam, to more recent attempts to create similar icons in figures like *24*'s Jack Bauer, an indestructible superhero for our own era.

"*Truth, Justice, All That Stuff...*"

Few superheroes have consistently embodied aspects of American identity as long or as successfully as Superman has. As the first major figure in popular fiction to combine mythological elements with superhuman abilities that made him virtually indestructible, he was also the first of the Golden Age comics icons to cross over successfully into other media: from the 1940s Max Fleischer cartoons to post-war B-movies, and from radio serials to the popular 1950s television show. But it wasn't until his appearance in *Superman: The Movie* that he would become the ubiquitous figure that would help define post-classical blockbuster cinema.

It is relevant to note that this first true A-list superhero film franchise, made up of four films that appeared from 1978 to 1987, was extremely lucrative during the Reagan era. Like so many other popular films from this decade, the series displayed a strong tendency towards nostalgia from its very start: throughout the films, we see jaded, cynical feminist Lois Lane being won over by Superman and his alter ego Clark Kent as the embodiment of the traditional values of a more innocent, less complicated age. Like *Back to the Future* (Robert Zemeckis, 1985), *Happy Days*, and many other popular films and TV shows from the early 1980s, this film seeks the answers to the post–Watergate, post–Vietnam sense of malaise in the romanticized patriarchal values of the 1950s. As defined by Fredric Jameson, these nostalgia films serve to de-historicize the postmodern present by continuously referring back to a glorified past that never truly existed in the first place. *Superman: The Movie* fits the bill perfectly, as the past to which it refers is nothing short of a postmodern pastiche of elements from fondly remembered childhood comic books and TV serials.

Given the resurgence of superheroes in blockbuster cinema since 2001, the Man of Steel's long-awaited return to the silver screen soon became all but inevitable, especially when one considers the fact that the Bush administration adopted the Reagan era as the very model of political and economic policy. Following several abortive attempts to re-imagine Superman in a radically updated guise, he finally appeared in the 2006 summer blockbuster *Superman Returns*. But instead of the originally envisioned update, this franchise reboot proved to be an exercise in nostalgic one-upmanship. In a strangely Baudrillardian twist, Singer's picture goes out of its way to recreate the experience of the 1978 film, thereby fashioning itself into the ultimate simulacrum: an identical copy without a true original. After all, if we can safely establish that *Superman: The Movie* cannot be considered an "original" in any sense of the word, the fact that *Superman Returns* enshrines it as its nostalgic object of desire becomes doubly odd.

From its opening credits, which re-use the earlier franchise's rousing orchestral score, to the casting of Brandon Routh first and foremost for his uncanny resemblance to Christopher Reeve, this 21st-century blockbuster seems overtly nostalgic for the pre–9/11 days of 1950s-inspired Reaganomics. In a remarkable plot twist, the film updates the Superman chronology with the notion that Superman abandoned earth (or rather: America) "five years ago," which works out as the year 2001, upon which Lois Lane published the Pulitzer Prize–winning editorial "Why the World Doesn't Need Superman." Returning at the start of the film from his self-imposed exile, the first thing Superman does is watch TV, which shows us news footage familiar from recent conflicts in the Middle East. The prospect is tantalizing: will Superman take it upon himself to assist in the War on Terror now that the film so clearly links his return to America's current sense of failure and abandonment? And given Kal-El's well-documented roots in Jewish culture, how would he attempt to solve the Israeli-Palestinian conflict?

Surprisingly, however, this idea is jettisoned almost immediately, serving only to establish a sense that things have gone badly wrong in his absence. Superman's return is made known to the world by his last-minute, media-friendly rescue of an airliner that was about to crash into a sold-out baseball stadium in a scene that serves as the movie's first major action set-piece, while simultaneously offering up a remarkable rewriting of 9/11. The potent image of an airliner hurtling with seemingly unstoppable momentum towards such an archetypically American landmark on a sunny day is eerily reminiscent of that moment of national trauma. The crucial difference is that Superman uses his death- and gravity-defying power to actually stop the plane before it wreaks havoc on this stadium that so clearly embodies an iconic American pastime. The location also turns this remarkable last-minute rescue operation into a moment of sheer spectacle that is immediately followed by rapturous applause, thereby managing to turn a moment of disaster and trauma into a celebration of heroism.

9/11: Reshaping Heroism

This moment in the film fits in perfectly with a wider form of cultural discourse that has been dedicated to rewriting the events of 9/11 as an emblem of heroism rather than of defeat. The first major 9/11 fundraiser, a star-studded telethon broadcast worldwide a week after the attacks, was already titled *Heroes: A Tribute to America*, featuring a host of mournful pop icons alternating with Hollywood stars commemorating the acts of heroism that occurred on that day; Marvel Comics' special commemorative issue of original work by a who's-who of major-league comics authors was similarly titled *Heroes: The World's Greatest Super Hero Creators Honor the World's Greatest Heroes— 9-11-2001*. This compendium depicted members of the police force and fire department using the aesthetics and iconography of superhero comics. Similarly, *World Trade Center* (Oliver Stone, 2006), the only Hollywood film to focus explicitly on the attack on the eponymous Twin Towers, devoted its running time to the heroic survival of its two protagonists trapped under the rubble at Ground Zero, its poster and trailer bearing the tag line "A True Story of Hope and Survival."

All of these texts, as diverse as their media, authors, and audience might be, continuously re-emphasize two major points related to the events of 9/11. First, they insist that the United States as a nation had been the innocent victim of these attacks. Secondly, they show that in spite of this victimization, America had made heroes out of its survivors. This tendency of pop culture texts to focus so specifically on a combination of American heroism and victimization from late 2001 onwards is strong and widespread enough to constitute a Foucauldian discursive formation that extends far beyond the borders of texts that deal specifically with the actual events of 9/11. Discursive formations come into existence whenever "between objects, types of statement, concepts, or thematic choices, one can define a regularity (an order, correlations, positions and functionings, transformations)" (Foucault, 2002: 41).

One particularly telling example of how swiftly 9/11 was transformed from a collection of historical events into a discursive formation with a clearly identifiable political-ideological agenda is the film release of *Black Hawk Down* (Ridley Scott, 2001). Unlike many other action films that were immediately shelved in the aftermath of 9/11 on the grounds that this particular brand of destructive fantasy was suddenly deemed inappropriate and possibly offensive, the release of this war film, originally scheduled for late spring 2002, was quickly rushed ahead to December 2001.

Since the film's subject matter is the embarrassing military defeat suffered by American elite troops in Somalia in 1993, one might wonder in what sense a big-budget action film about these events would be any less insensitive to release in the traumatized cultural climate directly following 9/11. An analysis of the film, as well as its immense commercial success, however, does bear out the distributor's decision. For unlike the much more balanced account in Mark Bowden's book, on which the film was based, Ridley Scott's immaculately produced movie jettisons all but the most basic explanation of the reasons behind the armed conflict pictured in the film, focusing instead on the American soldiers' experience in the thick of the battle. With political and military policy conveniently reduced to the briefest of text captions that bookend the undeniably exciting nonstop barrage of gunfire and bloodshed, the film's actual import is summed up by main character Scott Eversmann (played by Josh Hartnett) in the film's closing scene:

> I was talking to Blackburn the other day, and he asked me "What changed? Why are we going home?" and I said "Nothing." That's not true either; I think everything's changed. *I know I've changed.* You know a friend of mine asked me before I got here; it's when we were all shipping out. He asked me "Why are you going to fight somebody else's war? What, do you think you're heroes?" I didn't know what to say at the time, but if he'd ask me again I'd say no. I'd say there's no way in hell. *Nobody asks to be a hero.* [beat] *It just sometimes turns out that way* [my emphasis].

Either unable or unwilling to comprehend the complex social, political and economical reasons behind American military policy, nor this specific intervention and his own role in it, the character defines the experience (and therefore the film's entire narrative) as some-thing that is meaningless beyond its effects upon the individual: the only thing that has been changed by the experience is himself. Therefore, the characters who died in the film were the victims of unfathomable forces beyond anyone's command, allowing the events to leave in their wake only two kinds of subjects: victims and heroes. By focusing exclusively on the soldiers' individual experiences of these events, they are simultaneously de-histori-cized and de-politicized. The enemy responsible for the American bloodshed on the battlefield is defined only by its otherness, informed by Orientalist characteristics like religion — assassins on the street screaming out "Allah-u akbar!" — and ethnicity — only one of the American soldiers is African-American, while the Somalis, all but a rare few of which are seen only from a distance, have dark skin that functions as a strong visual "bad" contrast to the "good" white American soldiers. Therefore, traumatic military con-flict from the American point of view is presented as unavoidable, with reasons that remain unfathomable, in which Americans are both innocent victims and heroic protagonists.

These examples, and many others besides, seem to bear out the most pessimistically-minded postmodernist theorists, such as Fredric Jameson and Jean Baudrillard, and their central thesis that postmodernist (popular) culture serves first and foremost to sever the public's active connection with history by offering up continuous representations of events that are deliberately made unhistorical. These simulations, or, indeed, simulacra, do indeed "endow present reality and the openness of present history with the spell and distance of a glossy mirage" (Jameson, *Postmodernism*: 21). These words apply equally to *Superman Returns* and its deliberately unrealistic representation of such events, especially as pictured in the airliner sequence first described above.

Superman's reintroduction is followed by a number of scenes detailing his successful efforts to stop the enemies of capitalism from robbing some of New York's largest banks. Combining in his actions and general demeanor the nation's vaguely formulated ideals along with the power and the mandate to enforce them, he seems to embody Louis Althusser's dual notions of ideological and repressive state apparatus conveniently rolled into one. Superman's final challenge in the film is once again to save Metropolis from an attack by arch-villain Lex Luthor, who seeks to create a new continent in the middle of the Atlantic.

The creation of the continent causes shockwaves that surge through the recognizable streets of Manhattan, shattering skyscraper windows as the tall buildings of Metropolis teeter and sway realistically, their occupants and passers-by alike helpless in the face of their predicament. Generically speaking, this part of the narrative is all but a requirement for the Superman franchise, referring back not just to the original *Action Comics* panels, but also to the iconic Fleischer brothers animated shorts, which "give one the sense that the city is a fragile vessel, constantly under attack, crashing, breaking, bending" (ibid.: 98). Much of the pleasure in *Superman Returns* results from the film's determination to satisfy these expectations, providing new spectacular imagery of Superman dashing around the city in a number of last-minute rescues that update the visuals effects while remaining true to the basic formula.

But images of New York City under attack can no longer be perceived as they were before in texts that were created after 9/11. Especially given the amount of attention that has been devoted in special tributes and throughout pop culture to the disappointment that superheroes had been powerless to stop those real-world attacks, a surprise attack on Manhattan in a new Superman film can only be read through the prism of 9/11 and the many wish-fulfillment fantasies we have encountered since. This strange dissonance between the unavoidable associations with recent history and the Jamesonian "perpetual present" of postmodernism that typifies this sequence in generic terms is one of the most interesting theoretical issues raised by this film: how can this film simultaneously de-historicize while drawing its significance from clear references to historical events?

This paradox comes into sharper focus when Superman finally confronts his nemesis in the middle of the surreal landscape of Luthor's newborn continent, where he discovers that his extraordinary powers have unexpectedly abandoned him. And it is here, in a scene that has outraged avid Superman fans more than any other, that this iconic embodiment of truth, justice and the American Way faces his harshest moment of defeat. In this desolate continent that seems eerily reminiscent of the familiar photos of the rubble at Ground Zero, he is beaten savagely by Luthor's henchmen, strangely noticeable for being the only ethnically diverse group in the film, and finally stabbed in the back by the villainous mastermind himself. He stands up bravely to face his attackers, but teeters and falls powerlessly off the edge of an immense precipice. In what may be the film's most provocative image, the following shot shows "flying man" transformed into "falling man." Few images have been as disturbing a summation of America's sense of helplessness and defeat as those of the people falling or jumping from the towers after the attack, and literary works such as Jonathan Safran Foer's *Extremely Loud and Incredibly Close* and — obviously — Don DeLillo's *Falling Man* deliberately mobilize this icon of national emasculation as a powerful metaphor:

> [W]e are all, DeLillo suggests, in free fall. The plots, myths, institutions we once relied on to provide meaning and purpose are suspended. Our idols have fallen too: "God is

the voice that says, 'I am not here'" [Falling Man: 236]. Like Alzheimer's patients, all we can do is watch in suspense for what is ever-impending. And one man keeps popping up — like a puppet or a mime — to remind New Yorkers of the catastrophe. He calls himself Falling Man, a performance artist who appears unexpectedly around Manhattan, suspended from various structures, dangling upside down from a harness, dressed in suit and tie [Kauffmann: 372].

But not only must Superman experience this fall from grace along with us; he must also somehow reverse time — as he has been known to do before, and which is another narrative trait we can recognize in several of the 9/11 novels — and change the past to save our future. And indeed, after his inevitable moment of messianic resurrection, he lifts up the whole of Luthor's new continent into space, and playing on the film's innumerable references to Atlas and Jesus Christ, saves mankind by bearing the weight of the world for us, before plummeting once more back into the streets of Metropolis.

Superman, the picture seems to say, as the embodiment of America's true spirit, must return to relieve the country from the burden of the past by ridding the nation of the trauma of 9/11. Through its reliance on nostalgia for its hero's Reagan-era incarnation, Singer's film seems to propose that the answer to our current problems lies — once again — in a return to the values of an earlier era of innocence and purity. But rather than appealing directly to sentimentalized visualizations of Eisenhower-era Americana, Singer's film seeks this coveted sense of security by enshrining 1980s superhero blockbusters, already postmodern nostalgia films, as the object of ultimate desire.

Batman Begins

Batman Begins offers a similar 21st-century retooling of an indestructible Golden Age superhero, but as the title indicates, with a different twist. For, unlike *Superman Returns* and its only moderately revisionist continuation of an existing chronology and an established film franchise, Nolan's film presents itself as an origin story. It reinvents its already familiar character for a contemporary audience by resorting, re-shifting, and re-defining narrative elements that make up the Caped Crusader's long and contradictory history.

Drawing heavily on elements from Frank Miller's late–1980s graphic novels *Batman: Year One* and *Batman: The Dark Knight Returns*, the latest franchise re-establishes its protagonist as a troubled, reluctant hero operating in a murky, gritty Gotham City far less visually fantastic and stylized than its previous screen incarnations. *Batman Begins* was released in the summer of 2005, not long after the first two Spider-Man and X-Men features had re-established the superhero film's viability as a box office force. But more than any of the previous films in this genre, Nolan's picture builds on themes and imagery strongly associated with 9/11 and its aftermath.

Unlike *Superman Returns* and its repeated restaging of familiar catastrophes with triumphant heroic endings, *Batman Begins* provides a different kind of avenue into familiar 9/11 discourse and iconography. The film reintroduces Bruce Wayne as an embittered young man, deeply traumatized by the death of his parents. Still suffering from the loss of his father as a young adult, Wayne proves susceptible to the temptations of a fundamentalist terrorist group led by arch-villain Ra's Al-Guhl, who may not be portrayed as a Middle-Eastern Muslim, but whose appearance and attitudes answer to all the classical stereotypes that make him the archetypal Orientalist enemy of western values. This sect leader, played by Japanese actor Ken Watanabe, is later revealed as an empty figurehead meant to distract from the actual villain: Wayne's charismatic Caucasian mentor, Ducard (Liam Neeson).

Like *Iron Man*, the TV series *24*, and many other popular 21st-century narratives, *Batman Begins* trades effortlessly in familiar Orientalist stereotypes, only to make a last minute about-face that recasts the film's most aggressive father surrogate as the true source of evil and villainy. What on the surface would appear to be politically correct efforts to avoid suspicion of racist stereotyping could actually be regarded as a more troubling type of oblique racism than that of pre–9/11 action movies — from *Into the Night* (John Landis, 1985) to *True Lies* (James Cameron, 1994) — in which the villains were rabid Arab caricatures. For not only do these post–9/11 pictures use patronizing stereotypes to establish the antagonist's otherness, but the initial villain's unmasking as a red herring robs the character of agency, thereby effectively emasculating the stereotype without dissolving the negative connotations that surround his figure.

These connotations come to the fore when Bruce Wayne arrives at the League of Shadows' headquarters, where he undergoes his combat training in *Batman Begins*. These headquarters, located in a remote Asian mountain range, recall the headquarters of terrorist organization Cobra in GI Joe comics, which are described as "designed architecturally to resemble a temple hidden in a Himalaya-like region" (Norlund: 8). Like Cobra's leader, the head of the League of Shadows, Ra's Al Ghul, is also "a terrorist personality [portrayed] as a disingenuous religious leader, suggest[ing] that no terrorist or religious leader is authentically devout" (ibid.). This connection between terrorism and Eastern mystical religion is made explicit in the film by the League's headquarters' resemblance to a temple. It is further solidified by the presence of signifiers such as Buddha figurines on prominent display in the first interior shot. Bruce Wayne is successfully recruited, trained and indoctrinated by the League of Shadows, but later rejects the organization when he is assigned the task of executing a criminal as a required rite of passage. Wayne decides to reject the League's absolutist ideology, defining a subtle but crucial difference between revenge and justice, terror and fear. He immediately thereafter makes his separation complete by blowing up the temple where he has undergone the training that will later help make him a superhero.

Wayne's rejection of the League of Shadows and its ideology becomes even more evident when he exchanges his Eastern ninja garb for high-tech American military armor, which he reappropriates and transforms into his superhero costume. Thus, by portraying Bruce Wayne as someone whose childhood trauma has made him vulnerable to recruitment and indoctrination by a foreign and therefore "Other" terrorist organization, this revisionary superhero narrative and its re-imagining of Batman's origins breaks explicitly with Batman's established tradition of facing "a different and independent villain each issue, since a variety of them reside in Gotham City" (Norlund: 2). This break with tradition, relocating the main threat from inside Gotham to a sectarian rebel militia in the Far East, is the first element that connects *Batman Begins* with post–9/11 discourse, a connection that is further developed in the narrative once Ra's Al Ghul's scheme becomes clear.

Although he is at first taken in by the group's charismatic and elusive leader, he balks at the League of Shadows' true purpose: a destructive attack on Gotham City, another alternate-universe representation of New York. This motivation, which sounds remarkably similar to the oft-quoted "they hate our freedoms" rationale with its emphasis on New York City as the pinnacle of decadence, takes a form that makes it especially objectionable to Batman. For as the plot later reveals, the attack will focus on Gotham's skyline-defining skyscraper, which is also the city's trade center and infrastructural centerpiece. As Ra's Al Ghul reveals:

> Gotham's time has come. Like Constantinople or Rome before it the city has become a breeding ground for suffering and injustice. It is beyond saving and must be allowed to die. This is the most important function of the League of Shadows. It is one we've performed for centuries. Gotham ... must be destroyed.

The League's plot to destroy Gotham City, Batman's fictitious city of residence since 1941 that "for all intents and purposes is still New York, and more specifically Manhattan" (Brooker: 48), ultimately involves an attack that is to culminate in the destruction of Wayne Tower, Gotham's skyline-defining skyscraper and the symbolic and infrastructural heart of the city. The similarity to recent real-world events could hardly be more obvious. As Kim Newman has described it in his article "Cape Fear," Gotham City is attacked "by a fanatic eastern sect with a charismatic but impossible-to-catch figurehead which is bent on crashing a mode of transport into a skyscraper to trigger an explosion of panic that will destroy society" (21). Again, this climactic attack represents a departure from both primary sources, neither of which includes any reference to a skyscraper as a target singled out for destruction by the villain.

But since Gotham's major skyscraper was built by the hero's sainted father, a billionaire businessman, doctor and philanthropist, and therefore a model capitalist, the attack on Wayne Senior's phallic legacy also constitutes a direct assault upon patriarchal masculinity. Like Superman, Batman succeeds in saving the city at the last possible moment, but in this darker film, the memories of recent traumas are not lifted by a messianic hero so easily: part of Gotham is lost in the attack, Wayne Manor is burnt to the ground, and the democratic institutions continue to fail to address the problems that face them on any noticeable level. As the more recent sequel *The Dark Knight*

(Christopher Nolan, 2008) and the public debate surrounding its many references to contemporary social and ethical quandaries illustrated, this particular comic book world is one in which post–9/11 tensions and concerns are not so much solved as they are magnified.

Conclusion

As I have demonstrated in my reading of the way these two films draw on recognizable real-world concerns, *Superman Returns* and *Batman Begins* can both be understood as attempts to find relevance for familiar pop icons by investing their narratives and iconography with the strongest elements of 9/11 as a discursive formation: heroism and victimization. The fact that these films do so in distinctive ways is obviously due in large part to the traditions that developed them and set them apart as the two dominant superhero icons for over seventy years: Superman's garish optimism and messianic associations, and Batman's gothic skulking in the darkness of his cave.

But as different as their methods, narratives and aesthetics may be, their politics are ultimately similar in the ways they represent ideology in the Althusserian sense: as "a representational structure which allows the individual subject to conceive or imagine his or her lived relationship to transpersonal realities such as the social structure or the collective logic of History" (Jameson, *The Political Unconscious*: 14–15). By drawing on the iconography and thematics of contemporary public and political discourse while situating their narratives in an explicitly fantastical realm, these superhero films can be easily related to the genre of romance literature. And as Fredric Jameson observed so memorably in his analysis of this type of text and its ideological subtext, this genre "does not involve the substitution of some more ideal realm for ordinary reality[...], but rather a process of *transforming* ordinary reality" (ibid.: 97). In other words, films like *Superman Returns* and *Batman Begins* offer models for interpreting our own world and its history that serve to systematically dehistoricize the events to which they so obviously refer. By representing 9/11 metaphorically as part of a battle that takes familiar narrative categories ("hero," "villain," "victim," "resolution," etc.) as its basic components, the genre provides an assertive view that denies its passive spectator both understanding and any sense of historical agency.

Both *Superman Returns* and *Batman Begins* display ambivalent attitudes towards the desire to retreat into a romanticized past on the one hand, and the wish to understand how to respond to and make sense of traumatic contemporary events on the other. In doing so, they serve as further illustration of the persistent anti-democratic tendencies in American culture. But rather than utilizing this familiar narrative paradigm to recycle propaganda, both films do allow for other readings as well: *Superman Returns* through its mournful, ambivalent nostalgia, and *Batman Begins* in its more nuanced reflection on current events and ideological conundrums. And although these films demonstrate the wistful desire to resurrect our most familiar popular icons, they also show us that we will not be able to rely on superheroes to save the world in the 21st century.

Works Cited

Amis, Martin. *The Second Plane*. London: Jonathan Cape, 2008.
Bardwell, David, and Kristen Thompson. *Minding Movies: Observations and the Art, Craft, and Business of Filmmaking*. Chicago: The University of Chicago Press, 2011.
Brooker, Will. *Batman Unmasked: Analyzing a Cultural Icon*. London: Continuum, 2000.
Burton, Tim (Dir.). *Batman*. Warner Bros., 1989.
Cameron, James (Dir.). *True Lies*. 20th Century Fox, 1994.
Campbell, Joseph. *The Hero with a Thousand Faces*. 1949. London: Fortuna Press, 1993.
Dawson, Jeff. "Has the New Batman Plundered Its Plot from 9/11?" *The Sunday Times*, July 20, 2008. September 5, 2008. http://entertainment.timesonline.co.uk/tol/arts_and_entertainment/film/article4352512.ece.
DeLillo, Don. *Falling Man*. New York: Scribner, 2007.
_____. "In the Ruins of the Future." *Harpers Magazine*, December 2001: 33–40.
Donner, Richard (Dir.). *Superman: The Movie*. Warner Bros., 1978.
Eaglestone, Robert. "'The Age of Reason Is Over ... an Age of Fury Was Dawning': Contemporary Anglo-American Fiction and Terror." *Wasafiri* 22.2 (July 2007): 19–22.
Foucault, Michel, and Tavistock Publications Limited (Trans.). *The Archeology of Knowledge*. 1969. London: Routledge, 2002.
Jameson, Fredric. *The Political Unconscious: Narrative as a Socially Symbolic Act*. 1981. London: Routledge, 2002.
_____. *Postmodernism, or, The Cultural Logic of Late Capitalism*. Durham: Duke University Press, 1991.
Kauffmann, Linda S. "In the Wake of Terror: Don DeLillo's 'In the Ruins of the Future,' 'Baader-Meinhof,' and *Falling Man*." *MFS Modern Fiction Studies* 54.2 (Summer 2008): 352–77.
Klavan, Andrew. "What Bush and Batman Have in Common." *The Wall Street Journal*, July 25, 2008. September 2, 2008. http://online.wsj.com/public/article_print/SB121694247343482821.html.
Klock, Geoff. *How to Read Superhero Comics and Why*. New York: Continuum, 2002.
Landis, John (Dir.). *Into the Night*. Universal Pictures, 1985.
Lawrence, John Shelton, and Robert Jewett. *Captain America and the Crusade Against Evil: The Dilemma of Zealous Nationalism*. Grand Rapids, MI: William B. Eerdmans, 2003.
_____. *The Myth of the American Superhero*. Grand Rapids, MI: William B. Eerdmans, 2002.
Maggio, J. "The Presidential Rhetoric of Terror. The (Re)Creation of Reality Immediately After 9/11." *Politics and Policy* 35.4 (2007): 810–835.
McEwan, Ian. *Saturday*. London: Vintage, 2006.
Miller, Frank, with Klaus Janson, and Lynn Varley. *Batman: The Dark Knight Returns*. New York: DC Comics, 1986.
Moore, Alan, and David Gibbons. *Watchmen*. New York: DC Comics, 1986–1987.
Newman, Kim. "Cape Fear." *Sight and Sound* (July 2005).
Noland, Christopher (Dir.). *The Dark Knight*. Warner Bros., 2008.
Norlund, Christopher. "Imagining Terrorists Before Sept. 11: Marvel's GI Joe Comic Books, 1982–1994." *ImageText* 3.1 (2006).
Scott, Ridley (Dir.). *Black Hawk Down*. Columbia Pictures, 2001.
Stone, Oliver (Dir.). *World Trade Center*. Paramount Pictures, 2006.
Wright, Bradford W. *Comic Book Nation: The Transformation of Youth Culture in America*. Baltimore: The Johns Hopkins University Press, 2001.
Zemeckis, Robert (Dir.). *Back to the Future*. Universal Pictures, 1985.

AUTHENTICATING THE REEL
Realism, Simulation, and Trauma in United 93
Frances Pheasant-Kelly

Introduction

Of the four planes highjacked during the September 2001 attacks on America, only three struck their intended targets. Two destroyed the Twin Towers while another hit the Pentagon. The film *United 93* (2006) follows the fourth plane, reconstructing the heroic efforts of its passengers to overthrow the highjackers, and tracing their doomed trajectory. Because there were no survivors of the crash, the film inevitably generates considerable emotional impact for the viewer. Contemporary reviews (Dargis; Doherty; Pavlus) of *United 93* suggest that much of its effect derives from a high degree of realism, involving the painful exploration of the ways in which ordinary people became heroes.

In reconstructing the events of 9/11, director Paul Greengrass has achieved a visually conservative, yet intense film. Departing from many of the usual spectacular devices of the Hollywood disaster film, he deploys *mise-en-scène*, cinematography, sound, and lighting in ways that both sustain authenticity and provoke powerful emotive affect. The film deviates from standard Hollywood narratives in several ways. It fundamentally de-glamorizes aspects of everyday life in an attempt to maintain authenticity. Moreover, its narrative structure is devoid of the usual order, disorder, and order restored format that often characterizes classic Hollywood narratives. It does not fit easily into typical genre categories, and lacks closure in the traditional sense. Romantic interludes are absent, and it avoids obvious use of computer-generated imagery (CGI) and special effects, such as high impact explosions, that might feature in a typical disaster movie. Instead, *United 93*'s early foregrounding of the mundane makes its later events seem even more horrific. The depiction of the ordinary and un-spectacular aspects of people's lives mediates particular realism. The use of actual individuals involved at the time as central characters, and the inter-cutting of documentary footage of the Twin Towers' attacks further intensifies the film's credibility. Cinematography, as well as *mise-en-scène*, breaks with the conventions of fictional film in its realist tendencies. These aspects, together with a lack of stars and a general absence of formal aesthetic devices result in "simulation," understood in relationship to Baudrillard's theory, appearing close to reality. Consequently, the film sustains particularly significant emotional impact, and functions, not only as a tribute to those on the flight, but also as a mode of catharsis.

While *United 93* lacks spectacular effects, many writers have commented on the similarities between the dramatic aspects of some Hollywood narratives and media images of 9/11 (Baudrillard, *The Spirit of Terrorism*; Dixon, *Visions of the Apocalypse*; King, *Spectacle of The Real*; Lockwood; Rodney; Smith; Žižek, *Welcome to the Desert of the Real*). These resemblances lend themselves to postmodern analysis, particularly in relation to Baudrillard's concept of simulation and simulacra. Baudrillard explains that, in recent times, the reproduction often has more currency than the original and in some cases has replaced it. It is possible to explain some of *United 93*'s emotional impact using this model. The trauma that arises when viewing the film also relates to Lacan's concept of the Real. In this case, Lacan uses the term "Real" not so much to explain lived reality, but to describe aspects of existence that cannot be symbolized. The Real generally involves needs or desires and can only exist as sensations or feelings rather than objects. It is therefore not possible to represent them with an image. In examining the realist aspects of *United 93*, this essay will engage with Lacanian concepts of the Real and Baudrillard's theory of simulation.

9/11 and the Disaster Film

United 93 is one of several recent films that recount the events of September 11, 2001 (9/11). Some, such as Michael Moore's *Fahrenheit 9/11* (2004), are documentary in nature; others, including Oliver Stone's *World Trade Center* (2006), marshal fragments of evidence into coherent fictionalized narratives. As noted, while *United 93* also attempts to reproduce real events, it is mostly devoid of the conventional devices of the Hollywood blockbuster. Inevitably, however, the dramatic events of 9/11 have elicited comparisons with several other mainstream disaster films that preceded, and indeed, seemed to anticipate, the Twin Towers' attacks. As King notes, "The spectacle of high-profile American buildings being severely damaged or entirely blown to bits became a familiar one in the 1990s, especially in action-disaster-scifi hybrids such as *Independence Day* (1996) and *Armageddon* (1998)" (King, *Spectacle of the Real*: 47). King draws specific parallels between the fireballs of the Twin Towers and similar scenes from films such as *Die Hard* (1988) and *Armageddon* (1998). While he acknowledges the potential for postmodern reflection in the parity of these images, he also attempts to textually analyze them more closely and explain the effects of audience exposure to them in the immediate aftermath of 9/11. Although he argues that Hollywood's fictionalized scenes of disaster provide pleasure in their "sheer spectacle" (King, *Spectacle of the Real*: 49), and "the notion of a cleansing destruction of centres of government and urban decadence, against which certain powerful notions of American-ness have often been defined" (King, *Spectacle of the Real*: 49), such pleasure is displaced by confrontation with scenes of genuine devastation. While admitting the visual similarities between these fictional and real disasters, King goes on to explore their differences that, in the case of 9/11, manifested clearly in "the nature of a 'breaking' live news event" (King, *Spectacle of the Real*: 49) and the fact that images of the Twin Towers were screened on all television networks simultaneously. The reality of the disaster, he continues, was also evident in the relative dearth of imagery, especially the lack of footage of the first plane impact, and an absence of close-ups. He also notes that the actual events of 9/11 unfolded relatively slowly in comparison to the rapid intensity of images associated with the conventional Hollywood disaster movie. As more footage became available, the media attempted to organize the sequence of images to make sense of them, with standard narrative devices implemented to assist this construction. King maintains that this filling in of the gaps imposes "a form of *continuity*, a restoration of some kind of order" (King, *Spectacle of the Real*: 55).

Another form of confronting trauma arguably arises in repeated viewing of the endless repetition of images of the two planes colliding with the Twin Towers, closely followed by their collapse. Smith refers to Freudian psychoanalysis to explain how pleasure in watching fictional disaster derives from the ability to re-watch it and attain a certain mastery over it. In a similar way, she observes that

> in terms of repetition compulsion, the connection between Freud's theory and the media representation of September 11 is clear. One of the lasting images of the events of September 11 is the image of the second plane impacting on the second tower, replayed again and again [...] in a global attempt to admit its possibility and to come to terms with the act [Smith: 67].

However, she also notes that while such models of pleasure transiently come into play in relation to 9/11, the "ability to frame became temporarily inadequate" because of the overwhelming nature of its events (Smith: 66). In contrast, Lockwood observes that "media coverage aestheticized and numbed down the tragedy of 9/11" (76). Thus, in various ways, the autonomy of these images and their repetitive display and viewing seem to provide a means to effect containment of the trauma they incite.

Exploring the integration of such imagery and taking account of visual and narrative representation, this essay will examine realism and realist aesthetics in *United 93*. It will show how the film deviates from the predictable patterning of more conventional Hollywood cinema and how representation intersects with reality, blurring the boundary between them.

Realism in Film

Realism is a complex term and it is beyond the scope of this essay to explain its theoretical aspects in detail.[1] However, in film it generally operates at several different levels, either as a mode of recording events in documentary, to sustain believability in fiction, to enable the re-enactment of real events, or to persuade through propaganda. Therefore, it is a usual component of many films, whether documentary or otherwise, although some *avant-garde* films may be devoid of realistic aspects. Even fictionalized film requires some verisimilitude in order to suspend the audience's sense of disbelief and suture them into the narrative. Fictional film achieves this through the deployment of a credible *mise-en-scène* and a style of cinematography and editing that encourages identification with on-screen characters. Bordwell and Thompson discuss this approach extensively in their book *Film Art*, in which they assert that narrative film generally displays conventions of cause-effect logic and temporal-spatial coherence, negotiated through adherence to certain cinematographic codes. Documentary film, in contrast, often sustains realism through its seemingly indifferent recording of events and non-interventionist approach. Although such recording may seem naturalized, it may still depend on careful direction and coordination.

However, there are myriad variations between the classic narrative fiction film and the "true" non-interventionist documentary. The dramatic reconstruction or "drama based on a true story," falls somewhere between the two. It depends on some typical narrative conventions, such as continuity editing, while engaging with the 'naturalizing' aesthetics of the realist documentary. There has been extensive critical debate around the nature and form of realism in film (Bruzzi; Hallam and Marshment; Nichols; Ward) and the difficulties of its definition. Ward discusses the problems of taxonomy in relation to attempts to categorize its various forms. Examining the relationship between documentary and non-fiction, he observes that "the key distinction is never one of form or style, but rather of purpose and context" (Ward: 7).

The purpose of *United 93* is patently not to overdramatize or render spectacular the events of 9/11. Its visually conservative nature and conspicuous lack of special effects substantiate this. While it can never re-tell the full story, its intention is clearly to reconstruct events as close as possible to those that actually occurred. Some journalists and academics, however, question its intention. One reviewer of *The New York Times*, Manohla Dargis, asks "why [...] this particular movie was made. To jolt us out of complacency? Remind us of those who died? Unite us, as even the film's title seems to urge? Entertain us?" Its production seems to be, as stated in the closing titles, "dedicated to the memory of all those who lost their lives on September 11th, 2001." Like the repetition of images that replayed in the immediate aftermath of 9/11 and the later first-person documentaries of survivors, this film is both cathartic and pays tribute to those who died. It achieves this emotional impact and sensitive depiction through realistic and constrained style, particularly evident in its final scene, which avoids re-enacting the fatal crash of the highjacked plane. Instead, the screen cuts to a blank final image, provoking a real sense of loss for the viewer. This is not to say that *United 93* does not engage with some editing conventions of the disaster film, but utilizes them in an attempt to retell the facts rather than to make them spectacular.

Realism and United 93

United 93's realist aesthetic is especially apparent in its *mise-en-scène* and cinematography. Its *mise-en-scène* is visually unremarkable, consisting principally of airport lounges, air-traffic control scenes, and interior airplane shots. The opening sequence begins in a hotel room with the sound of several Muslim men praying in Arabic, leading the spectator to assume these men to be the 9/11 terrorists. They are young, clean cut, and dressed in western costume, departing centrally from the Eastern stereotypes often presented in American cinema. Their prayers form sound bridges over the following scenes in which crane shots track over the cityscape of New York, and which inter-cut with the terrorists preparing themselves physically and mentally for their ensuing task. A long shot of the New York skyline at sunrise is especially ominous to the spectator since, rather than signaling the start of a "beautiful day for flying" (Captain Dahl *verbatim*), it heralds impending disaster. It is one of several moments in the film when ordinary visual motifs become highly meaningful and hence emotionally charged for the spectator. Such scenes occasionally create a transient, futile hope for a different kind of ending, even though the spectator has prior knowledge of the film's inevitable outcome.

The mundane *mise-en-scène* also consists of bored-looking passengers dragging their suitcases and using their mobile telephones. Interior shots of the airplane show late arrivals and passengers typically ignoring the cabin crew's safety procedures. These familiar scenes are important in formulating a credible version of reality, and offer the spectator points of identification with the passengers that differ from typical filmic conventions. While narrative film usually depends on subjective camera or the close-up to encourage such identification, *United 93* utilizes the everyday aspects of characters' lives to engage its audience. As the film progresses, it captures fragments of the personal lives of the cabin crew, pilots and passengers. In this way, the film affords the development of emotional engagement without melodramatic effect, while allowing a circumspective distance for the spectator that sustains the illusion of reality. Similarly, in line with a realist trajectory, the lack of known actors contributes to this credibility since any star appearance calls attention to the fictional nature of film.

Nevertheless, one aspect of the *mise-en-scène* is significant and alerts the spectator to the ensuing tragedy. From the air-traffic control center, a brief incidental shot of the Twin Towers appears center frame on screen. It is another visual motif to which the characters in the film pay no attention but one whose appearance is highly emotive for the spectator. Such images serve to suture fiction to reality and consolidate the realism of events.

Like the routine aspects of the *mise-en-scène*, framing and cinematography are also intentionally restrained. The deliberate ordinariness of camerawork continues throughout the early part of the film, with a montage of city shots framing mundane aspects of the unfolding day. While the camera inter-cuts between cabin crew, terrorists, and passengers using a slow-paced editing style, as the film develops, a pattern emerges of scenes that oscillate between moments of trivial detail and extreme horror. Early on, however, the unspectacular and realist aspects of the film persist in almost every shot, with framing that appears random and characters that walk in front of the camera. The handheld camerawork constructs a series of unsteady shots that appear to lack the usual dexterity of the standard Hollywood film. For example, focus is erratic, and out-of-focus shots and partially obscured faces appear frequently, with obvious camera adjustments and jerky zooms that are suggestive of amateur video footage or reality television. These break fictional conventions, and construct a documentary aesthetic, although, in one sequence, this shaky camerawork contrasts with the smooth tracking shot of the take-off and ascent of Flight 93, perhaps signifying its inevitable, fateful trajectory.

Moreover, in the earlier part of the film, there are few extreme close-ups, particularly of key characters. This is consistent with King's discussion of the real event in which he observes a similar lack of close-ups (King, *Spectacle of the Real*: 50). One significant exception arises as the air-traffic-control team attempts to decipher the exact words spoken in a recording of a terrorist's voice. There is an extreme close-up of one character's mouth as he utters the words "it's planes, *planes* ... plural definitely!" This moment defines the point at which the air traffic controllers realize that they are under siege. The emphasis and repetition of the word "planes," together with the extreme close-up, indicates the gravity of the highjack situation. Usually, however, close-ups in the early part of the film tend to focus on seemingly unimportant aspects of the airport, such as the gauges and the flight paths visible on the radar screen. Again, while these visual motifs significantly fuel the trauma of the spectator, narrative progression suggests an apparent recording of events, especially as it occurs in real time.

As the narrative unfolds, however, the cinematography begins to change. Frequent whip pans rather than cuts prevail, and faster editing indicates the increasing urgency and confusion of the situation. The use of whip pans imitates the effect of an omniscient character turning to look at other characters. So it is used here as a tool of realism, suggesting the confusion of the situation, rather than as the high-speed technological spectacle of its fictional counterpart. The unfolding and escalating drama of the Twin Towers inter-cuts with scenes of the minor anxieties of the passengers aboard Flight 93. This device recurs repeatedly. In another example, crosscutting shows one terrorist apparently constructing a homemade bomb in the toilet while the cabin crew distribute breakfast to the passengers.

As the film progresses, a further feature of the cinematography is the increasing use of close-ups. While the handheld camerawork becomes more erratic, close-ups of the radar screens at the air traffic control center, followed by extreme close-ups of individual planes on the screen, now dominate the imagery. One view of the radar screen that shows the disappearance of flight "American 11" from view indicates to the viewer the first plane crash into the Twin Towers. This occurs several minutes before the Twin Towers appear on screen, casually shot through the control tower window, and initially framed un-dramatically in the scene. In one of the film's few point of view shots, attention focuses on the Twin Towers, seen in long shot through binoculars and framed centrally. Several scenes later, footage of the Twin Towers appears on "breaking news," now in close-up, and then in full frame as the horror of the situation begins to emerge. This close-up, and the reaction of the characters provides another juncture of reality and representation that sustains the film's authenticity. While King asserts that "spectacle in film may disrupt narrative" (King, *Spectacular Narratives*: 3), the effect here instead consolidates and authenticates it.

The earlier glimpses of the intact Twin Towers are thus replaced by documentary footage of smoke billowing out from the first tower. The spectator observes this scene at the same time as the air traffic controllers, who display both shock and disbelief. Rather than mediated through point of view shots, the spectator sees reaction shots of characters. The spectator again identifies with the on-screen characters without getting to know them, especially as the passengers, cabin crew and air traffic control remain mostly anonymous. This departs from typical Hollywood disaster scenarios where the personal lives of key characters are usually prominent. As the air-traffic control team attempt to piece together the information, their gradual realization of the situation seems slow paced. The shock of the second airplane hitting the Twin Towers thus elicits a similar response for the air traffic controllers as it may have done on initially witnessing the real event and sustains similar incredulity for the spectator, perhaps an effect of the temporal distance of 9/11, and its fresh re-viewing. At the end of the film, the distinctive blank screen and lack of imagery in the final frame differs significantly from fictional film, which would likely present the crash in a spectacular and special effects–laden long shot.

Realistic sound and lighting effects also support these cinematographic aspects. The restrained deployment of extra-diegetic music and the apparent use of natural and ambient light help to authenticate the film as real. Diegetic sounds also tend to be those that resonate familiarly with the spectator, such as the increased revving of the engines ready for take off. Rather than the musical crescendo that fictional film usually deploys, Greengrass here utilizes the alternation of diegetic noise and silence as a device to mediate moments of extreme shock and grief. This occurs at several points in the film. During the emergence of facts about the disappearance of the first two airplanes, there is intense background noise. As the scene of the first tower appears, the noise gradually falters and then completely halts at the air traffic controllers' realization of events. A potential mid-air collision detected on the radar provokes another escalation of shouting, followed by a hiatus as the planes narrowly miss each other. Before the second plane hits the second tower, there is again intense diegetic noise which abruptly ceases as the camera cuts to the "news" footage and then to reaction shots of the air traffic controllers and military personnel. The pattern of these sound effects anticipates the film's closing sequence where the screams of the passengers again abruptly cease, coinciding visually with the blank final frame.

The closing sequence is another feature that deviates from the typical Hollywood film. Closure usually follows the restoration of order with all enigmas made transparent and narrative strands resolved (Bordwell and Thompson: 354). In the first half of *United 93*, the narrative unfolds slowly with few moments of tension, although the pace of the film gathers momentum as it progresses. The narrative trajectory, however, becomes one of exponentially increasing tension that does not resolve until the final blank screen, abruptly signaling the death of the passengers. The film stops rather than ends, its absolute finality, after the highly tense and rapidly edited previous scenes, provoking an acute sense of loss with no sense of explanation or resolution. The intensity of the final scene thus differs from fictionalized narratives that generally provide relief or resolution, and thus reinforces the realist aesthetics of *United 93*. Indeed, such traumatic events exceed experience, and, as Lacan suggests, resist representation. The final scene of *United 93* respects this unrepresentability and is thus unable to offer any closure.

Baudrillard and Simulation

Baudrillard's concept of simulation is salient here because the events that *United 93* depicts have played out fictionally in earlier films. His writings are extensive, ranging from discussions of postmodernism to notions of symbolic exchange. Whilst he also refers specifically to terrorism and 9/11, this essay is more concerned with his concept of simulation and simulacra, an important theoretical perspective when considering "authenticity" and affect in regard to *United 93*. In *Simulation and Simulacra*, Baudrillard examines the pastiche and argues that the copy has attained more currency than the original. His concept of simulation and simulacra is readily applicable to film and particularly lends itself to science fiction. For example, films that center on the cyborg or replicant, such as *Terminator 2* (Cameron, 1991) and *Blade Runner* (Scott, 1982), often raise questions about the nature of humanity, and suggest the proximity of humanness to the cybernetic organism. This has particular resonance in an era of prosthetic body parts and the growth of artificial intelligence. The nature of identity and alternate realities also forms the central concept of *The Matrix* (Wachowski Brothers, 1999) which has therefore been subject to Baudrillardian debate. Although there is little discourse on the relation of Baudrillard's theory of simulation to the disaster film, the congruity of cinematic images with those documenting 9/11 has more recently prompted such discussion. This often centers on the idea that the plot of 9/11 derives from prior cinematic images. While it is possible that terrorists *have* drawn upon such images, and therefore fulfill the prophecy of Baudrillard's hypothesis, this essay offers a different approach to the phenomenon of simulation.

Baudrillard explains that simulation operates at different successive levels. First order simulation relates to obvious representations of the real, such as the painting, while second order simulation "*blurs the boundaries between reality and representation*" (Lane: 84). In third order simulation Baudrillard states that the image "masks the absence of a profound reality" (Baudrillard, *Simulation and Simulacra*: 6) and finally "has no relation to any reality whatsoever, it is its very own simulacrum" (Baudrillard, *Simulation and Simulacra*: 6). Baudrillard's concept of second order simulation is clearly relevant to a discussion of *United 93* as a copy that blurs the boundaries between reality and representation. However, his argument proposes that the original from which second order copies derive, still exists. This therefore suggests that imagery of the Twin Towers and their destruction has become hyper-real — they have replaced the real and become detached from it. While these representations clearly have their origins in the real, the Twin Towers now only exist as imaginary or cinematic monuments. Arguably, they therefore verge on third order simulation with their destruction inherent in their depiction.

While the images of 9/11 are signs, and obviously *not* the real thing, they have in some respects taken the place of the original. Such images, unlike the painting, which may be a product of imagination, are closer to the real. Barthes agrees that the photograph is different other forms of representation because it is

> not the *optionally* real thing to which an image or sign refers but the *necessarily* real thing which has been placed before the lens, without which there would be no photograph. Painting can feign reality without having seen it. Discourse combines signs which have referents, of course, but these referents can be and are most often "chimeras" [Barthes: 76].

For Barthes then, "[t]here is a superimposition here: of reality and of the past" (76). In some cases, he suggests that the photograph has potential to become the thing itself. Describing one particular photograph by Kertèsz, he notes that "here, the photograph transcends itself: is this not the sole proof of art? To annihilate itself as *medium*, to be no longer a sign but the thing itself?" (45). Barthes' work is relevant to film footage of the Twin Towers. These filmic sequences have a temporal and spatial dimension, and are thus even more "real" than the punctuated nature of the static photograph. Not only do these images supplant the original, but they also differ in both meaning and appearance. The originals, the real towers, formed part of the generic Manhattan skyline and thus contributed to the identity of the city. Meaning was also inscribed in the towers' title; as William Pawlett notes, they were named "not the U.S. Trade Center but the *World* Trade Center" (145). In contrast, 9/11 footage of the Twin Towers shows them in isolation, in close-up, as raw, compelling evidence of violation and vulnerability. The spectator has also gained new knowledge, in part through news media and through the production of documentaries, about the inhabitants of the Twin Towers. For many, the World Trade Center has become a more personal, familiar space than its former real counterpart. The condensed sequences of images of the towers' destruction and collapse have created an endless repetition that has thus become autonomous of the real towers and has taken on a life of its own. Baudrillard himself comments, "In all these vicissitudes, what stays with us, above all else, is the sight of the images. This impact of the images, and their fascination, are necessarily what we retain, since images are, whether we like it or not, our primal scene" (*The Spirit of Terrorism*: 26). Stella Bruzzi asserts that the images "ha[ve] been used as a collective site of national and global trauma" and that they "came to represent the wounding of an entire nation if not the western world" (21). However, the re-contextualization of these images within the narrative of *United 93* as simulation resurrects some of the original trauma in its close approximation to the real. While the film's construction and articulation through aspects of film form sustain realistic effect, the inclusion of real footage anchors authenticity. Such moments provide a nexus at which representation and reality coalesce and revive the emotions wrought by the original trauma. It is thus both *United 93*'s re-narrativizing of actual footage, and its overall realist aesthetic that recreate its harrowing effects.

Lacan and the Real

The concept of these images standing for something that no longer exists also relates to Lacan's theory of the Real. While Baudrillard's work concerns the relationship between the image and its origin, Lacan's considers psychoanalytical aspects of the Real. These two approaches are therefore quite distinct from each other, but here find intersection in their respective considerations of trauma, especially in relation to terrorism. While several writers refer to Baudrillard's work in relation to terrorism and 9/11, and Lacan refers more generally to trauma, this article suggests that the trauma depicted in *United 93* relates to both.

Lacan divides psychosexual development into the imaginary, the symbolic, and the Real. For Lacan, the imaginary is the infantile world associated with the mirror stage. The symbolic is that of language and other modes of signification that include the image while the Real exists at the periphery of the symbolic world. In his earlier work, the Real is a pre-linguistic state of need in relation to the infant. One example is hunger, and is a need that cannot itself be symbolized; it is pre-symbolic but may be signified through crying. Lacan's later concept of the Real still resists symbolization, but shifts from the notion of biological need to become primarily associated with trauma. Like hunger, trauma cannot be symbolized, only signified through expressions of grief or shock.

Several writers, including Todd McGowan, Sheila Kunkle, and Slavoj Žižek, are renowned for their application of Lacanian theory to cinema. While Žižek, perhaps the most significant scholar in this field, tends to focus on the films of Alfred Hitchcock and David Lynch, he also explores narratives as diverse as *Eyes Wide Shut* (1999), *Casablanca* (1942), and *The Matrix* (1999). These lend themselves readily to Lacanian analysis in relation to their various themes of desire, reality and fantasy. More recently, Smith utilized Lacanian theory to relate the trauma of 9/11 to its documentary record. She noted how these images provided

> moments when the representation was exceeding the frames of reference provided by our culture, and moving beyond our horizon of imagination, moments when — in Lacanian terms — the spectator was momentarily experiencing something outside of the symbolic, something in the Real [Smith: 68].

The narrative of *United 93*, especially in its use of reaction shots, which consistently reveal the shocked expressions of the characters, repeatedly signifies trauma. In returning viewers to the reality of September 11, it remobilizes traumatic memory. However, the re-contextualization of 9/11 footage and sense of loss generated through its tangible *lack* of spectacle and special effects, recreates some of the original trauma generated by these images. The final blank screen is testament to this sense of loss, and the impossibility of symbolizing the trauma of the Lacanian Real. The very emptiness of the screen, like the inserted footage of the Twin Towers, provides a final point of authentication. Arguably, the notion of terrorism itself, and the "War on Terror," because of their intangible nature and the anxieties they incite, also resist representation and therefore lie within the realm of the Real.

Conclusion

The use of cinematography, lighting, sound, and *mise-en-scène* in *United 93* produce highly realistic effects. The close integration of documentary footage of the destruction of the Twin Towers further consolidates this aesthetic, rather than drawing attention to the film's artifice, as earlier films representing traumatic events have done (for example, *Sands of Iwo Jima*, 1949; *JFK,* 1991). Rather, this interweaving of footage intensifies its authenticity and further blurs the boundary between reality and representation. 9/11 imagery, because of its multiple replaying, both in early post–9/11 media footage and in documentaries made since, does not merely signify the Twin Towers, but has come to stand in for them. The film, through using these images, collapses the boundary between representation and reality, and for some spectators, these images of the Twin Towers *are* the twin towers. Arguably, the film exemplifies Baudrillard's third order of simulation where the image is self-sustaining and autonomous of the original, while its re-narrativization provokes a sense of the original distress. The film's lack of stars and spectacular effects, and use of reaction shots furthers its sense of realism, while the empty final screen also remobilizes the trauma of the Lacanian Real.

These authenticating strategies place *United 93* in a unique position to contribute to the memory-making process of the events of 9/11. Aiming to re-enact the fate of the fourth highjacked plane, it differs from previous films that depicted shocking events, such as Vietnam movies, which tended to support specific political agendas. As Tony Williams comments, the majority of Vietnam films were "old fantasies [which] became cosmetically reworked to fit the circumstances of an era far removed from their original applicability" (118). In contrast, *United 93* seems to take an impartial standpoint and refuses to assume the "mythic trajectories" that Williams ascribes to previous traumatic narratives. Its consistent claims for truthfulness and authenticity, dependent on relatives' accounts and the *9/11 Commission Report* (Greengrass) indicate that this was a serious attempt to narrativize historical fact, providing a tribute to those who died, and a measure of catharsis for those left behind. Arguably, it achieves this not only by making visible some of the victims of 9/11, and indeed, revealing them as heroes, but also by giving form to the invisible face of terrorism. While perhaps at risk of compounding the pro-masculine rhetoric that Faludi claims permeated the media post 9/11, particularly the hyperbole surrounding Flight 93 (46–64), *United 93* insists on a commitment to veracity and collective endeavor. This is important since, as Faludi further comments, "Identifying acts of courage and acknowledging people whose heroism gives solace to others is an essential part of any war effort" (63). Made implicit in its title, *United 93*'s equal valorizing of all passengers was therefore not only important to relatives as part of the grieving process but was highly significant to a society immersed in a "War on Terror."

(*An earlier version of this essay appeared in* The International Journal of the Arts in Society, *Vol. 4, Issue 1 (2009): 95–106.*)

Notes

1. For further reading, refer to Bruzzi, Hallam and Marshment, Nichols and Lane.

Works Cited

Barthes, Roland. *Camera Lucida*. London: Vintage, 2000.
Baudrillard, Jean, and S. Glaser (Trans.). *Simulation and Simulacra*. Ann Arbor: University of Michigan Press, 1994.
Baudrillard, Jean, and C. Turner (Trans.). *The Spirit of Terrorism*. 2002. London: Verso, 2003.
Baudrillard, Jean, in M. Gane (Ed.), and I. Grant (Trans.). *Symbolic Exchange and Death*. 1976. Los Angeles: Sage, 1993.
Baudrillard, Jean, in D. Pettman. (Ed.), and P. Beitchman (Trans.). *Fatal Strategies*. 1983. Cambridge: MIT Press, 2008.
Bay, Michael. (Dir.) *Armageddon*. Touchstone Pictures, 1998.
Bordwell, David, and Kristin Thompson. *Film Art: An Introduction*, New York: McGraw-Hill, 2001.
Bruzzi, Stella. *New Documentary*. (2nd ed.). London: Routledge, 2006.
Cameron, James (Dir.). *Terminator 2*. TriStar Pictures, 1991.
Curtiz, Michael (Dir.). *Casablanca*. Warner Bros., 1942.
Dargis, Manohla. "Defiance Under Fire: Paul Greengrass's Harrowing *United 93*." *The New York Times*, April 28, 2006.
Dixon, Winston Wheeler. *Visions of the Apocalypse: Spectacles of Destruction in American Cinema*. London: Wallflower Press, 2003.
_____. (Ed.). *Film and Television After 9/11*. Carbondale: Southern Illinois University Press, 2004.
Doherty, Thomas. "United 93." *Cineaste* 31. 4 (2006): 73–75.
Dwan, Allan (Dir.). *Sands of Iwo Jima*. Republic Pictures, 1949.
Faludi, Susan. *The Terror Dream: What 9/11 Revealed About America*. London: Atlantic Books, 2007.
Greengrass, Paul (Dir.). *United 93*. Universal Pictures, 2006.
_____. *United 93 DVD Bonus Features*. Universal Studios, 2006.
Hallam, Julie, and Margaret Marshment. *Realism and Popular Cinema*. Manchester: Manchester University Press, 2000.
Homer, Sean. *Jacques Lacan*. London: Routledge, 2005.
Jaafar, Ali. "United 93." *Sight and Sound* 16. 7 (2006): 80–82.
King, Geoff *Spectacular Narratives: Hollywood in the Age of the Blockbuster*. London: I.B. Tauris, 2000.
_____. (Ed.). *The Spectacle of the Real: From Hollywood to Reality TV and Beyond*. Bristol and Portland: Intellect, 2005.

Kubrick, Stanley (Dir.). *Eyes Wide Shut*. Warner Bros., 1999.
Lacan, Jacques, and B. Fink (Trans.). *Écrits*. 1966. New York: W. W. Norton, 2002.
Landesman, Cosmo. "A terrifying flight back in time." *The Sunday Times*, London, June 4, 2006: 13.
Lane, Richard. *Jean Baudrillard*. London: Routledge, 2009.
Lockwood, Dean. "Teratology of the Spectacle." *In* G. King (Ed.). *The Spectacle of the Real: From Hollywood to Reality TV and Beyond*. Bristol and Portland: Intellect, 2005: 71–81.
Marcks, Greg. "A Credible Witness." *Film Quarterly* 60.1 (2006): 3.
McGowan, Todd, and Sheila Kunkle (Eds.). *Lacan and Contemporary Film*. New York: Other Press, 2004.
McTiernan, John (Dir.). *Die Hard*. 20th Century Fox, 1988.
Moore, Michael (Dir.). *Fahrenheit 9/11*. Lions Gate Films, 2004.
Nichols, Bill. *Representing Reality*. Bloomington: Indiana University Press, 1991.
Pavlus, John. "Revisiting Flight 93." *American Cinematographer* 87. 6 (2006): 26–30.
Pawlett, William. *Jean Baudrillard*. London: Routledge, 2007.
Pizzato, Mark. "Beauty's Eye: Erotic Masques of the Death Drive in *Eyes Wide Shut*." *In* Todd McGowan and Sheila Kunkle (Eds.). *Lacan and Contemporary Film*. New York: Other Press, 2004: 83–110.
Rodney, Lee. "Real Time, Catastrophe, Spectacle: Reality as Fantasy in Live Media." *In* G. King (Ed.). *The Spectacle of the Real: From Hollywood to Reality TV and Beyond*. Bristol and Portland: Intellect, 2005: 37–46.
Scott, Ridley (Dir.). *Blade Runner*. Warner Bros., 1982.
Smith, Kathy. "Reframing Fantasy: September 11 and the Global Audience." *In* G. King (Ed.). *The Spectacle of the Real: From Hollywood to Reality TV and Beyond*. Bristol and Portland: Intellect, 2005: 59–70.
Stone, Oliver (Dir.). *JFK*. Warner Bros., 1991.
_____. *World Trade Center*. Paramount Pictures, 2006.
Wachowski, Andy and Larry (Dir.). *The Matrix*. Warner Bros., 1999.
Ward, Paul. *Documentary: The Margins of Reality*. London: Wallflower Press, 2005.
Williams, Tony. *Enjoy Your Symptom!* London: Routledge, 2001.
_____. *How to Read Lacan*. London: Granta Books, 2006.
_____. "Narrative Patterns and Mythic Trajectories in Mid–1980s Vietnam Movies." *In* M. Andereggn (Ed.). *Inventing Vietnam: The War in Film and Television*. Philadelphia: Temple University Press, 1991: 114–139.
Žižek, Slavoj. *Welcome to the Desert of the Real*. London: Verso, 2002.

Films Cited

Bay, Michael (Dir.). *Armageddon* (1998). USA.
Cameron, James (Dir.). *Terminator 2* (1991). USA.
Curtiz, Michael (Dir.). *Casablanca* (1942). USA.
Dwan, Allan (Dir.). *Sands of Iwo Jima* (1949). USA.
Greengrass, Paul (Dir.). *United 93* (2006). France/UK/USA.
Kubrick, Stanley (Dir.). *Eyes Wide Shut* (1999). UK/USA.
McTiernan, John (Dir.). *Die Hard* (1988). USA.
Moore, Michael (Dir.). *Fahrenheit 9/11* (2004). USA.
Scott, Ridley (Dir.). *Blade Runner* (1982). USA/Hong Kong.
Stone, Oliver (Dir.). *JFK* (1991). USA/France.
Stone, Oliver (Dir.). *World Trade Center* (2006). USA.
The Wachowski Brothers (Dir.). *The Matrix* (1999). USA/Australia.

CONNECTING IN THE AFTERMATH
Trauma, Performance, and Catharsis in the Plays of Anne Nelson

James M. Cherry

In 9/11: *The Culture of Commemoration*, David Simpson proposes that the terrorist attacks on the World Trade Center and the Pentagon on September 11, 2001, resulted in a "compression" of the national narrative: "[t]he time of memory and commemoration evolved from the start alongside the time of revenge" (4). The national media covered the attacks unrelentingly for weeks, but the subject matter of the coverage inevitably shifted from the attacks themselves to the invasion of Afghanistan that soon followed. A widespread public demand for a swift and total retribution for the attacks coincided with the Bush Administration's media push for war. Less than a month from the attacks, the United States and its allies invaded Afghanistan, and the trauma from 9/11 was "made secondary to the initiation of new states of emergency" (4). With the pursuit of "Infinite Justice"—the original name of the operation in Afghanistan—dealing with the national trauma became less important than the persecution of war and the expansion of executive powers.[1] In the months and years that followed, the public discourse on 9/11 would become intertwined with the wars overseas, and the larger War on Terrorism. It would be a discourse often defined by bellicosity and jingoism, accenting the need for military reprisal rather than dealing with the complicated, emotional aftereffects of the attacks domestically. It is small wonder that nearly a decade later, the United States has managed to fight two wars in direct response to the 9/11 attacks, yet the chasm in lower Manhattan remains.

Anne Nelson's 2001 play *The Guys* is set, and was written and performed, in the cultural moment before the narrative irrevocably shifted from mourning to retribution and war. It was written by a New Yorker in a time of great uncertainty and fear, a time before the 9/11 attacks became rhetorically entangled with the foreign adventurism that followed. Based on Nelson's own experiences in the days after the attacks, *The Guys* is a simple one-act play with two characters. They are an unlikely pair, two people thrown together by happenstance, an experience likened in the play to subway trains "jumping tracks" (16). Joan (the stand-in for Nelson), an Upper West Side writer, looks for a way to resolve what she terms a "crisis of marginality": an awful, staggering act has changed the world, and there appears to be nothing that she can do about it (9). In a time of world-shaking crisis, she tells the audience, it is always "[p]lumbers and carpenters first[...]. Intellectuals to the back of the line" (8). She finds a way to contribute to the effort to rebuild and heal her stricken city by helping Nick, a Brooklyn fire captain, write the eulogies for his lost firemen. The main action of the play concerns the difficulty of finding the language to express trauma as the two struggle with the words that articulate Nick's feelings, and help the grieving families begin to heal. In the end, the stories that Nick tells Joan about his men show how we use language, and the public expression of that language, to cope with loss. In this way, *The Guys* is about the potential for language and performance to connect people in the aftermath of trauma. As a play intended to help a theatre recover financially from the attacks, it gives voice and a physicality to trauma as a way to begin to resolve it.

Nelson elaborates on the theme of connectedness and trauma in a later play, *Savages* (2007). *Savages* was prompted by the allegations of torture committed by the United States soldiers during the War on Terror, but also by what extreme nationalism means for a country that prides itself on its pluralistic ideals. Set during the Philippine Insurrection, the play depicts a war crimes trial of an American marine named Littleton Waller who gave the orders to water-board and massacre a group of Philippine prisoners following a bloody insurgent attack. In the day prior to the verdict, Hanley, the loutish American soldier charged with guarding Waller, and Maridol, a Filipina servant, argue the differences between their cultures, each equally ignorant of the other's. In the end, the marine is set free by the tribunal of his fellow soldiers, and his crime goes unpunished. Ironically, Waller is shown at the end of the play to be emotionally distraught and morally traumatized by his legal victory, because his crimes have been rendered irresolvable. In performance, *Savages* connects Waller's personal guilt to a collective — and seemingly irresolvable — national guilt in the wake of the various allegations of torture by American military and intelligence personnel during the War on Terror. But, in its final moments, the play points to a potentially brighter future by the sudden understanding reached between Hanley and Maridol. When Hanley discovers Maridol stealing much-needed Army medical supplies to bring to her village, he lets her go. For the first time, Hanley sees her and her countrymen as something other than "savages" and an intercultural connection is made.

This essay examines how ideas about connectedness and language manifest themselves in *The Guys*, and are further developed in the later play, *Savages*. With these themes, I argue, Anne Nelson's plays allow audiences to work through two of the most terrifying images of the modern era: the destruction of the World Trade Center and the atrocities that have taken place during the War on Terror, particularly the torture of suspected Iraqi insurgents at Abu Ghraib. A playwright who is also a journalist and academic, Nelson elides boundaries between performance forms, bringing into focus the performance of rituals that shape the way we cope in the wake of violent death (the eulogy) and reconcile unsanctioned military violence (war crimes tribunal). Nelson also suggests that it is through the dynamic of live performance and the resultant connection between performer and audience that the "crisis of marginality" in the face of trauma may be resolved, or at least ameliorated. And by focusing on the unseen, even unknowable connections between people, Nelson reveals how the true "crisis of marginality" is that there is no such thing as margins anymore. The neat distinctions between civilian and soldier, civilized and savage, global and local, guilt and innocence, are lost in the post–9/11 world.

The economic effects of 9/11 on the United States were severe, and the production history of *The Guys* illuminates the particularly deleterious effects of 9/11 on the New York theatre industry. As it happens, Nelson's play about New Yorkers trying to create closure and healing out of chaos, and its subsequent production at the downtown theatre, also went a long way to defining post–9/11 theatre. With the 9/11 attacks, New York's theatrical life, like much of the public life in the city, ground to a halt. Public spaces had become dangerous, the potential for repeated attacks inevitable. Broadway theaters reported massive losses. Within month of 9/11, City government and Broadway producers came to an arrangement that allowed for city money to be spent on marketing and ticket subsidies. The "Spend Your Regards to Broadway" campaign was part of a larger movement to bring tourists back into a city that once touted as safer than ever by the Guiliani administration, in order to infuse the city economy with needed tourist dollars. As Norman Adler, a New York–based political consultant observed: "The same way that nationally politicians gravitate toward Hollywood, New York politicians gravitate toward the [theatre] ... [h]elping the Met Museum is not as sexy as helping Broadway" (Pogrebin). At a time when George W. Bush suggested to Americans that they "[g]et down to Disney World in Florida" as a way to enact a "continued participation and confidence in the American economy," city lawmakers were suggesting the same in Disney-owned Times Square (Bacevich).

Smaller, off-Broadway theatres that always existed on the fringe of economic viability closed or played to tiny audiences. Lacking the political connections of Broadway houses, off-Broadway theatres were largely shut out of the political processes. Theatres in downtown Manhattan were particularly affected. *The Guys* premiered at the Flea Theatre, a downtown venue that is a short seven blocks from the site of the World Trade Center. The Flea staged 17 performances in the week before 9/11 and zero the following week; houses went from 90 percent full before the attacks, to 5 percent full when the theatre reopened (Yurgaitis). A chance meeting between Jim Simpson, the artistic director of the Flea, and Nelson at a benefit dinner led to Nelson writing the play. It opened in December of 2001, starring American film actors Sigourney Weaver (Simpson's wife) and her co-star from the film *Ghostbusters*, Bill Murray. It not only saved the theatre from insolvency — it ran to sold-out houses for 13 months — but became a downtown phenomenon, with actors Susan Sarandon, Tim Robbins, Swoosie Kurtz, Carol Kane, Bill Irwin, and others playing the two roles. It was performed script-in-hand, which allowed for short rehearsal periods, but also underlined the theatricality of the production. Audiences knew that they were watching a performance of famous actors playing the roles of Nick and Joan, but also speaking as themselves. Within a year, *The Guys* was adapted to film starring Weaver and another actor from the stage production, Anthony LaPaglia. The success of the play indicates the New York audience's deep hunger for and sympathy with representations of their own grief. The intimacy of the play, the immediacy of live performance, and the exchange between performer and audience member, combined to provide solace to people coping with their own "crisis of marginality."

Initial critical reaction to the play spoke to its unique position as a work of public mourning. In his review for the *New York Times*, Bruce Weber described *The Guys* as a piece that somehow works beyond standard conventions: "And though no one, I think, would describe it as an artful or literary piece (though it has its moments, believe me), it has the impact — half relieving, half-agonizing — of a chill salve on an open wound" (2002).

The play's seeming lack of polish can certainly be attributed to the fact that it was written in nine days, the sooner to get it in rehearsal and on stage. Weber implies that *The Guys* goes beyond the pretense of "art" or "literature" to do something significant — to give voice to grief and begin a public dialogue. But as Weber concludes, "[...] the real achievement of Ms. Nelson's play is that in the character of Nick, the fire captain, it gives credible and powerful voice to a very specific kind of pain that we crave these days to understand but from the outside seems only blindingly enormous and beyond sharing."

The "craving" to understand the pain of Nick and those who died in the attacks is natural, but also suggests a need for a differently-mediated response to the attacks, an alternative to American flag lapel pin-wearing cable anchors and flashy visual effects. *The Guys*, in Nelson's words, attempts to "revisit [9/11] in a way that is controlled and effective" (Marks). The revisitation of traumatic experiences in theatre is common in drama therapy, where participants act out personal traumas as a way of resolving them. As Ellen W. Kaplan has noted, theatre as a communal, participatory form "offers a singular opening for constructive intervention to relieve personal and communal distress" (173). The *catharsis* or "purgation" that Aristotle describes in *Poetics* as an after-effect of viewing tragedy might be seen as the result of such a "constructive intervention." But as Francis Fergusson has suggested, "Aristotle noticed (Politics, VIII) that, in religious rituals that he knew, the passions were stirred, released, and at last appeased; and he must have been thinking partly of that when he used the term 'purgation' to describe the effect of tragedy" (35). In Nelson's play, the ritual of the funeral eulogy allows for a public *catharsis*. In this way, *The Guys* foregrounds the need for a public ritual of release and cleansing in the wake of national trauma.

In a preface to the play, Nelson explains that "the theme, and the intent, of the play is to give comfort through language" (4). Language, and the potential for language to heal and restore, seemed critical in 2001, in a moment defined by repetitive visual imagery played on television of planes and towers, smoke and ash. Of these ever-present mediatized images, Harry Elam wrote that "through such representations, through the compulsive retelling of the story [...] we aspire to understand the 'real' event and its meanings" but do so unsuccessfully (103). In the graphic repetition of trauma, there is no real return to the event and no catharsis. *The Guys* is a reaction to the use of imagery "emanating from electronic media," a media that worked to codify the event in simple, nationalistic terms (Nelson: 4). In this way, the play has an old-fashioned, almost nostalgic, view of human connectedness before new media. There is no flag-waving in the play, or images of the towers being struck and falling; indeed, in a forward that precedes the text of the published play, Nelson forbids the use of any imagery from the attacks. Rather, the focus on the language and composition is meant to shift away from the visual and toward a eulogistic utterance and a communal experience. As director Jim Simpson acknowledged, "Theater's obligation is to be more than escapist. It should offer an opportunity for the community to come together to encounter the catastrophe on human terms" (Kadlecek, 2002). Outside of the theatre, a eulogy is just this opportunity for a community to come together, to encounter the catastrophe — the loss of a loved one — in human terms.

The structure of the play is straightforward, alternating between Joan's direct addresses to the audience, and her one-on-one writing sessions with the fire captain Nick. Joan's monologues reflect not only on the process of the composition of eulogies, but also about the city as self-created community. She tells the audience about how even though there are many people in New York, "no matter how big a city gets, the only way to live in it is to live in your village" (16). The densely populated city allows for anonymity and selectivity; creating a village is a matter of choice, personal preference, a space of one's own. But Joan goes further, explaining: "After September 11th, all over the city, people were jumping tracks" (16). In the aftermath of trauma, the individual villages, knots of people in the teeming city, become unraveled and intertwined. Columbia journalism professors meet Brooklyn fire fighters and downtown artistic directors. In the performance of a eulogy, these disparate figures come together to grieve. And new, more vital communities are made.

While *The Guys* was being produced, photographs of people killed and missing began to be taped to walls, lampposts, and street signs in lower Manhattan. The *New York Times* published "Snapshots of Their Lives, with Family and at Work," bringing together not only pictures of men and women lost in the attacks, but also anecdotes about their lives. The visual images of these people, often in situations in which they were happy and truly *alive*, serve as markers, the beginnings of dealing with their absence. What these markers and the stories in the *Times* do not reveal or replicate is the process of grieving. In a sense, *The Guys* stages the "Portraits of Grief" series that ran in the *Times*, but instead of documenting the victims' likes and dislikes, the play stages what it means to try to articulate what these people mean to a community. The significance of *The Guys* is that it uses the formal structure of theatrical performance to express suffering, creating a setting that frames expression of public sorrow. The play, like the eulogy, is meant to be a point of departure. Other conversations will happen later; first, we must honor and bury our dead.

The Guys is a play that is also deeply personal, not only to Nelson obviously, but as an expression of grief. In "Representing Atrocity," David Steritt concludes that the most affecting memorials to the dead of 9/11 eschewed the raucous extraversion of the coverage found on cable news networks:

> Such embarrassments contrast vividly with the appearance on Ground Zero's fences of point-and-shoot snapshots, Xeroxed drawings, informally scrawled poems, and other such items bearing the mark not of knee-jerk jingoism but of deeply personal responses to an ultimately incomprehensible event [77].

Nancy Miller in her essay "Portraits of Grief" notes that eulogies are meant to illuminate something vital and fundamental about the deceased, they "provide points of entry into the character," to introduce the figure to an assembly by "revealing something good, like virtue — often civic, or at least domestic, virtue" (117). The eulogy freezes the character in time and explains him or her to the audience. Nick has known his firefighters in a largely professional manner, through it is slowly revealed that he actually knows a great deal about the home lives of his men. The anecdotes that Joan encourages Nick to share throughout the play are woven into stories that illuminate the life of a person. Miller's idea of the "point of entry" into character becomes "the big thing," as Nick describes it, that can define his men, and give meaning to the assembly (24). Eventually we learn that Nick can tango, a dance seemingly at odds with his macho profession, and in a fantasy sequence Nick and Joan dance in the middle of the eulogy composition. Nelson asks that "the tango be played as an homage to the notion of craft and the beauty of synchronized movement — not as a seduction scene" (4). This unlikely synchronization of bodies returns to the image of the jumping of tracks and the potential of new communities to be formed in response to trauma. But it also points to the synchronization of language and performance in the deliverance of the eulogy, in which a person speaks for the community, and gives meaning to loss.

In *The Guys*, the climax comes in the ultimate transference of grief at the end of the piece. In the final scene, the stage is split as Nick gives the eulogy to the imagined collection of family members at a fireman's funeral, the rhetorical work that has been building throughout the play. According to the stage directions, Joan stands next to him and speaks to the theatre audience as she does in the monologues throughout. He speaks the eulogy, as she reflects on the process of grief. The audience becomes two things at the same time, a group of playgoers sitting in the dark, and a group of mourners at a firefighter's funeral. The two characters alternate in their addresses, and though in two separate spaces, their words mingle and reference each other. At one point, Nick describes the deceased firefighter's ability to make imaginative firefighting tools out of metal, and remarks, "When you are answering an alarm, every tool counts" (35). This eulogistic reference answers Joan's initial question about her place in a traumatized world — her "crisis of marginality." Writers are not always at the back of the line after all. But Joan is described as "distraught" and overcome by this resolution. Her work completed, she can now experience the grief that her physical (but not spiritual) distance from the tragedy denied her. Like the audience, she now knows these men, both in life and death. And like the audience, she is no longer marginalized. She grieves actively. Her concluding monologue begins by asking the audience how to cut a deal with God, one that allows for the images displayed on her television screen to be played backwards, in real life. For the towers to fall up, for the trucks to go back to the station, to have "them back, just the way they were" (35). This image of reversal is one that comes up repeatedly in literature tied to 9/11, the most significant example being in Jonathan Safran Foer's *Extremely Loud and Incredibly Close* (2005), which concludes with a flip book of images that reverses the descent of the unknown "Falling Man." One way that *The Guys* tries to "have them all back" is by registering the full implications of their loss in meaningful language. Moreover, the play's attention to the art of composition, the mental and emotional trauma of finding the magic words and speaking them, highlights the hard work and the pain rather than the ultimate and still elusive healing that they will hopefully bring. The play is a blue-print and a suggestion: if we work together in the new communities formed by trauma, we can help each other match words to experiences, create narrative out of chaos. And once we do that, we will have a common language with which to comfort each other and will depart from a vocabulary centered on revanchism and victimhood. This reversal of emotions at the end of the play leaves the story open ended. The trauma of 9/11 is not resolved. But this new connection between Joan and Nick leaves open the possibility of renewal. Trauma needs to be shared through language, through new communities that may bear it together. The tracks Nelson asks us to jump are not those separating the Upper West Side from Brooklyn, they are also those separating east from west, Christianity from Islam, and the various narratives, that nations, people, and religions tell themselves about their place in the world.

A film version of *The Guys*, starring Sigourney Weaver and Anthony LaPaglia, premiered at the Toronto Film Festival one year after the attacks. The film version is fairly close to Nelson's original play, though because of the translation to film it is more visual. The informality of the script-in-hand of the live performance becomes impossible, replaced by a more traditional cinematic realism. In the opening credits, we see what appears to be a security camera within the firehouse. A couple of firefighters are standing in front of the firehouse. Suddenly, a swarm of white paper floats into view. The firemen get into their trucks and drive away. It is the last we see of them, more of them than we ever see in the original play. It is the first and only time that we see "the guys" in *The Guys*. Seen from a distance through a grainy footage, the figures seem remote and unknowable. But this is the moment to which Joan wishes to have the tape rewound, the point when they, the guys, are all back again.

Another difference between the film version and the play occurs at the climax. In the play, the final image is that of Joan's distress and Nick's attempts to mollify her. In the end of the film, Nick's eulogy is given in an actual church in front of a group of actual mourners. The equivalency of audience members and mourners, as found in the theatre, is lost here of course, but so is the sense of transference. After the speech, Nick walks down the aisle toward the camera holding the fire helmet of the man his company lost. He makes eye contact with Joan on the way, and there is a moment of connection between them. What seems to be significant in the end of the play, the direct addresses to the audience and the moment of bonding, are lost in the film version. As befits a play about the potential of performance, the power of *The Guys* derives at least partly from the intimacy of actual live performance, of the experience of the community in the theatre.

While *The Guys* is a play that is about dealing with trauma it also delves into the politics of what 9/11 may come to mean, particularly about America's place in the world. Joan explains that on a trip outside of the United Sates, she yearned to be back in New York City where people "understood": "Everybody, all over the world, was talking about it. Writing about it. And they all — they all — thought it was about them. But it's not. It's about us! ... isn't it?" (30). Theatre historian Marvin Carlson refers to Joan's last question as "the beginning of the new post–9/11 political theatre in America" (7). She, like many New Yorkers and Americans, felt like 9/11 was *her* experience, a uniquely American experience, something that happened to us and only we can understand. In the process of articulating this strange pride, Joan is derailed by another thought. What if it isn't about us? What if 9/11 can only be understood in the context of a larger global relationship and history? It is a moment that illuminates how the Manichean dichotomies favored by the Bush Administration — a black and white world spinning on axes of good and evil — did not, and do not, suit the complexities of the moment.

In *Savages*, Nelson directly confronts the Bush Administration and the conduct of the War on Terror while further developing themes of connectedness and language. The playwright stages a military tribunal that resulted from atrocities in an all-but-forgotten corner of American military history, the Philippine Insurrection. The title of the play references how each faction in the conflict, Philippine and American, considers the other. And, in a direct parallel to the War in Iraq, American troops are fighting an insurgency against the very people they sought to free. The plot is based on actual historical events — an American Marine named Littleton Waller, acting under orders, water-boarded and killed a large number of Filipino civilians in reprisal for an insurgent attack. Both the crimes of the marine and his subsequent emotional turmoil are revealed slowly through the course of the day leading up to the trial, in conversations between the marine, who is sickened with malaria; Hanley, a naïve and gung-ho soldier from Oklahoma ordered to guard him; and Maridol, a Filipina nursemaid.

As in *The Guys*, Nelson's characters in *Savages* are "jumping tracks." Hanley and Maridol spend much of the play talking past each other, as language proves inadequate to the task of intercultural communication. Though both Maridol and Hanley are both Christians, they disagree about how even to describe their differences:

MARIDOL: Please explain to me, which tribe do you belong to? Are you Pres-bee-tee-rian like Doctor Miller?
HANLEY: Oh no, they're not tribes. They're *denominations*. And we're Church of Christ.
MARIDOL: (*She brightens.*) Oh, but so are we!
HANLEY: No, we're *The* Church of Christ.
MARIDOL: So ... you mean that we are not? [12]

We also discover that Maridol's Christianity is infused with Buddhist beliefs as well. As she tends to the sickened Major Waller, she sets two small figurines by his bedside: the Virgin Mary and the Buddhist goddess of mercy, Quan Yin. Hanley's reaction to this heresy is predictable, but Maridol explains that these two religions need not be mutually exclusive: "I used to work for a doctor on Kipuya Street. He taught me many useful things. Our Lady assists me. (*Beat.*) And Quan Yin assists her. (*She smiles happily.*) I think they are friends" (14).

The idea of peaceful coexistence of two different religious traditions is anathema to Hanley, even though it is perfectly natural to Maridol. Hanley's inexperience with local cultures of the empire is one that parallels with some unfortunate American actions in the War on Terror, highlighting the consequences of lack of knowledge of the Other. This disconnect is used to humorous effect in *Savages*. In one sequence, Private Hanley demands to sample Maridol's lunch, the Philippine dish *baluut*, not knowing that it mainly consists of fertilized duck egg. The result causes Hanley to spit small bones and feathers all over the stage. But this inability to identify with the Other also defines the American experience in the Philippines. In the beginning of the play, Waller explains to Hanley why America became involved in the Philippines to begin with:

> Once we whupped the Spaniards, our dear departed President thought that we should hold onto Manila, as a fueling station.... But one night, as he lay sleeping, God himself paid a visit. And God said: "William — not just Manila. I want you to take them all. And why don't you civilize 'em for me" [21].

Waller's anecdote is based in historical fact: in a 1903 interview with *The Christian Advocate*, President McKinley justified the occupation in this way:

> [...] there was nothing left for us to do but to take them all, and to educate the Filipinos, and uplift and civilize and Christianize them, and by God's grace do the very best we could by them, as our fellow-men for whom Christ also died. And then I went to bed, and went to sleep, and slept soundly, and the next morning I sent for the chief engineer of the War Department (our map-maker), and I told him to put the Philippines on the map of the United States (pointing to a large map on the wall of his office), and there they are, and there they will stay while I am President! ["Interview"].

McKinley's purposeful linking of religious duty and imperial conquest smacks of the "crusade" that George W. Bush invoked some days after the 9/11 attacks. In both cases, religious rhetoric informed the rationalizations that the leaders of all empires must make to sustain them.[2]

The trial at the climax of the play signifies the arbitrary justice that comes with empire. Maridol, the Filipino maid, accuses Handley that all occupying empires — be they Spanish or American — are the same: "The water cure [a euphemism used for water-boarding] and the firing squad. What is different? You say you 'bring the law'" (43). The civilizing elements of colonial occupation are used for the colonizer's own purposes, showing how the sources of rhetoric may be twisted. Like the eulogy in *The Guys*, the tribunal at the end is meant to resolve trauma — a trauma committed *by* the protagonist in the play — and put everything to right, but instead does precisely the opposite. As the judge of the tribunal tells Waller in the scene preceding the announcement of his sentence, "Some people think we can wage a clean war against an enemy who plays dirty. And Major, you spoil the picture." The trial sequence cleanses with rhetoric, but does not resolve the underlying trauma.

Lucy Winner has noted in her essay entitled "Democratic Acts: Theatre of Public Trials," that "trials, like rituals, function as a way for the public to confront chaotic, painful, and contradictory social issues" (151). Like a theatre, a courtroom is a sanctioned, liminal space. The tribunal in *Savages* is depicted in stark terms, a chair placed in the midst of a blinding spotlight. Waller tries to see through the brightness, his military bearing breaks down and, according to the stage directions, "he is not as unflinching as he would like" (48). The stage directions indicate a sound effect: "there is the sound of slow-dripping water. Rain?" (48). The sound of water dripping is an auditory referent to the waterboarding committed by troops under Waller's command. It also connects the trial situation to torture; man is isolated, afraid, trapped physically in the light, and at the mercy of an unseen, unknowable jury: the audience. Finally, the verdict comes down: "Major Waller, this court-martial finds you of all specifications and charges: Not Guilty" (48). Waller is relieved at first, described as "happy and proud" (48). But he is still alone in the pool of light. There is no applause. The scene ends with a sound of thunder in the distance. The water heralds a storm yet to come. Waller is isolated, not allowed to come to terms with his actions. He slumps in his chair, disoriented and staring. His guilt, and the lack of resolution, weighs on him. What Waller and the audience come to realize is that the official language of guilt and innocence does not suit the truth. The reality is "chaotic, painful, and contradictory" and the private ritual of the tribunal cannot provide the necessary public catharsis.

In his essay "Love Letter to America," Ariel Dorfman asks when America "will be able to look at itself in the racked mirror of history and join the rest of humanity[?]" (Hesford: 39). In *Savages*, Nelson underscores the repetition of that history, drawing connections between a century-old war, and the wars in Afghanistan and Iraq today. Waller sees himself and his country in that racked mirror at the end of the play, isolated, stuck by choice in the same track.

In wartime, guilt is seen as too expensive, and justice rendered moot, with no one to blame. The court's decision revokes any possibility of catharsis: we are left with no crime, no perpetrator, no victims — only uncertainty and the impossibility of closure. While the grief of the trauma is shared with the community through rhetoric in *The Guys*, in *Savages* the possibility for reconciliation is cut off. The trauma continues unabated, not only both at the end of the play set during the Philippine Insurrection, but also in our own time, in the aftermath of Abu Ghraib.

In the final moments of *Savages*, there seems to be the potential for catharsis and reconciliation. Hanley catches Maridol in the process of stealing medical supplies to take back to her village. In the scuffle that ensues, Hanley breaks Maridol's icon of Quan Yin, and Maridol is injured. Chagrined, Hanley uses the medical supplies to tend to Maridol's wounds. When she rises to go with the remaining provisions, Hanley appears ready to shoot her. When Maridol persists, Hanley, forced to choose between mercy and his intolerance, squeezes the broken fragments of the statue in his hand and "emits a long deafening bellow of pain and frustration" (52). Maridol leaves the room with the supplies, and Hanley "*looks at the fragments of Quin Yin in his hand. He doesn't know what to do with them*" (53). Throughout the play, Hanley and Maridol have skirmished, each lacking experience with the other's cultures. Finally, each is confronted with the humanity of the other. This is a painful moment, but one which points to the possibility of progress.

In comparison with the generally favorable reception of *The Guys*, critics gave *Savages* mixed reviews. Its initial run at the off-Broadway Lion Theatre lasted only a month. While Victor Gluck's review in *Backstage* called the play "riveting," Charles Isherwood in the *New York Times* claimed that "few will be entertained by a play that has too much information to impart and too many contemporary parallels to underscore to allow time for nuanced interpersonal drama to emerge." Isherwood's critique of *Savages*—that it is better punditry than playwriting—points toward what may be seen as the potency of Nelson's intention in writing her first play: social utility. *The Guys* was to offer a space where people could sit in close proximity and mourn. In doing so, Nelson could, like her avatar in the play, resolve her "crisis of marginality." Suffering in comparison with the visceral underpinnings of *The Guys*, *Savages* may feel like an exercise in historical and political analysis.

The lack of visual spectacle in both of Nelson's plays gesture toward a theatrical aesthetic that seems appropriate for a post–9/11 America. This minimalism can be found in many plays that concern the events of 9/11, like Neil LaBute's *The Mercy Seat* (2002) and Craig Wright's *Recent Tragic Events* (2004). In these plays and Nelson's, there seems to be an attempt on the part of playwrights to act as a contrapuntal force to the 24-hour news cycle that helped define 9/11 in the public imagination, and that shapes our current politics. The mediated image of the towers exploding and collapsing was, and continues to be, searing. As Nelson notes in her Preface to *The Guys*, those "images will be present in the minds of the audience for years to come" (4). But, as Nelson has shown, 9/11 may be represented outside the footage of the planes hitting the towers. And the intercultural connection that Nelson strives for in her plays is one that can also be the role that theater plays in a media-saturated age. In the work of Anne Nelson, the potential of theater to foster communion and contemplation is made manifest.

To varying degrees of success, Nelson describes, in both *The Guys* and *Savages*, how in the present global moment we are all "jumping tracks," moving outside of our spaces of comfort, blurring lines. The "crisis of marginality" that Joan experiences, her feeling of uselessness in the face of great public disaster, can be resolved through her participation in public rhetorical and performance situations where new communities may be created. In *Savages*, Waller is made marginal, allowed to go free with his, and his country's crimes, unpunished. There is no public catharsis possible. Thus, Anne Nelson's plays instantiate that it is through connection and exchange, through people and cultures and nations "jumping tracks," that trauma can be addressed. They articulate how in the aftermath of trauma, grief and opportunity always coexist.

Notes

1. Following protests from Muslim groups, the title of the invasion was changed to "Enduring Freedom" on September 25, 2001.
2. The quote in full: "This crusade, this war on terrorism is going to take a while." Bush's remark caused a sizable controversy at the time. See Jonathan Lyons' Reuters piece, "Bush enters Mideast's rhetorical minefield" (September 21, 2001).

Works Cited

Bacevich, Andrew J. "He Told Us to Go Shopping. Now the Bill Is Due." *Washington Post*, October 5, 2008. November 6, 2009. http://www.washingtonpost.com/wp-dyn/content/article/2008/10/03/AR2008100301977.html.
Carlson, Marvin. "9/11, Afghanistan, and Iraq: The Response of New York Theatre." *Theatre Survey* 45:1 (May 2004): 3–17.
Elam, Harry. "Response to 'A Forum on Theatre and Tragedy in the Wake of September 11, 2001.'" *Theatre Journal* 54 (2002): 102–104.
Fergusson, F. "Introduction." *In* S.H. Francis Butcher (Trans.). *Aristotle's Poetics*. New York: Hill and Wang, 1961.
Gluck, Victor. "Savages." *Backstage*, March 10, 2006. September 4, 2009. http://www.backstage.com/bso/esearch/article_display.jsp?vnu_content_id=1002157202.
Hesford, Wendy S. "Staging Terror." *TDR: The Drama Review* 50:3 (Fall 2006): 29–41.
"Interview with President William McKinley." *The Christian Advocate*, January 22, 1903: 17. *History Matters website*. March 31, 2006. http://historymatters.gmu.edu/d/5575/.
Isherwood, Charles. "The Consequences of War Can Be Deep and Everlasting." *New York Times*, March 11, 2006. September 4, 2009. http://theater.nytimes.com/2006/03/11/theater/reviews/11sava.html?scp=9&sq=savages&st=cse.
Kadlecek, Jo. "The WTC Tragedy Turned Journalism Professor Anne Nelson into a Playwright." *Columbia News Website*, December 12, 2002. September 6, 2009. http://www.columbia.edu/cu/news/01/12/anneNelson.html.
Kaplan, Ellen W. "Going the Distance: Trauma, Social Rupture, and the Work of Repair." *Theatre Topics* 15.2 (2005): 171–183.
Lyons, Jonathan. "Bush Enters Mideast's Rhetorical Minefield." *Reuters*, September 21, 2001.
Marks, Peter. "A Theatrical Candle in a Shrine to Sept. 11—A Small Play Offers a Focus for Solace." *New York Times*, May 1, 2002. September 8, 2009. http://www.nytimes.com/2002/05/01/theater/theatrical-candle-shrine-sept-11-small-play-offers-focus-for-solace.html?pagewanted=all.

Miller, Nancy. "'Portraits of Grief': Telling Details and the Testimony of Trauma." *Differences: A Journal of Feminist Cultural Studies* 14:3 (2003): 112–135.

Nelson, Anne. *The Guys*. New York: Dramatists Play Service, 2003.

_____. *Savages*. New York: Dramatists Play Service, 2007.

Pogrebin, Robin. "How Broadway Bounced Back After 9/11— But Downtown Theater Lacked the Right Ties." *New York Times*, May 22, 2002. October 3, 2009. http://www.nytimes.com/2002/05/22/theater/how-broadway-bounced-back-after-9-11-but-downtown-theater-lacked-the-right-ties.html.

Simpson, David. *9/11: The Culture of Commemoration*. Chicago: University of Chicago Press, 2006.

Sterritt, David. "Representing Atrocity: From the Holocaust to September 11." *In* Wheeler Winston Dixon (Ed.). *Film and Television After 9/11*. Carbondale: Southern Illinois University Press, 2004: 63–78.

Weber, Bruce. "Standing in for New Yorkers: Expressions of Grief Over Sept. 11." *New York Times*, January 28, 2002. October 10, 2009. http://theater.nytimes.com/mem/theater/treview.html?id=1077011432486&html_title=&tols_title=&byline=&fid=NONE.

Winner, Lucy. "Democratic Acts: Theatre of Public Trials." *Theatre Topics* 15.2 (2005): 149–169.

Yurgaitis, Daniel. "Notes on the NSU Theatre Presentation of *The Guys* by Anne Nelson." *Northern State University website*. February 24, 2004. October 10, 2009. http://www.northern.edu/wild/0304Season/Guys/Guy_nts.htm.

About the Contributors

Véronique Bragard received her M.A. from the University of Warwick and her Ph.D. from the Université Catholique de Louvain in Belgium, where she is a lecturer in contemporary and comparative literature. Her book *Transoceanic Dialogues: Coolitude in Caribbean and Indian Ocean Literatures* (Peter Lang, 2008) establishes new comparative dialogues between the Caribbean and the Mascarene Islands and between francophone and anglophone literatures. She has published on Indo-Caribbean literature, coolitude and the creative works of Ananda Devi and Khal Torabully in several journals in English and French. Her research interests include the representation of trauma and exile in literary texts and graphic novels.

Gerry Canavan is a James B. Duke Scholar in the Graduate Program in Literature at Duke University, specializing in twentieth-century American literature, film, and popular culture. His dissertation concerns the uses of futurity in culture and politics, with a focus on American science fiction during and after the Cold War. He is the co-editor of a special issue of *Polygraph* titled "Ecology and Ideology" and a special issue of *American Literature* on science fiction, fantasy, and myth.

James M. Cherry is the Byron K. Trippet Assistant Professor of Theater at Wabash College where he teaches classes in theatre history and film. He earned his Ph.D. in theatre from the City University of New York Graduate Center in 2005. James has published reviews and articles in *Theatre Journal* and *The Journal of American Popular Culture* and has contributed an essay for a book on dramatic parodies of the work of American playwright David Mamet.

Magali Cornier Michael, English Department professor and chair at Duquesne University, specializes in post–1960 British and American literature and feminist studies. She has authored two books, *New Visions of Community in Contemporary American Fiction: Tan, Kingsolver, Castillo, Morrison* (University of Iowa Press, 2006) and *Feminism and the Postmodern Impulse: Post–World War II Fiction* (State University of New York Press, 1996), and articles on authors such as John Fowles, Don DeLillo, Angela Carter, D.M. Thomas, Doris Lessing, Virginia Woolf, Margaret Atwood, Toni Morrison, Grace Nichols, and Ian McEwan.

Matthew J. Costello received a Ph.D. in political science from the University of North Carolina, and is a professor of political science at Saint Xavier University in Chicago. Since 1999 his research has focused on Cold War culture in film and comic books. Recent work has appeared in *American Studies* and the *Journal of American Culture*; his book, *Secret Identity Crisis: Comic Books and the Unmasking of the American Cold Warrior*, was published in 2009 (Continuum). A chapter titled "The New Superpowered Conflict: Re-Imagining the Cold War in Contemporary American Comic Books" will appear in *Cold War Representations* (ed. Kathleen Starck, forthcoming).

Aaron DeRosa's research focuses on trauma in Cold War and post–Cold War America. A critical work on E.L. Doctorow's *The Book of Daniel*, trauma, and 1950s "containment culture" is forthcoming in *Studies in the Novel*. DeRosa earned his B.A. at Bucknell University in 2003, his M.A. at Northeastern University in 2005, and is a Ph.D. candidate in English literature at Purdue University.

Christophe Dony received an M.A. degree from the Université Catholique de Louvain in 2007. He is a Ph.D. candidate in English literature at the Université de Liège. His research interests include the pedagogic potential of comics in the ESL classroom, hyper-visibility and postcolonial criticism in contemporary comics, and detective fiction and popular culture. He has published in such journals as *The International Journal of Comic Art*, *Postcolonial Text*, and *La Revue Nouvelle* and co-authored an essay on the implications of trauma in 9/11–related comics for the edited collection *The Rise and Reason of Comics and Graphic Literature* (McFarland, 2010).

Dan Hassler-Forest holds M.A. degrees in English literature and film and television studies, and has taught extensively in the Media Studies department and the English Literature department of the University of Amsterdam. He combines his teaching activities with ongoing work on his Ph.D. degree, which deals with the politics and rhetoric of superhero figures in (graphic) literature and film from a post–9/11 perspective. He regularly presents papers at international conferences, and serves on the advisory board of the journal *Studies in Comics*.

Timothy Krause is a Ph.D. candidate in the Department of English at the Graduate School of the City University of New York. He is an adjunct lecturer in the English departments of Hunter College, CUNY, and Stern College for Women at Yeshiva University. His field is twentieth-century and contemporary American literature, culture, and media. He specializes in crime, detective fiction and film noir; the postmodern and contemporary novel and long narrative; and New Wave science fiction. He is currently working on a study of the theme of failure in the works of Philip K. Dick.

Marc Oxoby completed his undergraduate work at San Jose State University and received his M.A. and Ph.D. degrees in English at the University of Nevada, Reno. He specializes in modern American literature, mass media, and culture. He currently works in the UNR Core Humanities program. He is the author of *The 1990s* (Greenwood, 2003), and has contributed to scholarly journals such as *Film & History* and *Critique*, as well as to *The St. James Encyclopedia of Popular Culture*, *The International Dictionary of Film and Filmmakers* and *New Paths to Raymond Carver*.

Stephan Packard is an assistant professor of comparative literature at Munich University. He focuses on semiotic and psychoanalytic media research and on issues of censorship, propaganda and textual control. He writes on sentimentalism and is an active member of the German Society for Comic Studies (ComFor). Publications include *Anatomie des Comics: Psychosemiotische Medienanalyse* (Göttingen, 2006); "Was ist ein Cartoon?" (in Ditschke et al., eds., *Comics: Zur Geschichte und Theorie...*, Bielefeld, 2009); "A Model of Textual Control: Misrepresenting Censorship" (in Dović, ed., *Literature and Censorship*, Ljubljana, 2008); and "Two-Dimensional Narrative Velocity," *Journal of Literary Semantics* 37, 2008.

Frances Pheasant-Kelly is a senior lecturer in film studies at the University of Wolverhampton, UK. Her research interests include abjection, gender and space, particularly in science fiction, spectacular film, and 9/11 narratives, and representations of medicine in media and film. She recently gained her Ph.D. at the University of East Anglia, with a dissertation that is the basis for a book, *Abject Spaces in American Cinema: Institutional Settings, Identity, Psychoanalysis* (forthcoming). Recent publications include a chapter, "In the Men's Room: Death and Derision in Cinematic Toilets," in *Ladies and Gents: Public Toilets and Gender* (Temple University Press, 2009).

Warren Rosenberg is a professor in and chair of the English Department at Wabash College in Crawfordsville, Indiana. His teaching specialties are American literature, film, gender studies, and Jewish and ethnic studies. He wrote *Legacy of Rage: Jewish Masculinity, Violence, and Culture* (University of Massachusetts Press, 2001), and a number of articles on a range of literary and cultural figures and texts. In 2002, he was a Fulbright fellow at the Université Catholique de Louvain.

Ulrike Tancke is a junior professor of English literature in the Department of English and Linguistics at Johannes Gutenberg-Universität Mainz (Germany). She has previously taught at Lancaster University (UK) and Universität Trier (Germany), where she was awarded a Ph.D. in English literature in 2006. She has published various essays on early modern women's writing and contemporary fiction. Her book *"Bethinke Thy Selfe" in Early Modern England: Writing Women's Identities* is forthcoming. Her current research focuses on violence, trauma and guilt in contemporary British fiction.

INDEX

Abu Ghraib 161, 170
Anderson, Benedict 13, 24
Armageddon 148
Auster, Paul 70; *Man in the Dark* 115
authenticity 8, 46, 102, 104, 105, 147, 152, 154, 156, 157
The Authority (characters) 36
The Avengers (characters) 36–37

Back to the Future 137
Barthes, Roland 155
Batman (character) 41, 134, 136, 144, 145
Batman (film) 135
Batman Begins (film) 7, 8, 135, 136, 142–145
Batman: The Dark Knight Returns 135, 142
Batman: Year One 135, 142
Battlestar Galactica (TV) 128
Baudrillard, Jean 103, 105, 119–121, 127, 140, 147, 148, 156; *The Gulf War Did Not Take Place* 103; *Simulation and Simulacra* 154, 157; *The Spirit of Terrorism* 121, 148; 155; *see also* simiation; simulacra
Benjamin, Walter 11–13, 103
Bhabha, Homi 22
Black Hawk Down 139
"Black Reign" 38
Blade Runner 154
Boyer, Paul 59–60, 70
The Boys 38–39
Bush, George W. 19, 31, 34, 38, 50, 55, 64, 69, 74, 126, 131, 132, 162, 168, 171; administration 15, 26, 30, 71, 73–74, 119, 130, 134, 138, 160, 167

caesura 45, 47–50, 53–55; *see also* Peirce, Charles S.
Campbell, Joseph 136
capitalism 16, 75, 76, 101, 120, 140; art 24
Captain America (character) 33–37, 39, 44, 52, 53, 55–56, 135, 137
Captain America (comics series) 32, 42, 53, 56
Caruth, Cathy 1, 63, 71, 135
Casablanca 156
catharsis 8, 16, 147, 157, 160, 163–164, 169–171

Civil War 3, 6, 39, 41, 44–45, 47, 50–51, 53–56
CNN 107, 122, 123, 126, 127, 132
Cold War 7, 32, 34, 35, 37, 42, 58–60, 64, 65, 67, 71; culture 59, 64, 66, 69
commemoration 3, 7, 13, 24, 160
communism 30, 32, 64, 66, 68, 69, 70, 134
connectedness 161, 164, 167
containment culture 59, 63–66, 149
counter-narrative 3, 70, 73, 74, 86
Coup d'État 35
cross-over 42, 44, 54, 56

The Dark Knight (movie) 135, 144
Debomy, Frédéric 1
Debord, Guy 27, 103, 120–122, 130
DeLillo, Don 6, 7, 58–59, 61–62, 64, 66, 68, 70, 73–86; *Falling Man* 7, 58, 59, 61, 64, 66, 69–70, 73–86, 115
Die Hard 148
documentary film 150
domesticity 59, 66, 68, 71, 86, 91; manifest 75

11'9"01 (film) 124, 126
"11 septembre" 1–2
Éulogy 161, 163–166, 168
Ex Machina 40–41
Extremely Loud and Incredibly Close 59, 62, 141, 166
Eyes Wide Shut 156

Fahrenheit 9/11 124, 126, 132, 148
falling man (trope) 49, 70, 87, 124, 134, 141, 166
Faludi, Susan 60, 67–68, 74, 75, 78, 127, 132,158
Faulkner, William 58–59, 70
fictionalized film 149
Foer, Jonathan Safran 6, 59, 62, 65–66, 68, 70, 115, 141, 166
foreign policy 4, 15, 30, 64, 66, 67, 71
Foster, Hal 11–13

Fox News 56, 130

gender 6, 26, 67, 83, 87
Gibson, William 6, 7, 102–111, 115–116; *Pattern Recognition* 7, 102, 103, 106–111, 114, 115
Ground Zero 63, 76, 89, 132, 139, 141; images 4, 125; installations 49, 131; naming and describing 61, 165
The Guys 8, 160–170

hero(es) 12, 18, 32, 38–41, 46–47, 51–54, 134, 139–140
Herogasm 39
Hersey, John 60, 62

ideology 25–26, 49, 53–54, 70, 100, 143, 145, 170
imperialism 3, 15, 20, 23, 99
Independence Day 49, 121, 125, 148
Iron Man (character) 36–39, 44, 52, 134
Iron Man (movie) 143

Jameson, Frederic 25, 105, 137, 140, 145
JFK (movie) 157
Joos, Louis 1
Justice Society of America 38

Kalfus, Ken 6, 59, 61–62, 65–66, 68–70; *A Disorder Peculiar to the Country* 59, 61
Kimmel, Michael 74–75, 78, 86
King, Geoff 148–152
kitsch 6, 11, 13, 14–16, 24–25

Lacan, Jacques 148, 154, 156–158
LaCapra, Dominic 59, 60, 63
Leavy, Patricia 30–32, 35, 39, 41, 42
"Letting Go" 38

Marvel (publisher) 3, 31, 38, 39, 41, 44, 46–47, 50, 53, 54, 56, 139
masculinity 73, 74, 75, 78, 81–82, 85, 86, 87, 144, 174
mass media 5, 7, 11, 16, 19, 26, 102–107, 109, 110, 114, 115, 116
The Matrix 154, 156

Index

May, Elaine 66–67, 70–71
McCarthy, Cormac: *The Road* 4
McEwan, Ian 6, 7, 8; *Saturday* 89–101
Melnick, Jeffrey 5, 61, 63
memory 8, 13, 17, 18, 24, 30, 42, 67, 70, 73, 77, 83, 113, 118, 121, 123, 124, 150, 160; collective 7, 118; construction 4–7, 157; cultural 12, 119; popular 11; traumatic 156
The Mercy Seat 170
mise-en-scène 1, 147, 150–151, 157
Muslims: culture 4; and Obama, Barack 25–26; protest groups 171; stereotype 19, 143, 151; violence against 19

Nadel, Alan 64, 67, 71
nationalism 3, 12, 18, 24, 26, 32, 34, 35, 37, 38, 41, 42, 161
Nelson, Anne 7, 8, 160–171
The New Yorker 5, 6, 9, 11–27
"New Yorkistan" 20–25, 27
The 9/11 Truth Movement 121, 132
nostalgia 118, 132, 137, 142, 145; Cold War 58–70; and myth 129–130

Obama, Barack 25–26
Orientalism 140, 143
the Other 8, 13, 18, 20, 23, 25, 168

patriotism 3, 13, 19, 25, 26, 69, 93
Peirce, Charles S. 48, 50, 56; *see also* caesura
"Portraits of Grief" 164–165
postmodernism 103, 105, 154

the Real 90–91
realism 6, 56, 147–158
Recent Tragic Events 170
"Red Zone" 36–38

Retort (protest group) 120, 122, 125, 132

Said, Edward 22
Sands of Iwo Jima 157
Savages 161, 167–171
Simpson, David 3, 4, 5, 61, 160
simulacra 7, 25, 90, 103, 112, 140, 148, 154; *see also* Baudrillard, Jean
simulation 102, 103, 140, 147, 148, 154–155, 157; *see also* Baudrillard, Jean
singularity 7, 107–108, 118–119, 125, 131
spectacle 90–91, 114–115, 124–131; aesthetics 7, 8; of mass media 5, 103; society 120–123
Spider-Man 46–47, 51, 134; "Black Issue" (*Amazing Spiderman*) 46–47, 50; movies 135, 142
Spiegelman, Art 5, 12, 70; *In the Shadow of No Towers* 9, 45, 53, 121, 133
Stockhausen, Karlheinz 119, 121
Sturken, Marita 14–16, 18, 25
Superman (character) 31, 34–35, 41, 42, 134, 137–138, 140–142, 144, 145; "Enemy" 32, 35; "The Harvest" 34
Superman Returns (movie) 7, 8, 134, 135, 136, 138, 140–142, 143, 145
Superman: The Movie 135, 137, 138
surrealism 11

T'Challa (character) 36
Terminator 2 154
terror 1, 4, 12, 58, 69, 87, 99, 113, 116, 118, 119, 120, 122, 123, 127, 133, 143; war on 3, 8, 30–32, 37, 68, 95, 129, 134–135, 138, 157, 158, 161, 167, 168
Thor (character) 38
trauma: collective 89–90, 103, 110; and connectedness 161–162, 165–166, 171; cultural 59, 63–66, 69, 74, 139; definition 1, 9, 63, 135; and Freud 149; individual 74, 76, 78–85, 103, 110, 163; kitsch 11–26; and Lacan 148, 156–157; mediated 102–116; national 59, 125, 135, 138, 160, 163, 167; nuclear 63; and repetition 7, 46, 62, 68, 164; and sign 48–50; and spectacle 123; and therapy 60, 71, 161, 163; and violence 89–100
24 (TV) 137, 143
Twin Towers 8, 11–12, 15, 23, 36, 40, 73, 108, 114–115, 119–121, 126, 127, 129, 139, 147–149, 151–153, 155, 157; *see also* World Trade Center

the uncanny 22
United 93 7, 8, 118–119, 123–124, 126–129, 131, 147–158

Wallace, David Foster 6, 8, 102–103, 106; "The Suffering Channel" 7, 12, 103, 111–116; "The View from Mrs. Thompson's" 106
War of the Worlds 128
Watchmen 135; movie 131
the West 3, 4, 8, 98–99, 121, 166
World Trade Center 30, 33, 40, 45, 49, 59, 69, 73, 77, 90–91, 106, 109, 113, 116, 118, 119–124, 126, 129, 132, 155, 160, 161, 162; *see also* Twin Towers
World Trade Center (movie) 7, 119, 123, 124, 126–130, 139, 148
World War II 31–32, 33, 36, 44, 53, 54, 58, 59, 61, 64, 71, 85, 130, 134

Žižek, Slavoj 3, 9, 46, 50, 90–93, 100, 101, 121–122, 124–125, 148, 156

www.ingramcontent.com/pod-product-compliance
Lightning Source LLC
Chambersburg PA
CBHW081600300426
44116CB00015B/2944